AF574626

F. SCANA

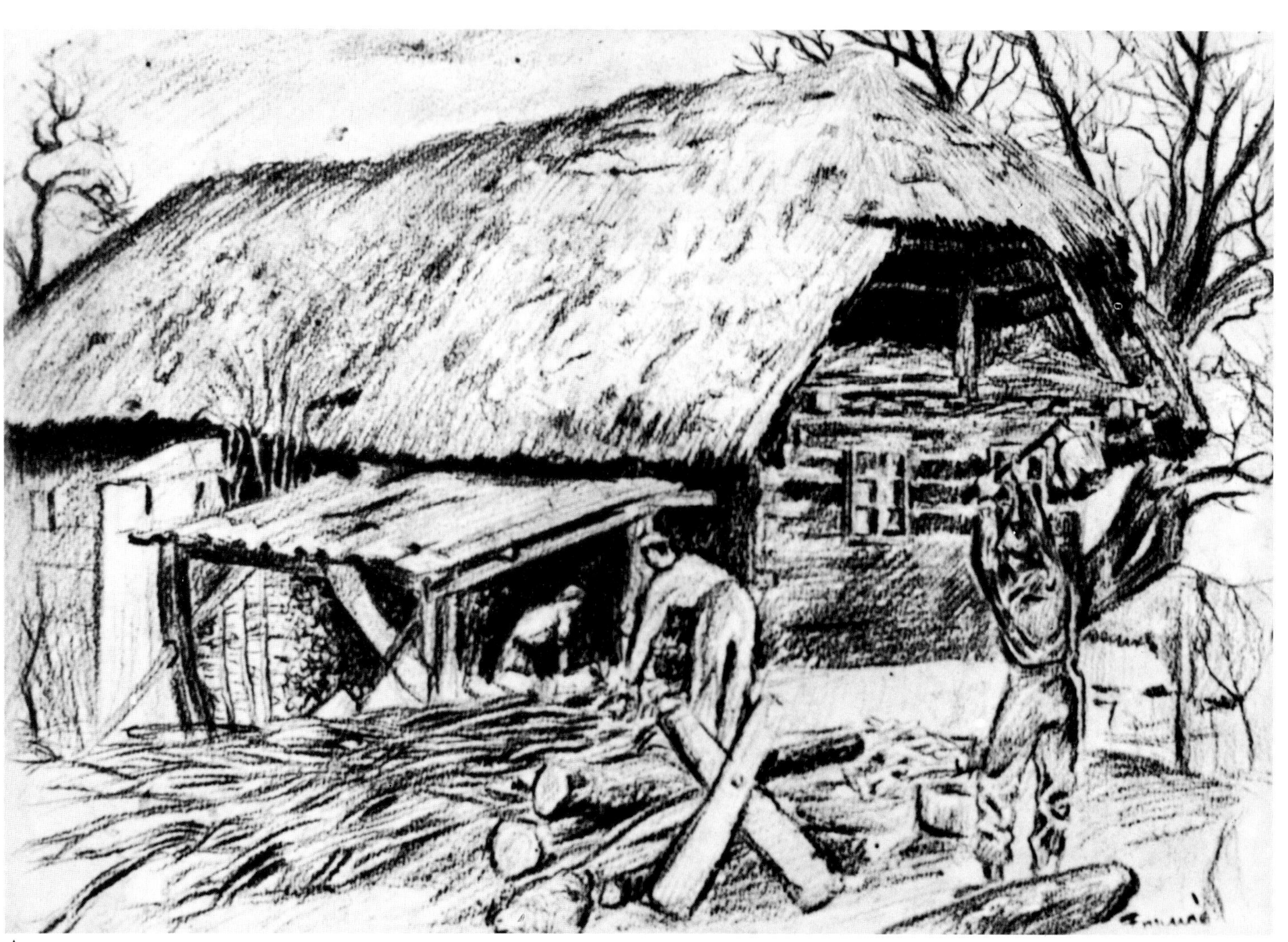

A

FRANCE SLANA

WATERCOLORS, PAINTINGS, AND DRAWINGS 1944–1980

by Janez Mesesnel

CONTROL DATA ARTS
a service of
CONTROL DATA CORPORATION

Minneapolis, Minnesota
1981

France Slana
Introduction by Emilijan Cevc
Text by Janez Mesesnel
Translated by Milan Mlačnik

Supervising editor: Iztok Bartolj
Designer: Jože Brumen
Coordinating editor: Tajka Ojdanič
Technical editor: Tadej Tozon
Photographers: Janez Kališnik and Miroslav Zdovc
Bibliographer: Melita Stele-Možina

Editor, English language edition: Susan Mattfeld Brown
Supervising editor, English language edition:
Pamela Lee Espeland
Designers, cover and text for English language edition:
Ned Skubic and Carol Evans

Library of Congress Cataloging in Publication Data

Mesesnel, Janez.
Slana.

Translation of Slana/J. Mesesnel
1. Slana, France I. Espeland, Pamela, 1951–
II. Title
N7253.S57M4713 1981 759.9497 81–3156
ISBN 0–89893–082–0 AACR2

First English Language Edition

Printed and bound in Yugoslavia

CONTENTS

FRANCE SLANA'S PICTORIAL BALLAD

When asked if I would write prefatory remarks for this book, I enthusiastically consented, for I have long been an admirer of France Slana and his art. I have chosen not to write a formal treatise, however. Instead, I have used simple words to discuss his compositions; I have tried to forget all of the artistic "rules" critics typically use to reduce a work of art to a formula or categorize it. For I believe that such "rules" only destroy the special human qualities of a painting and, thereby, its creative significance.

Every interpretation of a work of art threatens to undermine the artist's expressive intent. Explaining a picture somehow betrays the artist and destroys his or her message. At one time poets were the ones who wrote about paintings; today we too often allow them to be dissected by art theorists, and then we accept the leftover bits and pieces as laws we must abide by. I feel that this type of approach is useless and destructive, and prefer to respond to an artist on a personal, intimate level. And I believe that this is the best way to approach an artist of France Slana's caliber.

Thirty years ago Slana said this about his art: "I paint what is closest to me: houses, streets, a backyard surrounded by old walls, humble people with worried faces." At the time he was imbued with the feeling of hope that shaped his outlook as a member of the Partisan liberation forces during World War II. When this feeling began to fade, it was replaced by a darker, somewhat less optimistic vision reflected in the new approach to painting he voiced in 1970: "The point of departure of my painting is the revolt against the wasteland of today's technological society, which strives to cast man's personality into a mold. Since an artist is not a passive echo of his time and environment, but rather a critical personality, he must resist the process of dehumanization. For me, art is confession. I paint what I love and what disturbs me as a man. I think that an artist must be rooted in his country, in his surroundings, in a tradition . . . . Nowadays, when man's environment is, under the pretext of rationality, full of the dreary materialism of our consumer society, man needs more than ever the warmth and poetry which only art can provide."

Amid the mass of technological glitter that surrounds us, Slana seeks to create an art of simple truths, of the earth and the sea. He invents dream-like scenes which are akin to mirages and threaten to dissolve into nothing at any minute. His landscapes of plains stretching into the distance may be subconscious recollections of the vast fields along the Mura River, near where he was born; his seascapes recall the Adriatic coast where he spent his youth.

This new world which Slana opens to us seems as if it has been abandoned by humankind — or perhaps it is so pure that people simply do not belong there. For everything that bears the human stamp appears to be on the verge of collapsing and vanishing. Houses are vacant and dilapidated. A hay barn, no longer the keeper of the fruits of the earth, sits empty though still firmly anchored to the soil. A mill that once ground wheat into flour decays with idleness. Boats are broken and stranded on lonely shores. Cattle are mere skeletons roaming through space. Images of the past have been reduced to shadowy memories, disturbing symbols of the alienating effects of modern society.

Slana's romantic recollections are given form by a carefully controlled interplay of line and color. There is always a recognizable motif, as a point of departure, but the final work often verges on the abstract. The artist reshapes reality to mirror his own inner vision. A bunch of flowers appears in one work as a naturalistic bouquet (plate 99); in another the blossoms disintegrate into nothing more than a tonal association (plate 101); in yet another they are transformed into a shower of multi-colored shooting stars (plate 97). I once described his withered bouquets — a subject he paints often — as "abstract arrangements of tonal splashes and lines. Sometimes these elements assume the form of a decaying wall of a slum dwelling. At other times they surge upward in pallid colors akin to tarnished enamel; then again they swell up in immaculate white, like a ripe but damaged fruit — until at last they fade away into a shroud of thinnest gossamer that crumbles into luminous dust."

Spiritual content and overall pictorial expression are irrevocably linked in Slana's works. The stained stone of some ramshackle wall changes under his brush into a brightly colored gem. A lone flowery splotch is translated into a promise of new life among the ruins of a dead city. And everywhere is a sort of weird, inaudible music. Even the titles of his paintings sound as if they have been taken from ancient ballads: *Dark Sandbanks. Abandoned Houses. Wreckage. Decayed Boat. Jetsam on the Beach. Shapes on the Hayrick. Withered Blossoms. Remains of a Fish. House Against a Wall. Barn in Moonlight. Old Mill. Blue Shoal. Distant Landscape.*

His human and animal figures are impersonations of fate. A lean cat becomes a lurking phantom (plate 83); a horse is no longer a spirited steed but a forlorn, run-down jade (plate 89). The progression is thus from beast to symbol to creature of apocalyptic foreboding. His nudes are not Venuses emerging from the foam of a sunlit ocean, but rather passionate women who burst out of fiery backgrounds (plate 64) or spring from frosty moonlight.

In response to our troubled world, Slana creates a world of his own. This will be his refuge when technology has reduced nature to nothingness. He will sail away, though his craft may be decayed and barely seaworthy; perhaps he will take with him his "humble people with tired faces" or his weary horses. A cock will crow atop his mast; his fish will revive; and his dried flowers will bloom again. For in the kingdom of art all things are possible.

EMILIJAN CEVC is a Slovene art historian and expert on Slovene medieval sculpture. He also writes on modern art. Born in Kamnik in 1920, he received his B.A. in 1947 and his doctoral degree in 1951; he subsequently studied in Munich on a Humboldt Scholarship. He is currently a Fellow and Councillor of the Slovenian Academy of Sciences and Arts.

FRANCE SLANA

The new social and cultural ideas which emerged in Yugoslavia during the unsettled years following the second World War came into conflict with a nostalgia for the traditions and values of the prewar period. France Slana and the other artists of his generation were affected by the vitality as well as the dilemmas which this confrontation between the new and the old produced. The teachers at the Ljubljana Academy of Figurative Arts—where Slana and many of his contemporaries studied—still practiced the styles that had predominated before the war. The majority of them were *intimistes,* painters whose works were typified by middle-class subject matter, refined color, and balanced composition. But nearly all of them had also been active in the Partisan national liberation forces. So it is not surprising that they had difficulty reconciling their political activities with their continued allegiance to an art which seemed ideologically incompatible with the needs of the postwar era.

In an attempt to resolve this conflict, the professors at the Academy might have turned back to the minor prewar tradition of social and political protest art. This had previously been quite popular and successful, especially in the field of drawing. Instead, however, they focused on issues of craftsmanship and technique. Nevertheless, the contradictions between the requirements and aims of art and those of a rapidly changing society continued to influence the faculty and students of Slana's generation at the Academy well into the 1950's.

Like many of his colleagues, France Slana entered the Academy with some previous artistic experience. In early 1944 he had joined the Partisans who were fighting to free Yugoslavia from German occupation. During the year and a half he spent with them, the young artist had produced a large number of drawings (figures B-G and plates 1, 2, and 4) and painted his first watercolor. Although some of these early works exhibited traces of the novice's awkwardness, Slana's many-sided talent, particularly his feeling for the subtleties of light and dark contrasts, was already evident. While the subject matter of his drawings was frequently prescribed by the concerns of the resistance movement, it is apparent that themes were sometimes of less interest to him than the creative process itself (plate 6). Many of the drawings and posters produced by other artists involved in the Partisan cause were dominated by their content, but Slana was always more intrigued by the tonal harmony, the rhythm of the graphic elements, and the overall mood of the composition.

Slana enrolled in Ljubljana's newly-founded Academy of Figurative Arts in the autumn of 1945, and he and his fellow students soon became known as the "First Generation of Students of the Ljubljana Academy—Participants in the Liberation War." His training under Gabrijel Stupica added a firm foundation in craftsmanship and a proficiency in technical skills to Slana's natural ability; it supplied, in a sense, the skeleton to an organism which has since continued to evolve and grow on its own. The young painter was eager to learn and soon mastered the compulsory academic program. Even at this early stage in his artistic career, he displayed a remarkable facility, especially in his drawings. Like most artists of his generation, Slana had reached maturity and was already a morally and ideologically formed personality before he entered the Academy. All of the ideas which later found expression in his art were present then in either embryonic or fully-developed form. Consequently, when he graduated from the Academy in 1949, he did not find the transition from student

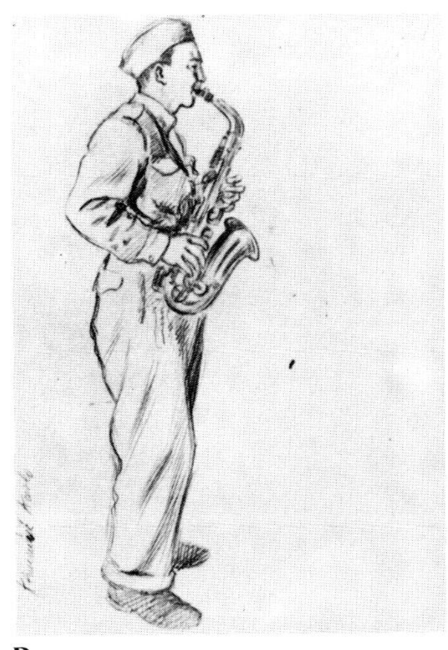

B

C

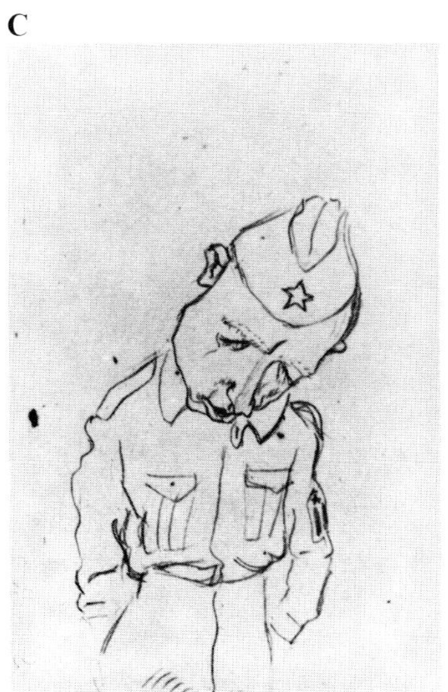

to independent artist a difficult one to make, nor did he find it necessary to effect any radical transformations in his artistic viewpoint.

The creative process, which starts with perception and evaluation and ends in artistic ordering and execution, consists of a variety of unrelated but equally significant impulses. The source of Slana's creativity is, of course, his inventive mind combined with his acute visual and plastic sensitivity. But the stimulus for the continuing evolution of his themes and modes of expression originates in his rare ability to preserve an intensely youthful responsiveness to everything that takes place around him. Since this openness is not quite conscious, it is therefore all-inclusive. This faculty is apparent in the moods and hues which pervade even his earliest watercolors. Later he incorporated an auditory component into his creative method as an extension of his appreciation of serious modern music. In his paintings, vibrations and experiences of sound take on visual qualities and are used to complement or alternate with color and graphic elements. In all of these aspects, although not in his artistic form, Slana clearly ranks among the spiritual heirs of the early twentiety-century Slovene impressionists—Rihard Jakopič, Matija Jama, Ivan Grohar, and Matej Sternen.

Slana's vehicles of expression are traditional: drawing, watercolor, and oil painting. His constant search for the full range of effects attainable in each of these media, however, has inspired him to use these materials in his own way. He is able to subordinate the technical aspects of a work to his refined sensitivity and visual conception of its subject, selecting a specific technique for a particular creative task.

Watercolor has always been the artist's favorite companion

on his many aesthetic journeys, the primary means by which he has recorded his impressions and documented his experiences. In the course of Slana's technical development, his use of this medium has undergone innumerable revisions and modifications, but it has remained throughout the most trustworthy vehicle for his artistic messages.

Slana's visit to the city of Skopje immediately after the tragic 1963 earthquake marked the beginning of his most important experiments with watercolor painting. His initial scenes of Skopje were simply realistic, documentary renderings in india ink. But soon he combined watercolor with drawing and his views became more stylized. He used color contrasts more and more expressively as he struggled to capture the drama of the city: the ancient and the modern, the ravaged and the preserved, the oriental and the European, the dead and the living (plates 20 and 28).

As his ideas increased in complexity, Slana's watercolor style also became more complicated until he settled on the combination of techniques he still uses today. He almost never employs the traditional method of wet-on-wet application of painting with the brush. Rather he pours the paint onto the paper, draws on it, and at the same time cuts into the paper surface, allowing the color to penetrate more deeply into the resulting grooves. He then washes or wipes or pours the excess paint off the sheet; draws on the dried pigment; sprays on additional color and wipes it off again; overpaints; and then lets the composition dry by sections and phases. In other words, Slana's watercolor technique ultimately melds the effects of painting with those of drawing and even of printmaking. The process remains carefully controlled in each phase, becoming in effect the tool through which the artist

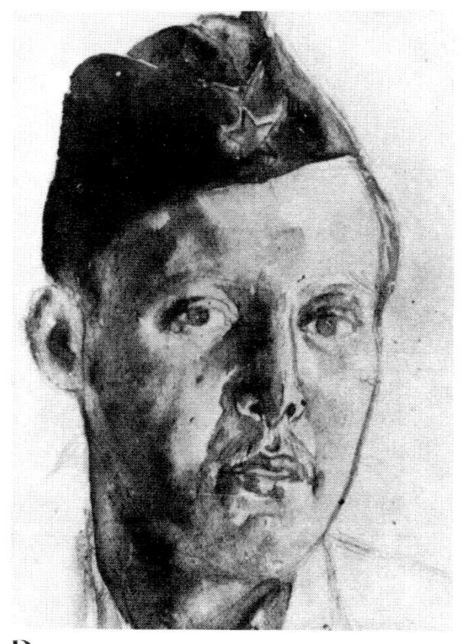

D

E

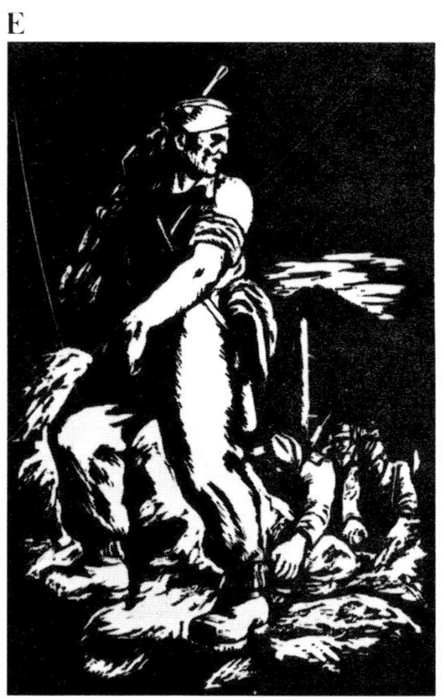

reproduces an entire spectrum of moods ranging from harshly expressionistic to playful to poetic.

Slana's great technical skill and control over the creative process are equally apparent in his works in oil. In some of his paintings the theme is dominant; in others optical effects are more important. His focus may shift from a general emphasis on an entire work to a special interest in a detail. A highly varied use of the medium enables Slana to create in one painting a refined surface vibrating with color and punctuated by a few outlines, and in another an image composed almost entirely of graphic elements. He always builds up his pictures synthetically, structuring the whole without neglecting the expressive possibilities of color or line as independent elements.

Slana has never lacked subjects to paint. Initially, artistic tradition led him to render conventional, classical motifs. Surprisingly, as his inventory of themes gradually increased, his sphere of interest became narrower for a while, and he concentrated mainly on what was closest to him: his immediate surroundings, his house, and his studio. Later, as a result of travel and a growing fascination with sports, this circle again widened to include more of the outside world, and this in turn was reflected in his paintings.

The period after 1950 was a bleak time for a number of Yugoslav artists. Confronted by the dramatic stylistic innovations of postwar European and American painting, many Yugoslavs suddenly felt as if they had been relegated to a subordinate position in world art. Slana, however, did not see this encounter as having negative consequences. Instead, he took advantage of these new ideas, redirected his attention inward into the organism of the picture, and began to elaborate the painting surface as something independent of the theme. Although he soon found this approach too restrictive and ventured again into representational subjects, he had by then assimilated these technical experiments into his mode of expression, thus enriching the decorative complexity of his compositions.

In the 1960's a wealth of new themes emerged in Slana's watercolors and oil paintings, and these motifs have continued to intrigue him up to the present day. This wide range of subject matter—which included seascapes (plate 41), lighthouses (plate 14), sandbanks littered with jetsam, boats (plate 45), fish, ancient barns, hayricks, rows of suburban gables, the woods during the spring thaw, cats, cocks, bouquets of flowers (plate 92), children, and nudes—consciously mirrored his human and artistic compassion and introduced an inobtrusive symbolism into his works.

While Slana is always experimenting and seeking new means of artistic expression, he is not a proponent of the various *avant-garde* movements in modern art. In his paintings there is no overt criticism of so-called revolutionary trends, but it is apparent that he is dedicated to the free, uninhibited growth of individual creativity within the framework of established artistic standards. He seems to feel that the achievements of the *avant-garde* are novel and interesting only for a moment and cannot reach the high level of personal expression he seeks.

An important dimension to Slana's art is his keen sensitivity to music. This appears in his paintings as an indefinable but ever-present force which acts on the organic configurations and orders them unconsciously according to some unseen principle. This musical energy aids the artist in

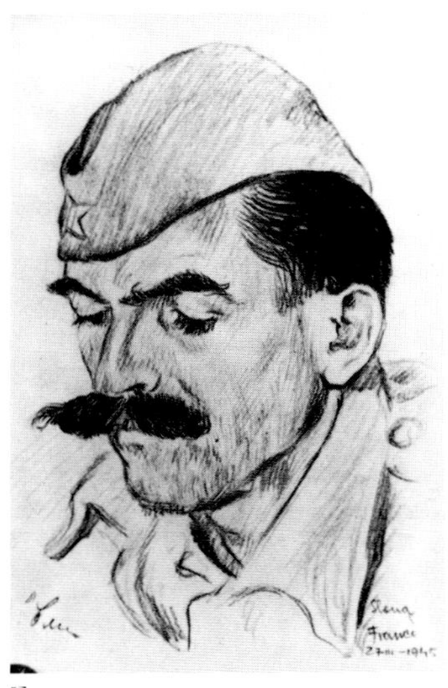

F

G

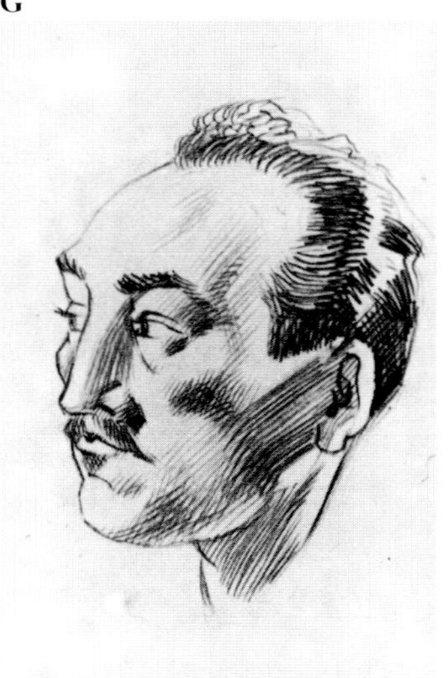

creating a synthesis of color and outline in his compositions: the optic vibrations correspond with the auditory ones, resulting in a structural harmony of the whole. Evidence of Slana's ardent appreciation of serious modern music is found in his series of portraits of musical performers (plate 32), instrumental soloists (figure H), and blues singers. In these works the musical theme serves as a stimulus for the complementary visual response. Sometimes a single detail or one figure in a group sets the mood for the entire piece by its weight or prominence in the design; at other times a solitary figure sustains the whole composition, and its shape provides a showcase for Slana's facile and playful draftsmanship. He skillfully delineates the forms of the bodies, dividing the painted surface into clearly defined sections, and then adds color. His strong and sometimes shocking hues do not merely fill the spaces left in the canvas, however; color is always the transitional element which links the surface and the design. The works in this series of portraits are notable for their refinement and their wealth of decoration. Their intricacy corresponds to the full range of the artist's sensual perceptions of and emotional reactions to both music and art.

Slana is in some respects on the forefront of modern Yugoslav art, but he also sustains a close and intimate relationship with his country's artistic traditions. A profound respect for the artistic heritage of his homeland is inherent in both his painting and in his concept of the role art should play in society. An examination of his oeuvre reveals that while he has continued the traditions of his teachers at the Academy, he has added an entirely new range of subjects to the poetic, middle-class themes of the *intimistes*. When he paints a picture, he is not only reproducing certain forms or motifs on paper or canvas; he is also voicing a deeply-felt personal response to the landscapes, flowers, animals, children, cities, old mills, hayricks, gardens, or barns he is depicting. He uses the lyrical palette of the prewar generation spontaneously and unprogrammatically, introducing richer, darker colors to achieve his own unique visual effects.

Interwoven with this thread of *intimism,* however, is a rougher, more somber hue. Although Slana does not produce prints, his harsh, often expressionistic compositions are linked stylistically with the socially critical graphic arts of the prewar era. The texture and surface structure of his paintings and the strong, expressive quality of the lines echo the mood of the earlier works. Slana's old people (plate 71), peasants, village paupers, stray cats, emaciated horses (plate 89), burned-out barns, abandoned mills (plate 50), and collapsing houses are not meant to proclaim an abrasive social message; visually, however, they are the immediate descendants of the art of the previous generation.

But even though his fluent, richly-colored paintings grow out of certain aspects of Yugoslavia's artistic tradition, Slana does not look to the past. The artist is interested in the objects which surround him and shape his immediate physical and spiritual environment and, thereby, his conscience and awareness. Nor does he speculate about the future; in fact, he refuses to believe any fantastic predictions about what tomorrow may bring, regardless of their scientific or pseudoscientific basis. Similarly, the themes in his paintings derive from his observations and impressions of actual objects. His images are formed against a background of real perceptions and through the feelings of real relationships. This does not mean that he must forgo all interest in things which are old or have vanished, though. In keeping with his persistently romantic spirit, Slana's scenes exhibit a special fondness for remnants of earlier times as well as for the realities of the present-day world.

For the past fifteen years, the paintings of France Slana have been clearly recognizable by their broad range of subject matter, vivid color, lush presentation, and untiring elaboration of the surface. He portrays everything he sees, hears, smells and feels. Unconcerned with modern artistic trends, he has persisted in the development of a highly personal style. His primary task has been to achieve a working relationship between his understanding of the world and his art. This is not to say that he has isolated himself or removed himself from the mainstream of contemporary art; in principle, his vision encompasses the entire world. To him, every object is worthy of being portrayed and everything deserves his close attention. He is continually observing, evaluating, and reacting to the wealth of stimuli around him.

The foundation of Slana's paintings is still, as it was in his earlier years, his emotional response to the subject matter. He never seems quite satisfied with a particular visual interpretation or definition, and he returns again and again to the same themes, each time exhibiting new energy and taking a fresh approach. He tirelessly explores an impression or expression under a certain light or in a certain mood. In one painting a coast or a landscape may look almost like a scene from a postcard; in another version, completed a year or two later, the same vista may appear as a structural study or a rhythmically arranged group of elements; in yet a third or a fourth or a fifth rendition it may reappear almost abstractly as simply the evocation of a mood. Over time, Slana may try out his whole color palette on an ancient, decayed, or burned-out barn; these works eventually become a catalog of an entire range of feelings from sentimentality to hopeless resignation.

The attitude Slana takes toward his subjects is worthy of note. Unlike many other contemporary artists, he repeatedly uses real objects that he has adapted from nature. He never imitates, as the realists do; yet he preserves a vital link between what he sees and what he paints. He is an aesthete who finds beauty both in the visual and in the palpable—in the agitated outlines of the curves of a woman's body and in the physical touch of the surface of her skin. In spite of his comparatively free interpretations, however, Slana never strays into total abstraction. One could almost speak of his works in terms of their naturalism, but on a modern, more personal level. Slana is well acquainted with European and Yugoslav traditions in figure and landscape painting, but although he is a great admirer of tradition he never duplicates past styles. He draws from them and occasionally summarizes them, but he never repeats them.

Slana's mature painting manifests great confidence, refinement, and expressiveness. Evidence of his self-assurance is found in the fact that his recent compositions, in contrast to his earlier ones, are built up with shades of color or even through the patina of a neutral, almost non-color. He never employs any traditional or programmatic color theories, as this would inhibit his artistic freedom. Instead, he regulates his use of color by means of an intricate combination of stylistic and cultural factors: his innate feeling for color itself, his sense of the melodic tension that exists between lines and shapes, his understanding of nature and its phenomena, his love of everything bequeathed by the past, and his fondness

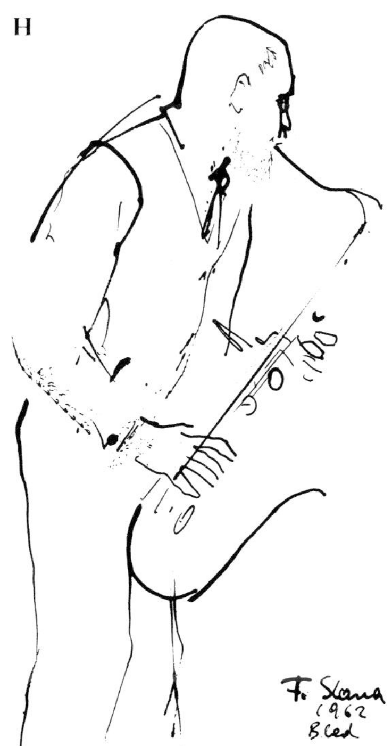

for all that human industry has shaped and designed.

Slana's belief in the permanence of these values and in their ennobling effect on the minds of men and women pervades the spirit of his mature works and instills them with a sense of serene optimism. The famous assertion by the nineteenth-century artist, John Constable, that he had never seen an ugly thing in his life applies as aptly to France Slana. All of his bouquets, townscapes, coastal views, nudes, and landscapes are infused with his unflagging faith in the beauty of his surroundings. Every painting teems with the energy of his countless perceptions, which are held in check by his efforts to order the objects and reduce them to forms which are both comprehensible and functional as elements in the composition.

Slana achieves such intensity of interpretation through a sincere and unconditional love of his subject matter. The natural components in his paintings, however, are no more than mere points of departure which form a general but unrestrictive framework for his vision. It is as if every blade of grass, every flower, tree, barn, animal, nude, cloud, shadow, or curve of the horizon has a special meaning for him that involves far more than its form or use; as if each object conceals something which is beyond human comprehension. Slana's work, in essence, embodies a pantheistic belief in the relationship between the divine and the forces of nature. In reevaluating the elements of nature, Slana elevates all of humankind, his own individuality, and his art.

Thus France Slana occupies a special place among the ranks of contemporary Yugoslav artists. His extensive oeuvre has grown out of the best Yugoslav painting traditions while at the same time extending them into new thematic areas and ranges of expression. Highly sophisticated draftsmanship and an uncommon sensitivity to color have become the hallmarks of his paintings and watercolors. The inner structure and content of his compositions are attractive, interesting, and even puzzling. The artist has developed from stage to stage, always setting goals for himself along the way, but his concern has continued to remain the sensual and emotional intensity of presentation. He attaches equal importance to visual impression and aesthetic effect on the one hand, and to expression and message on the other.

Slana invites and entices us into his colorful and musical world. And we follow him willingly, without noticing the moment when our own passive, realistic perceptions are transformed into his enchanted vision.

JANEZ MESESNEL is a Slovene art historian and critic. He was born in 1931, received his degree in 1957, and since 1967 has served as Director of Ljubljana's City Museum. He is the author of numerous reviews and articles on art.

I

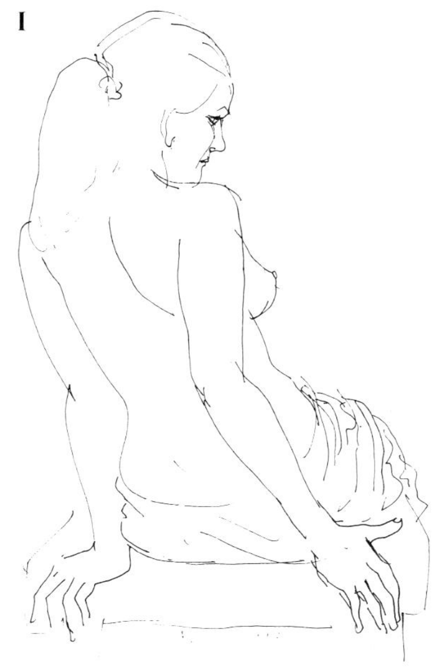

THE PLATES

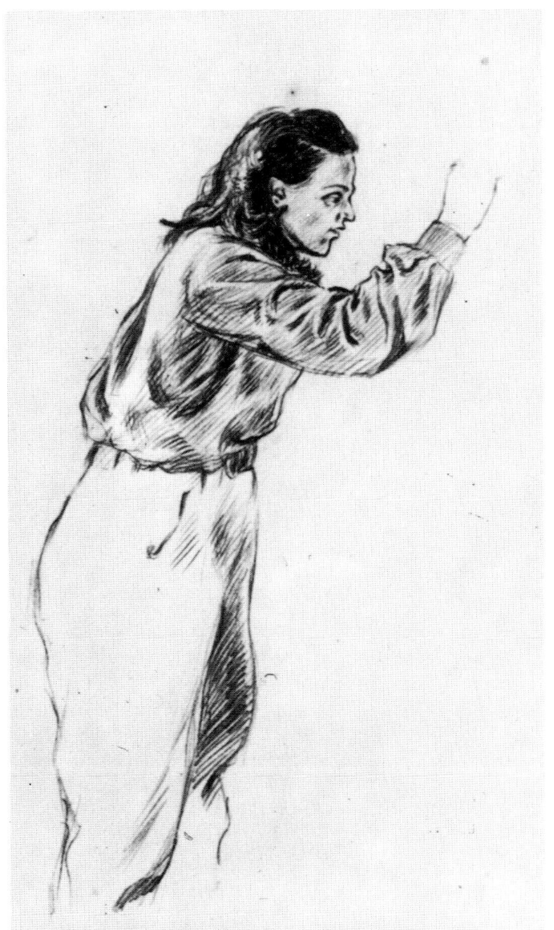

1

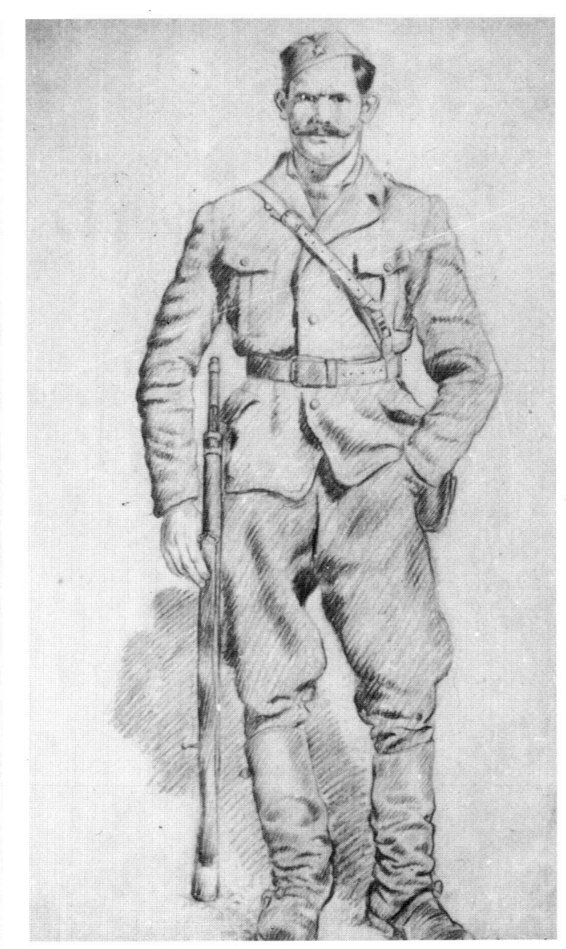

2

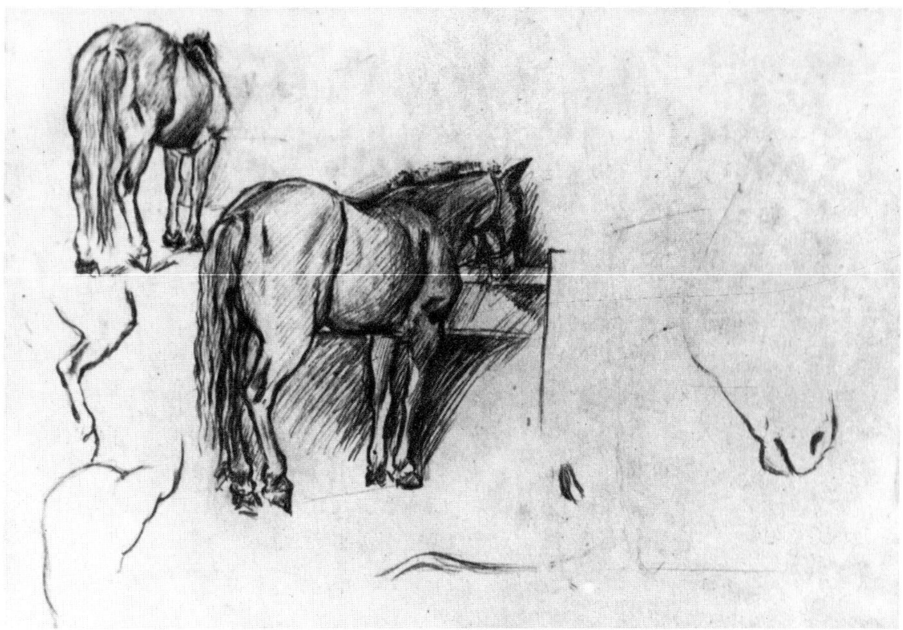

3

4

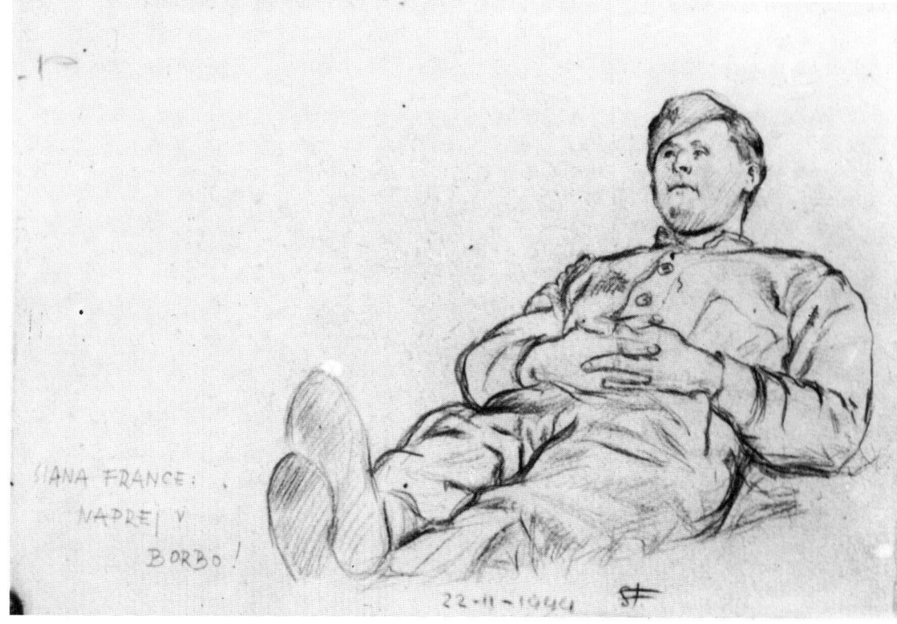

5

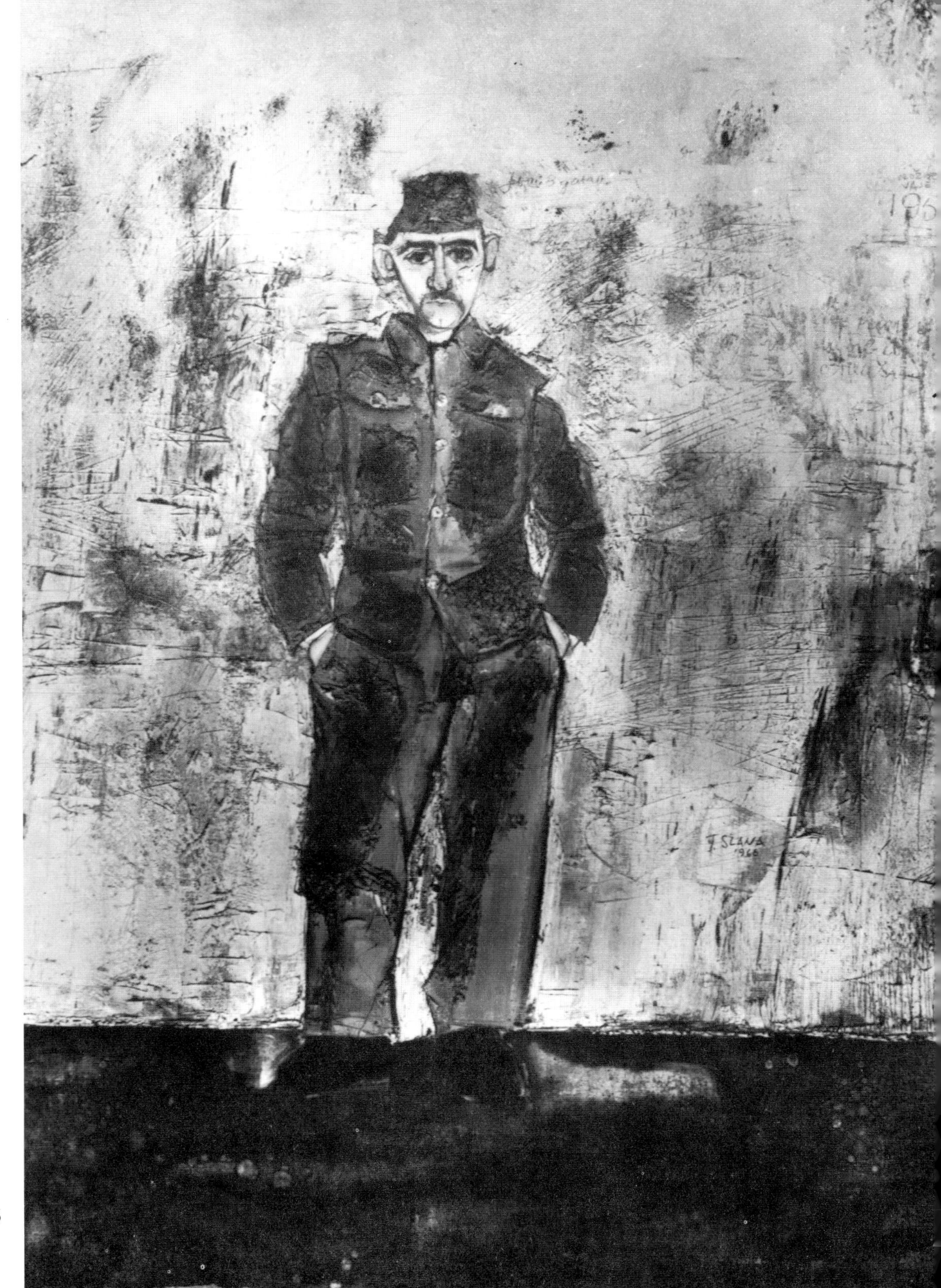

6

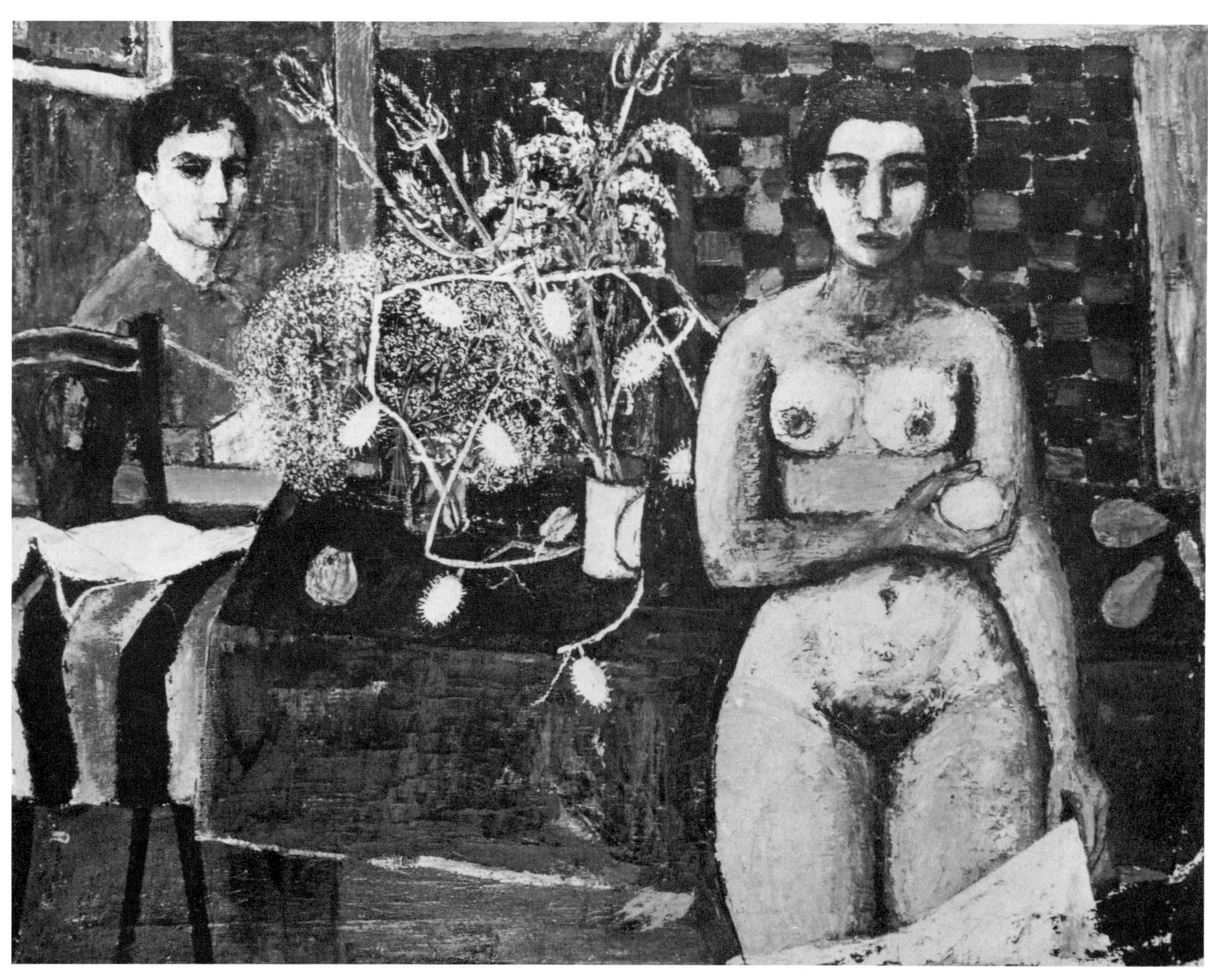

7

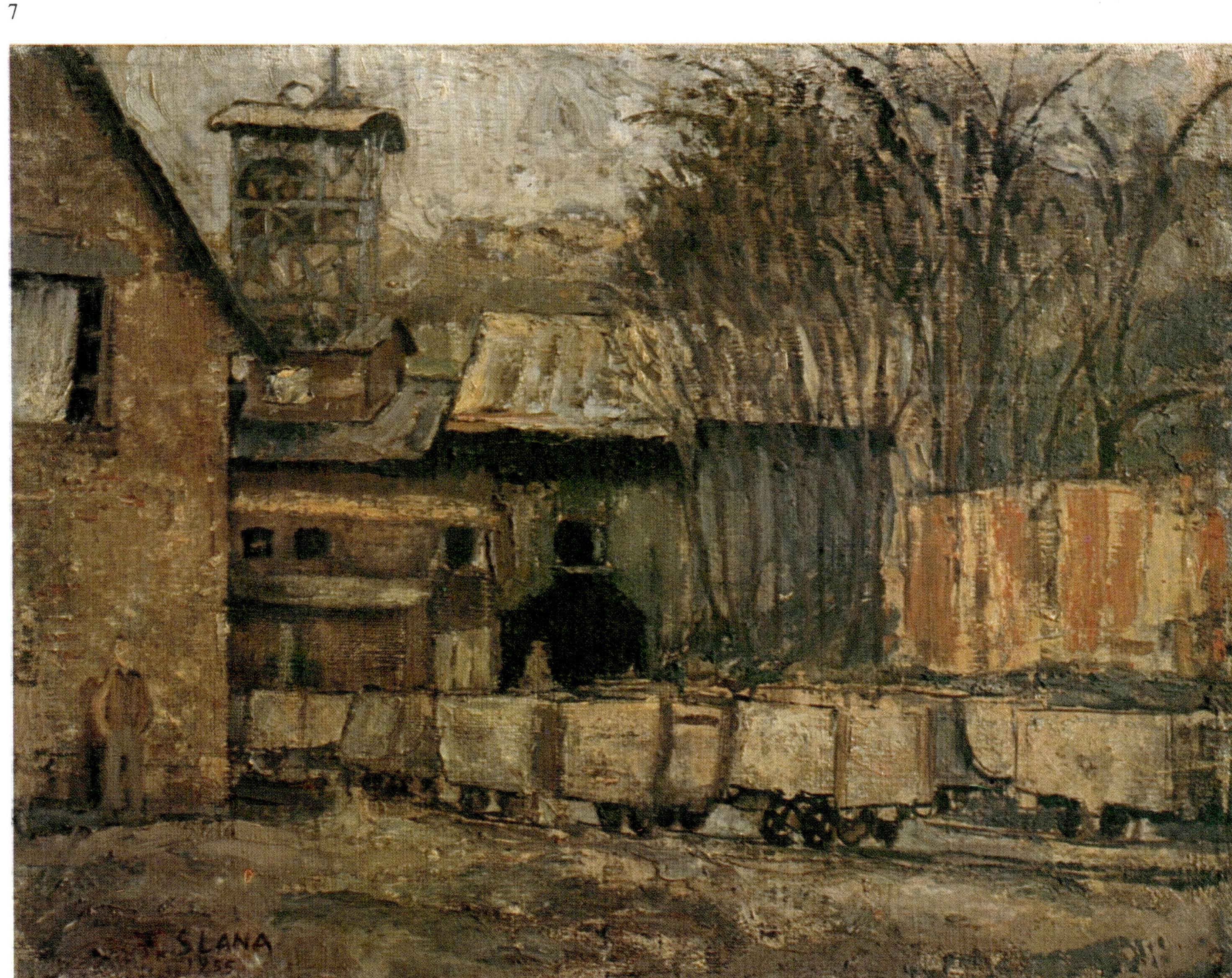

8

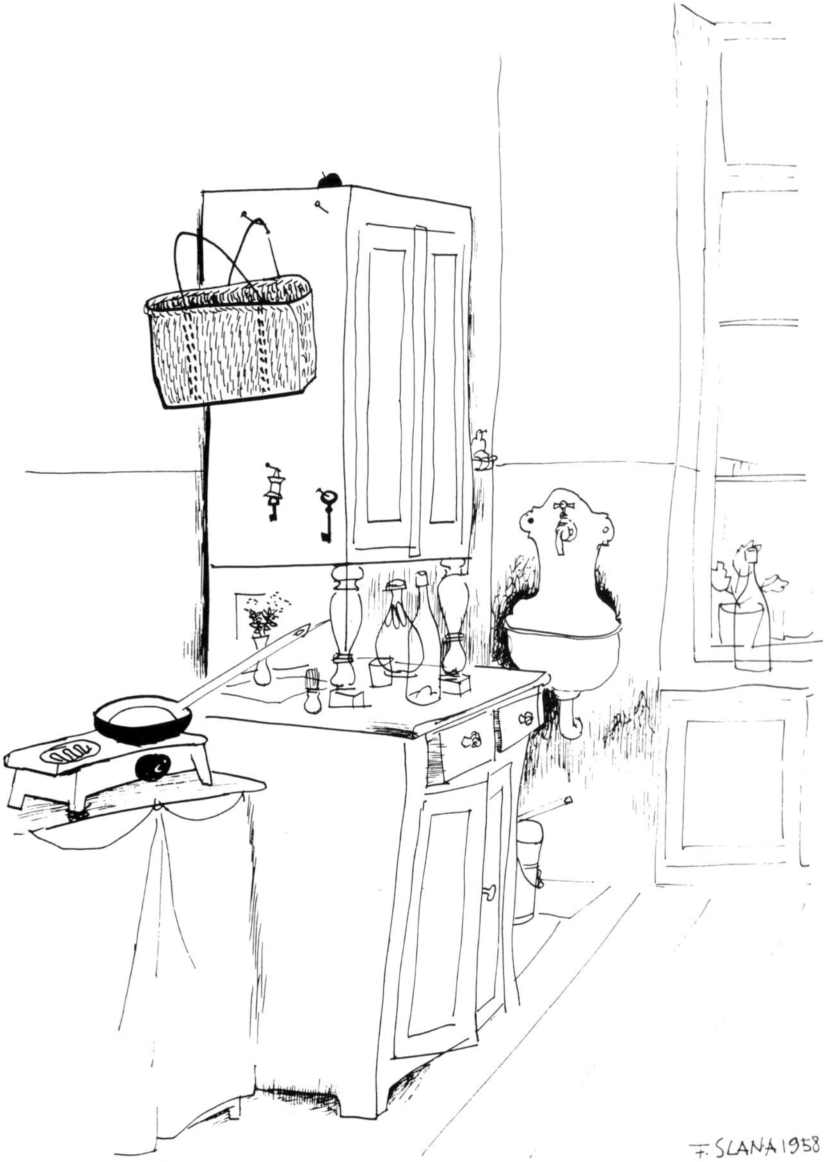

9

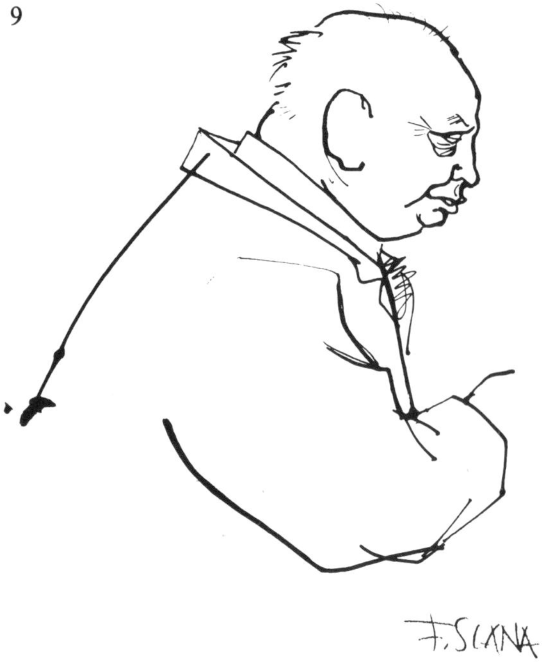

10

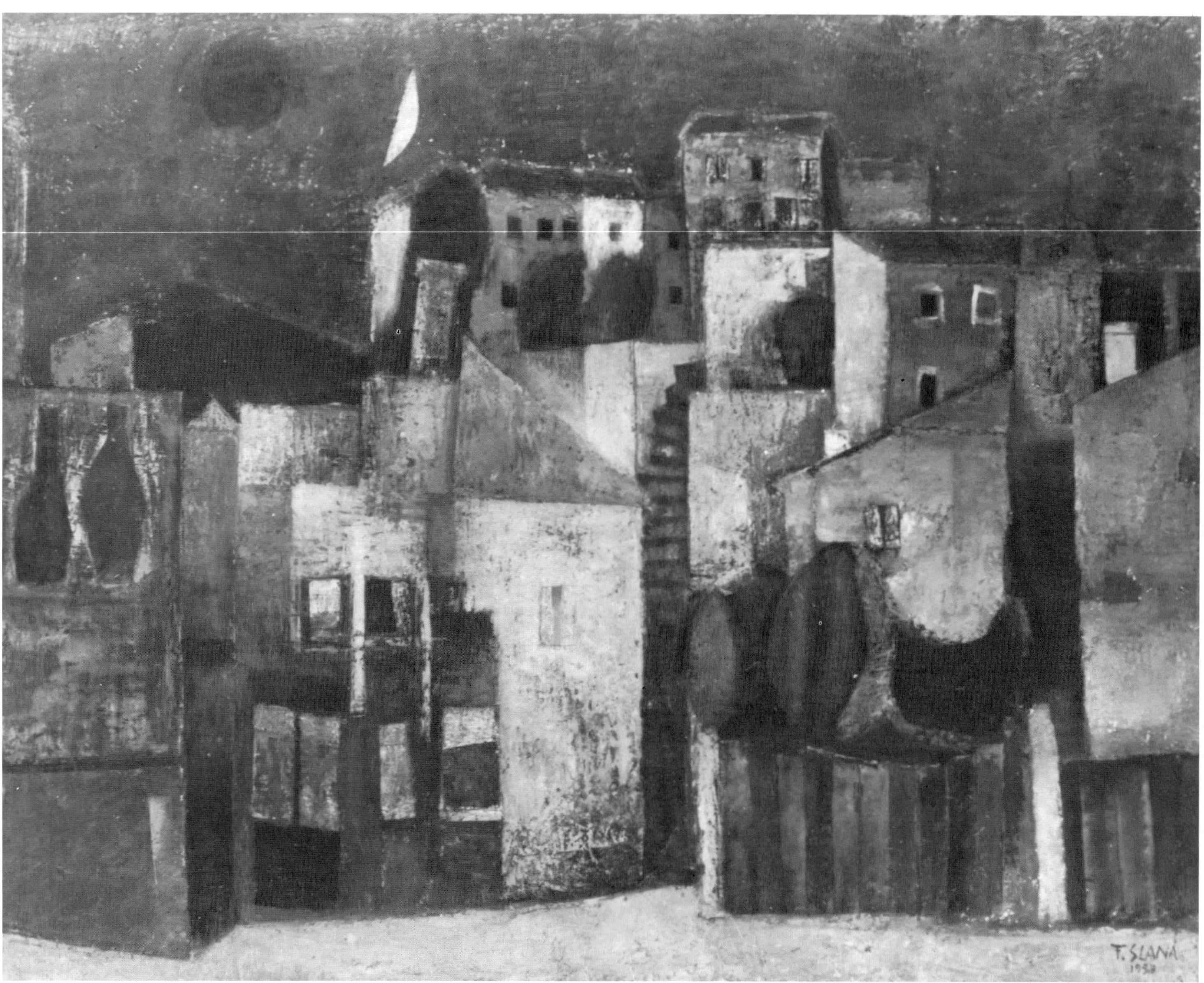

11

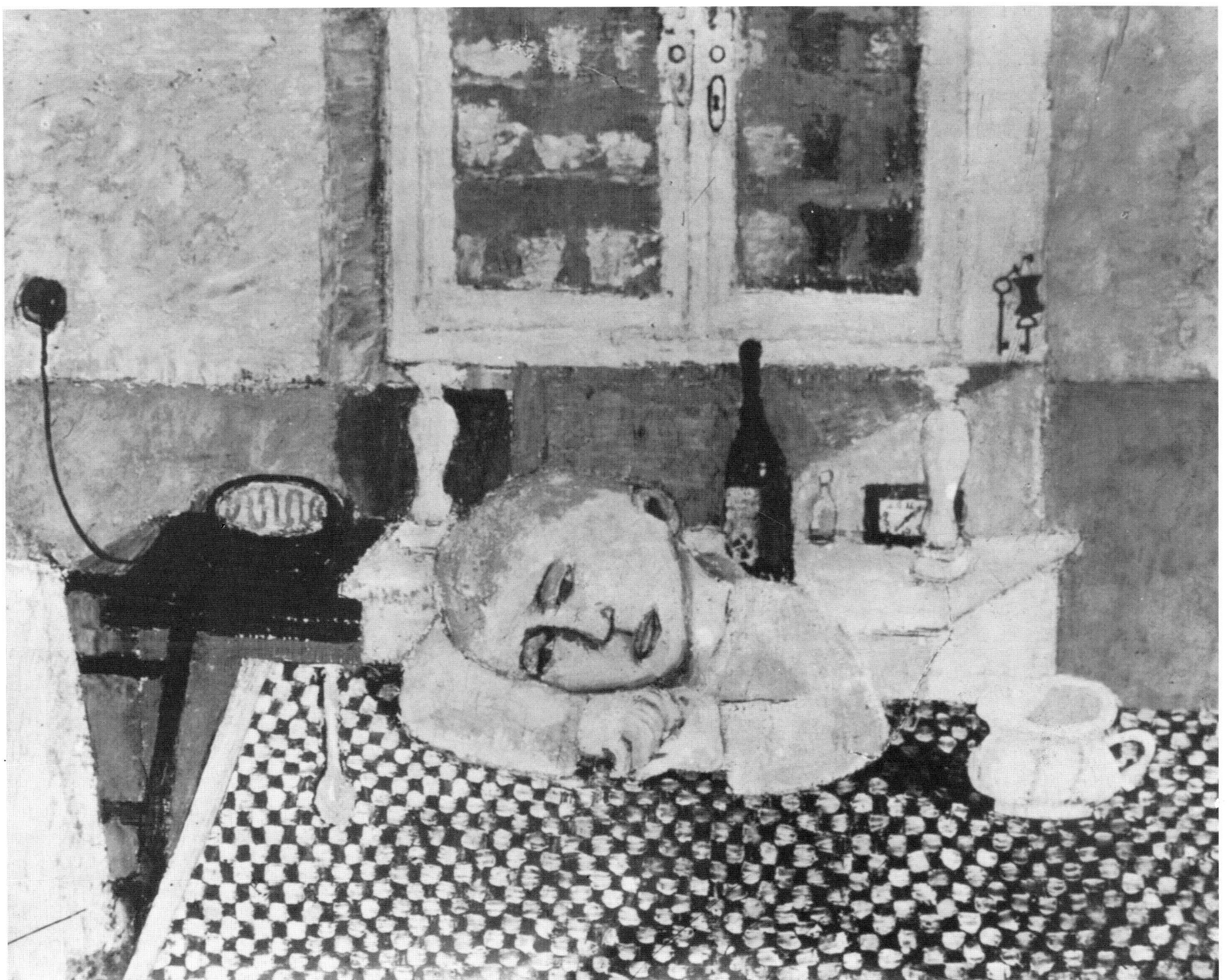

12

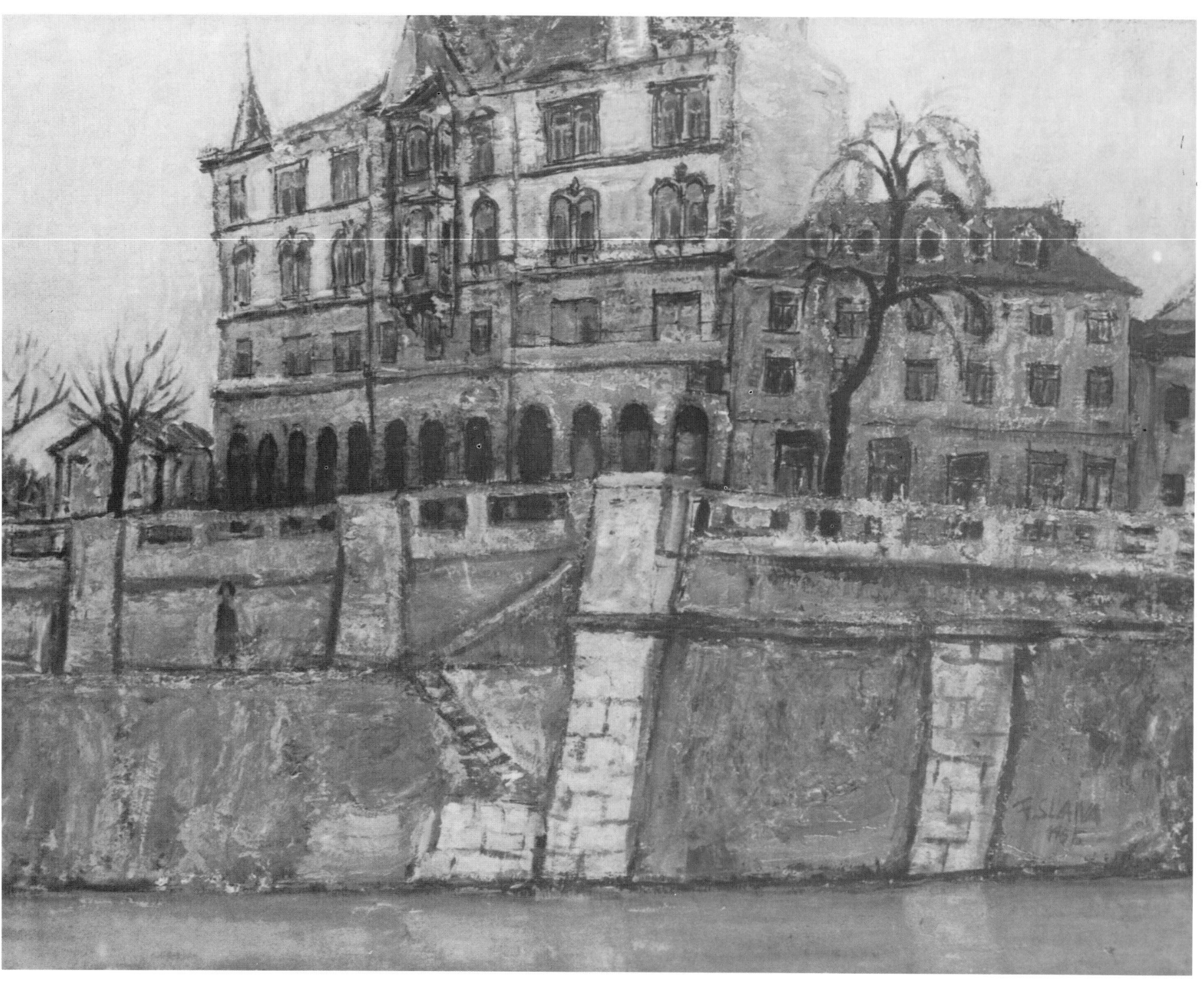

13

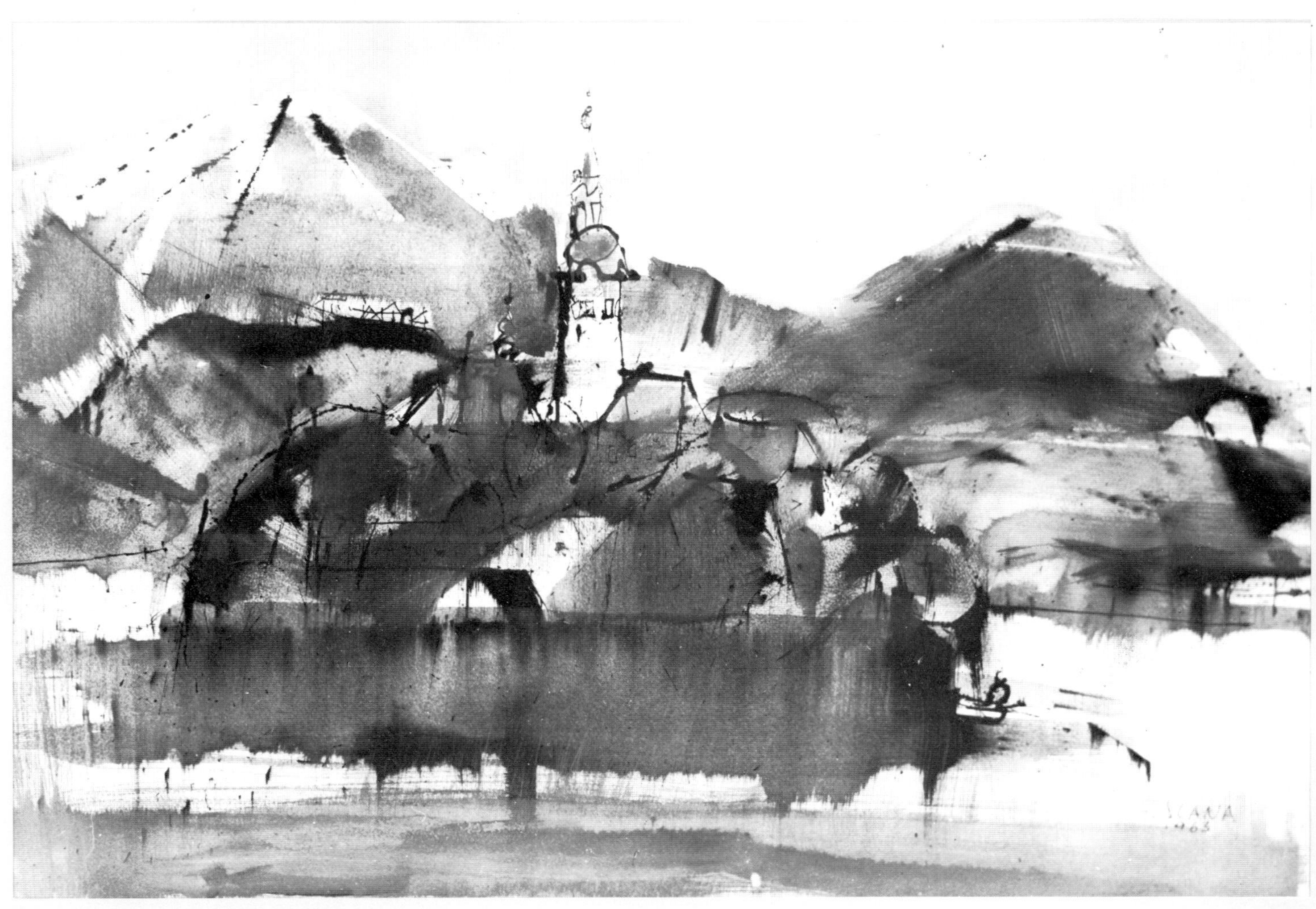

14

15

17

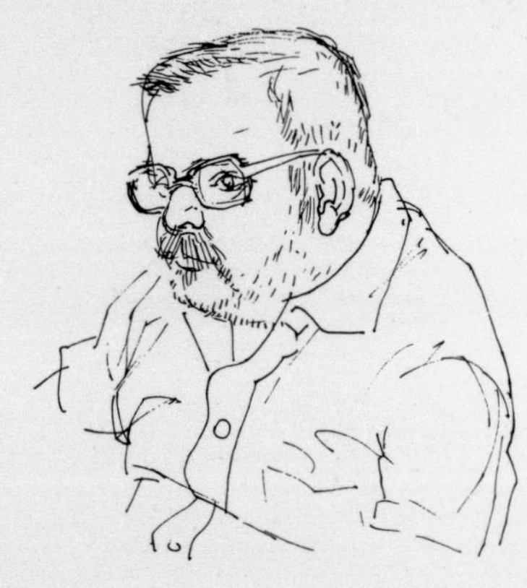

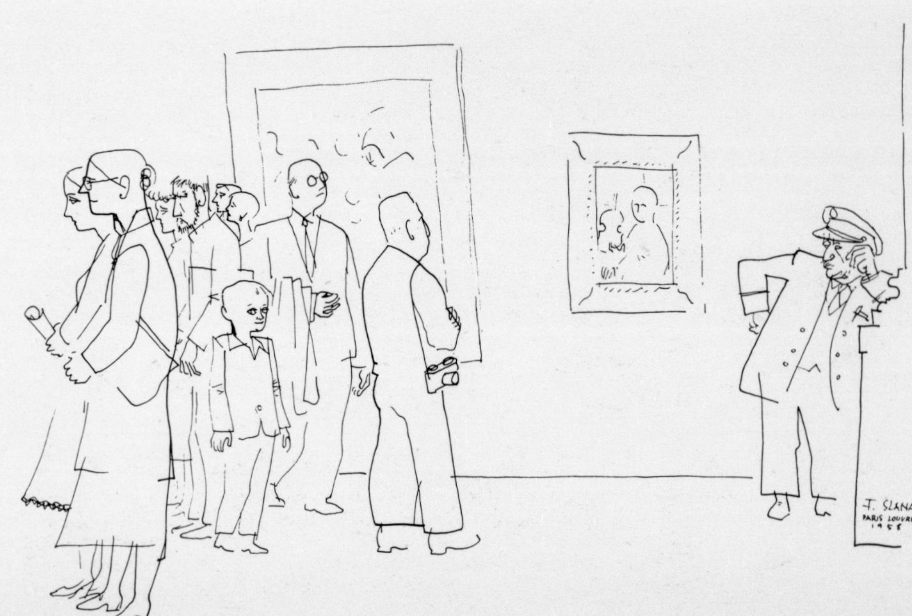

16

18

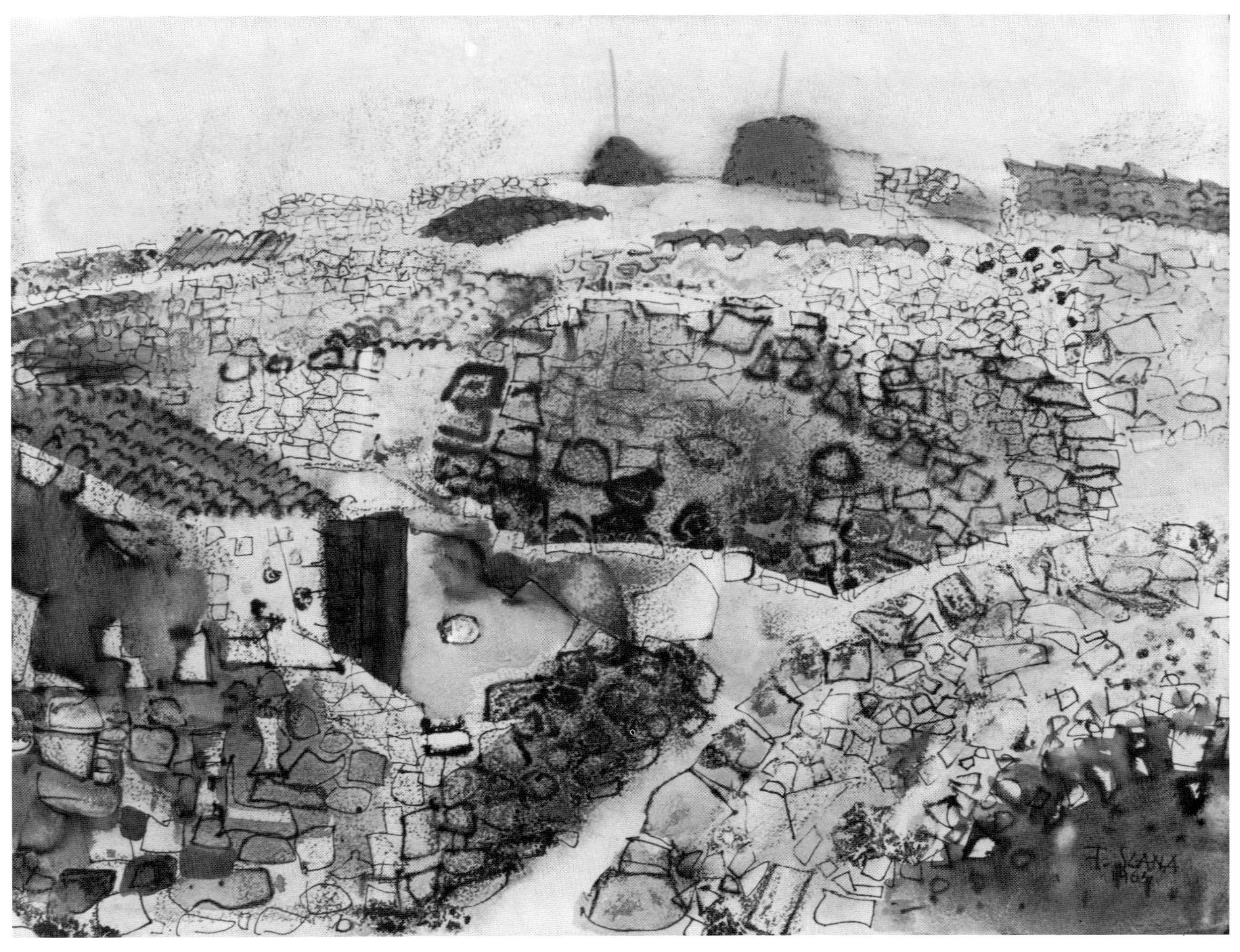

19

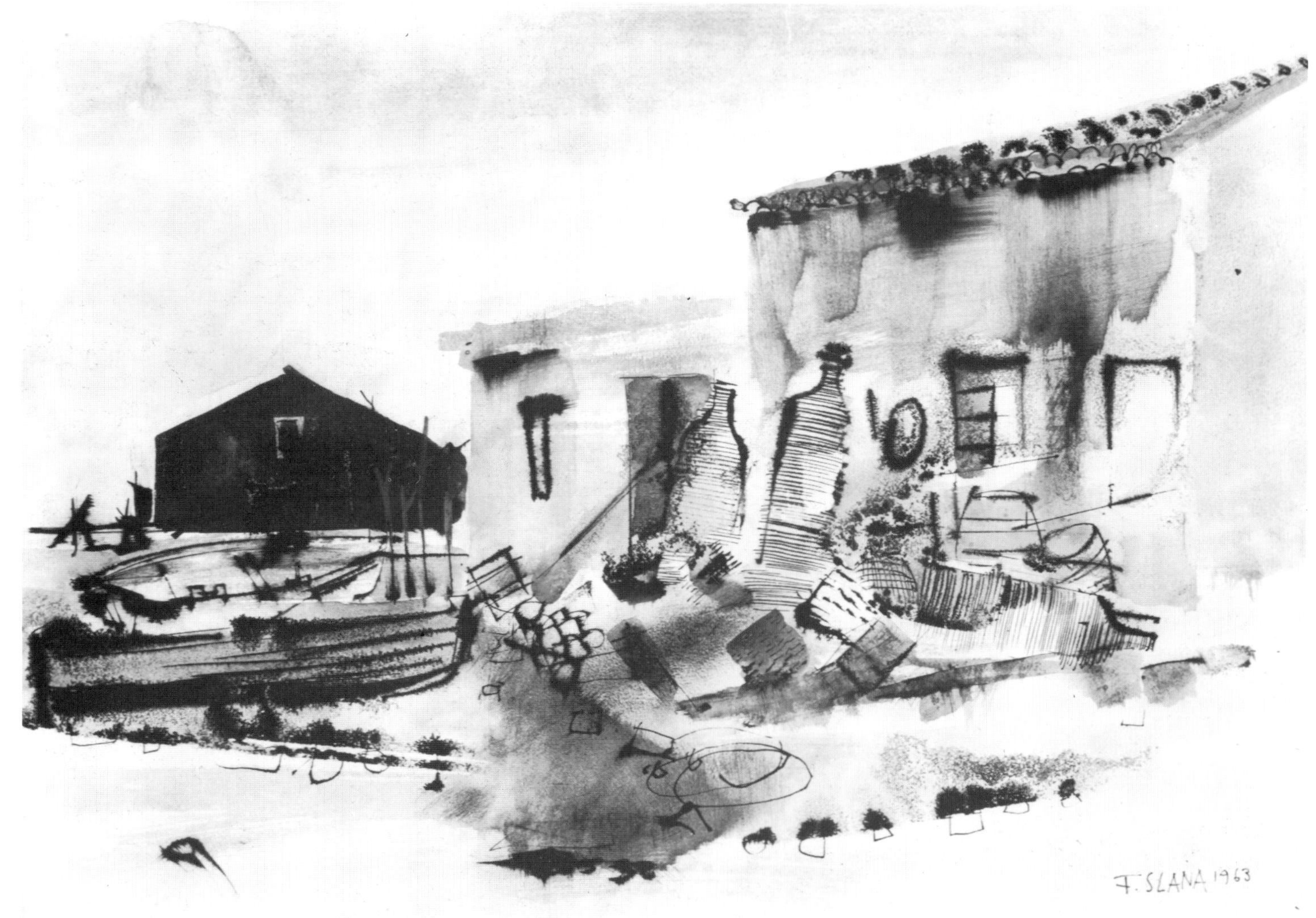

20

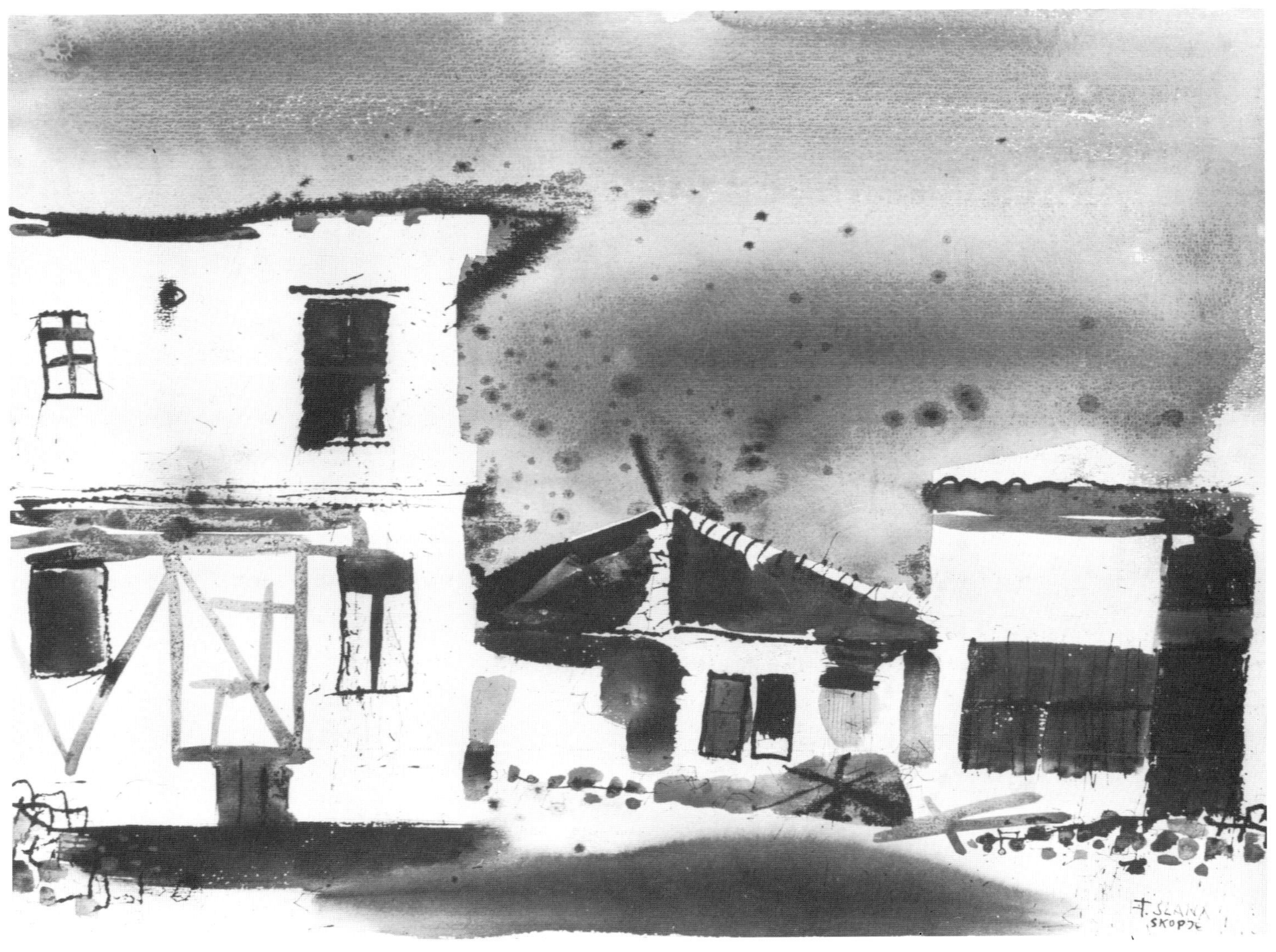

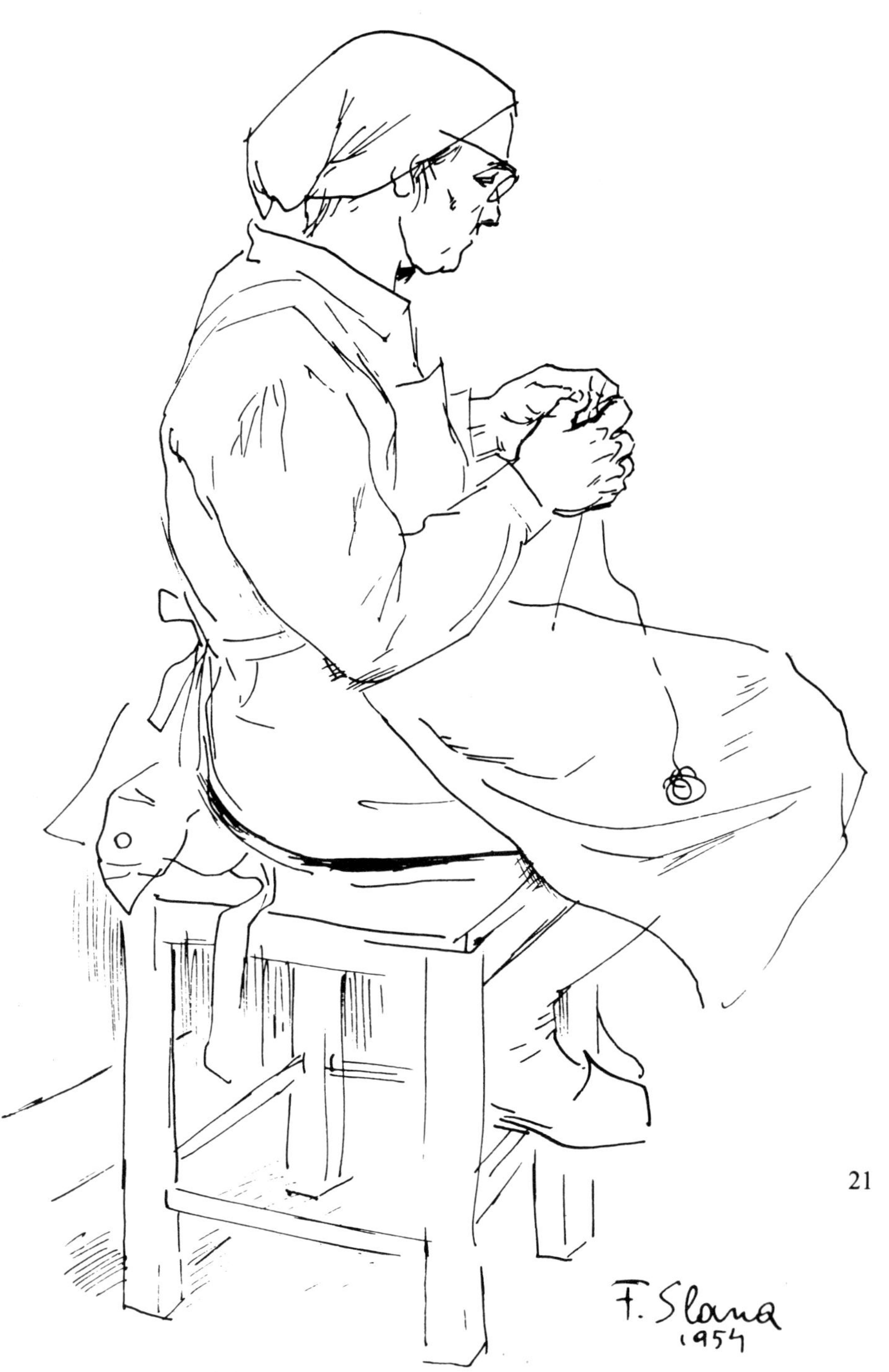
F. Slana
1954

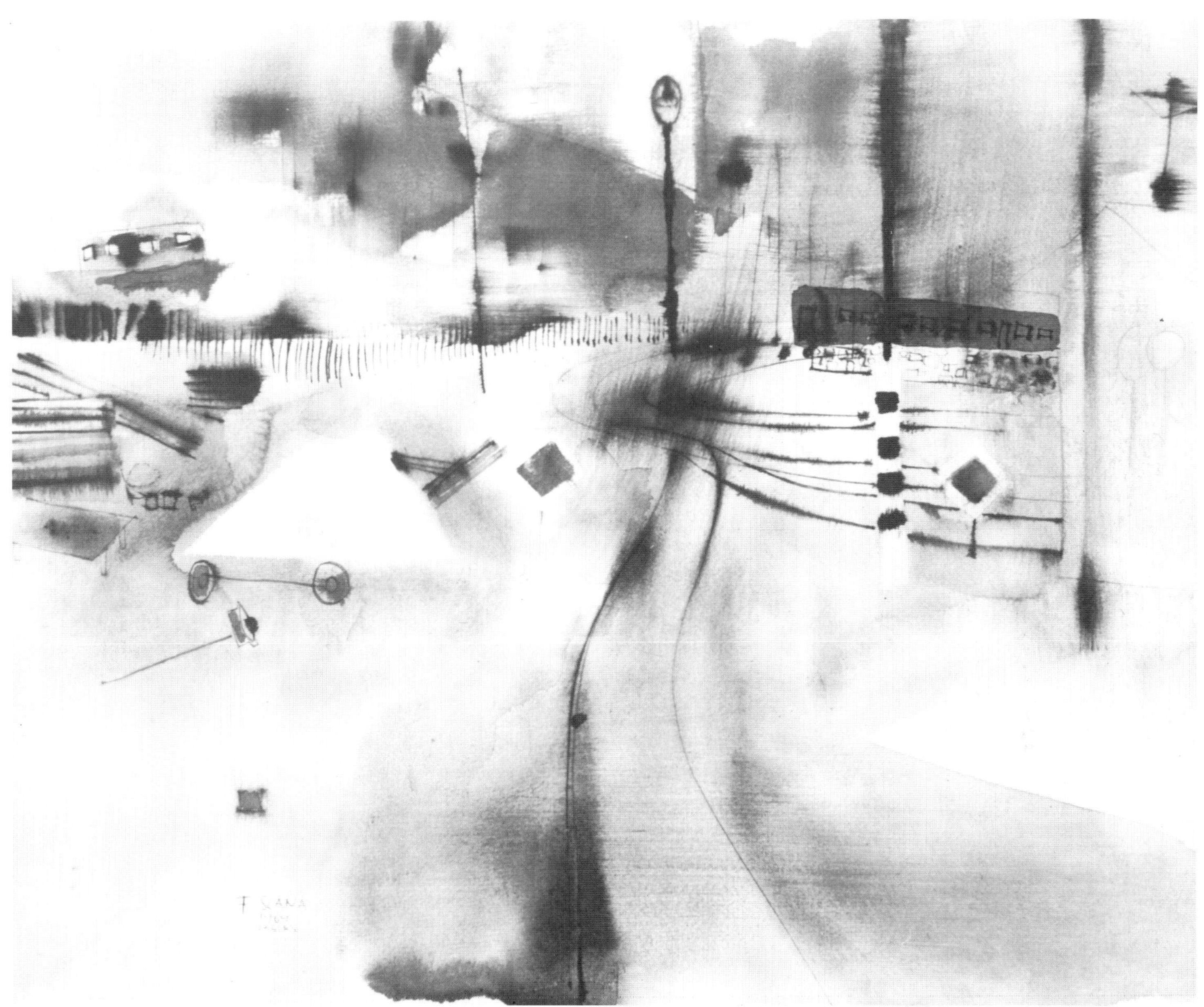

23

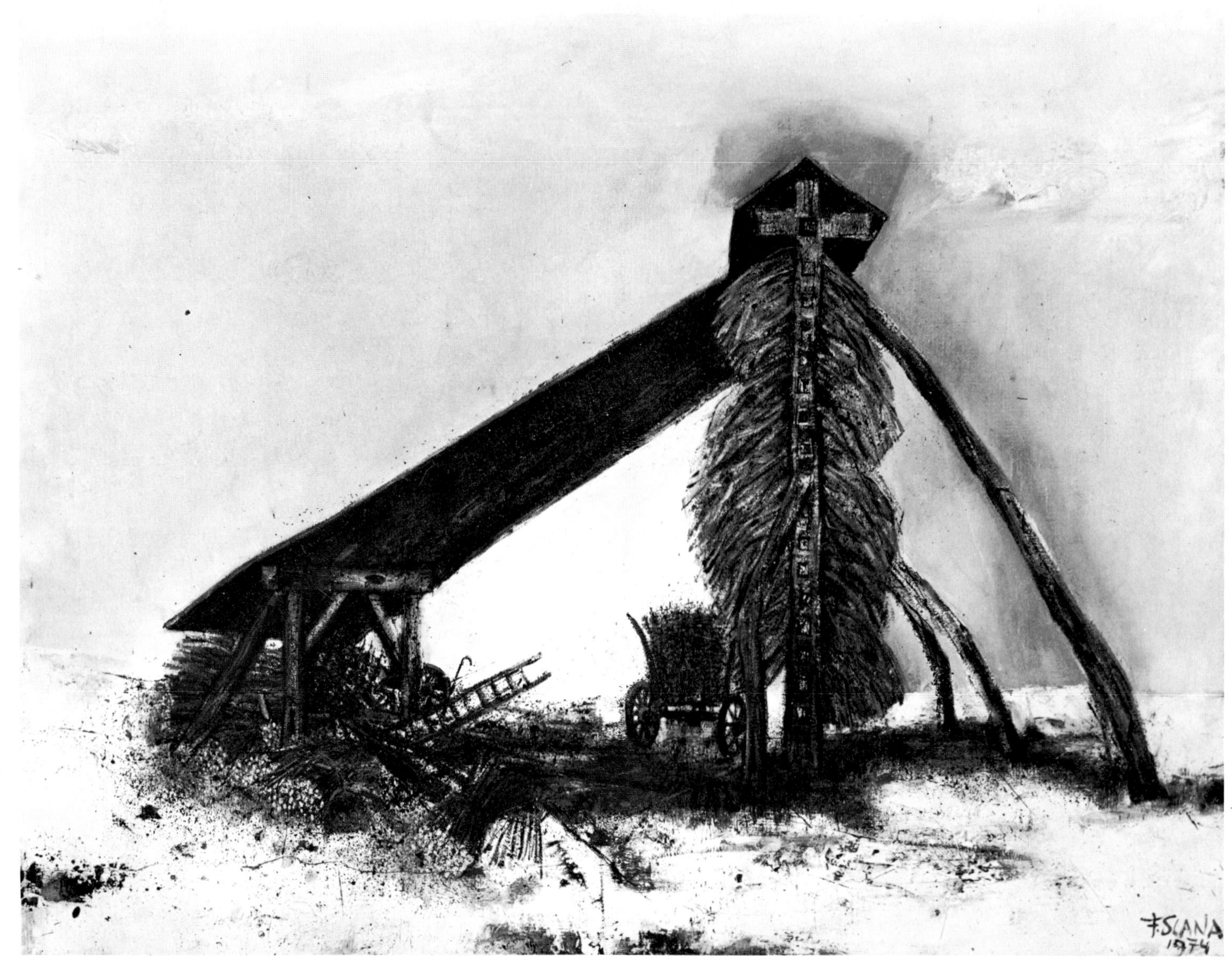

24

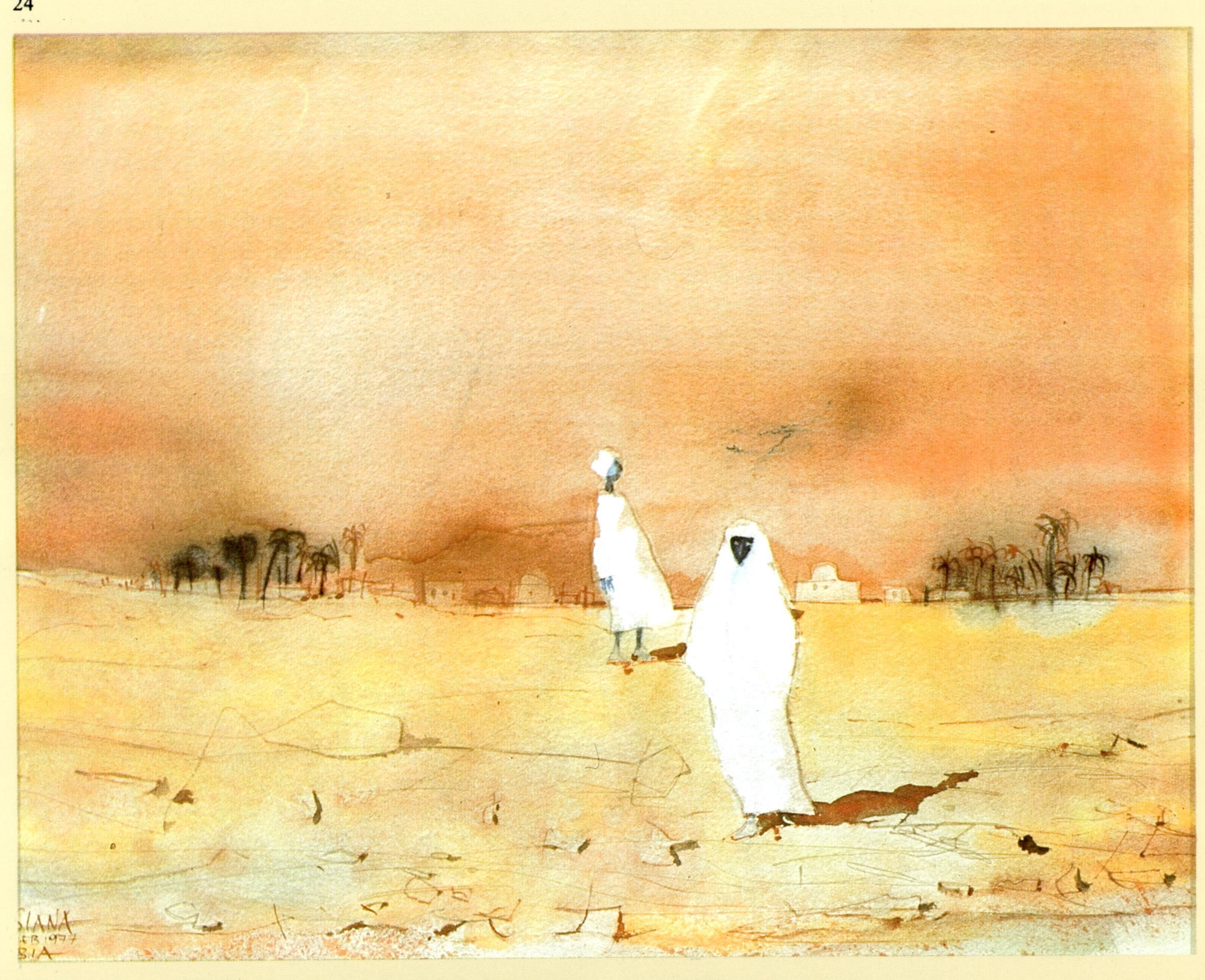

25

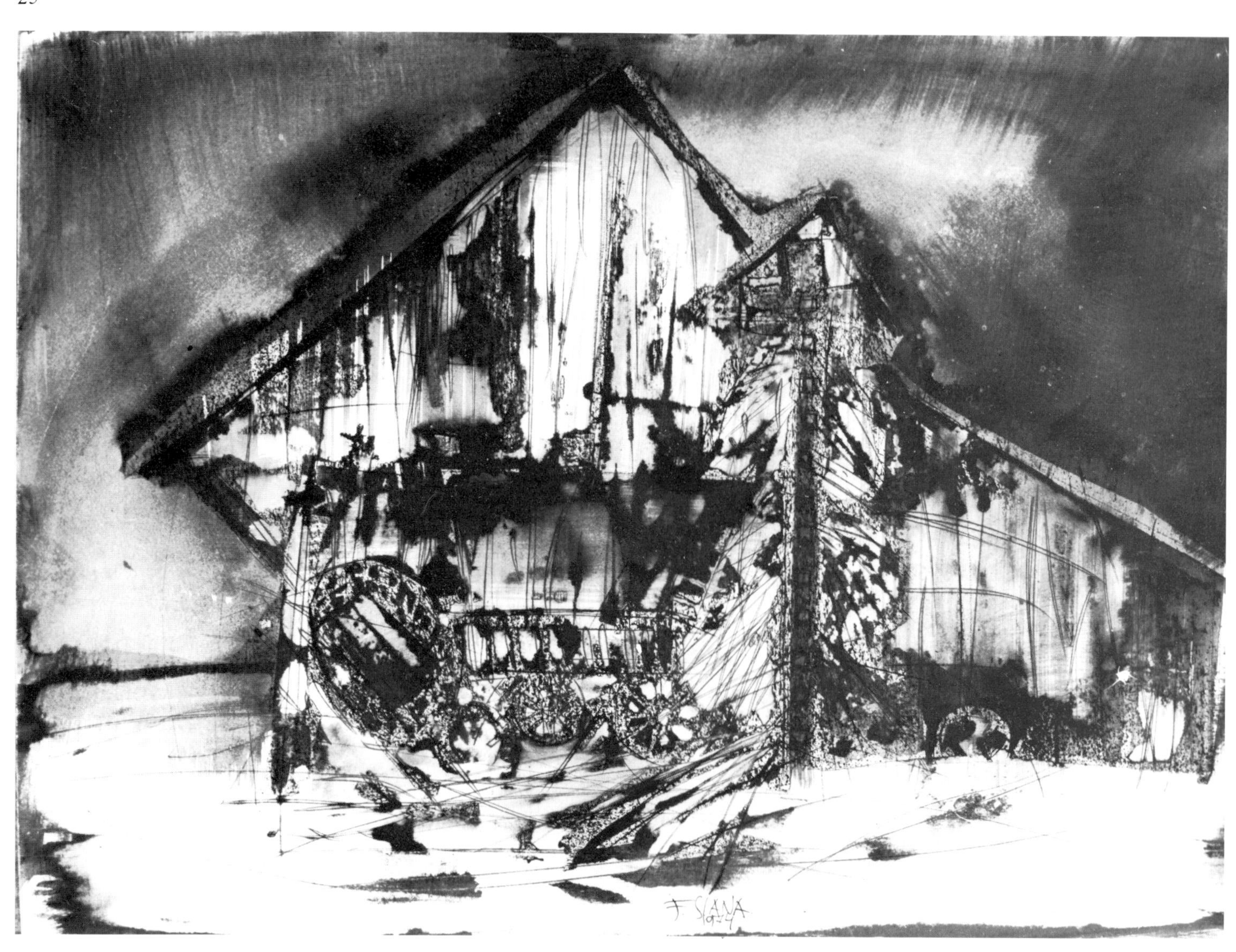

26

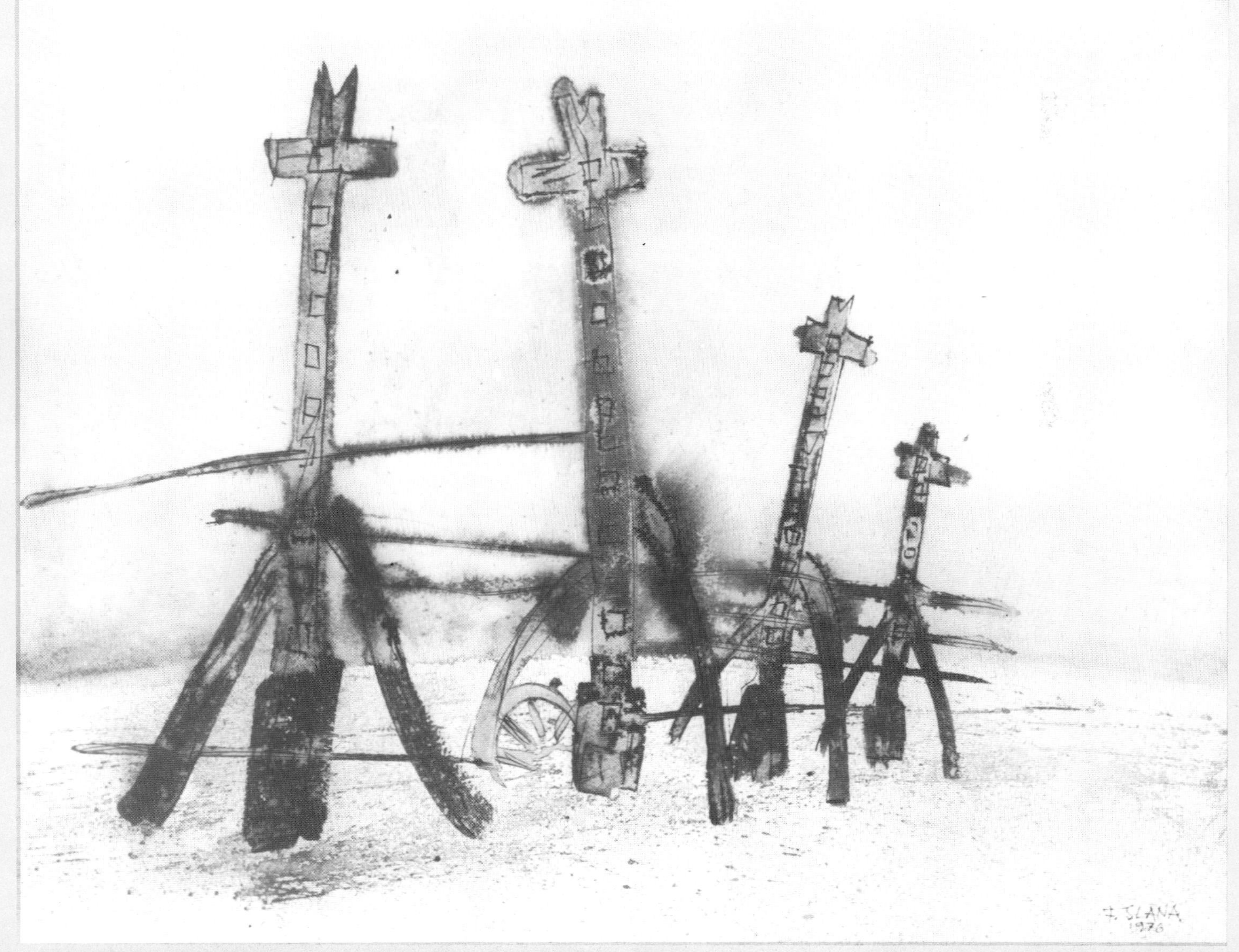

27

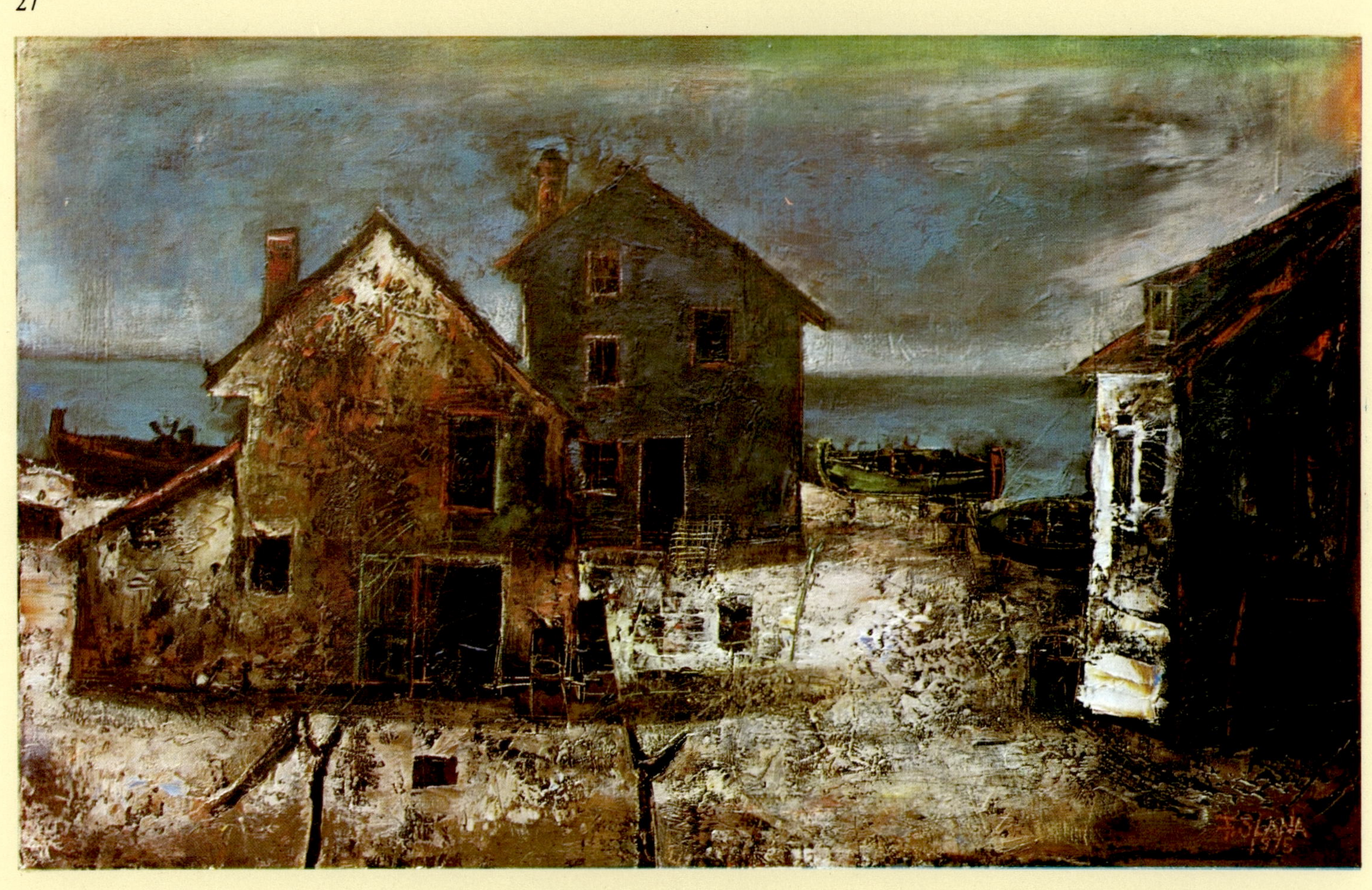

28

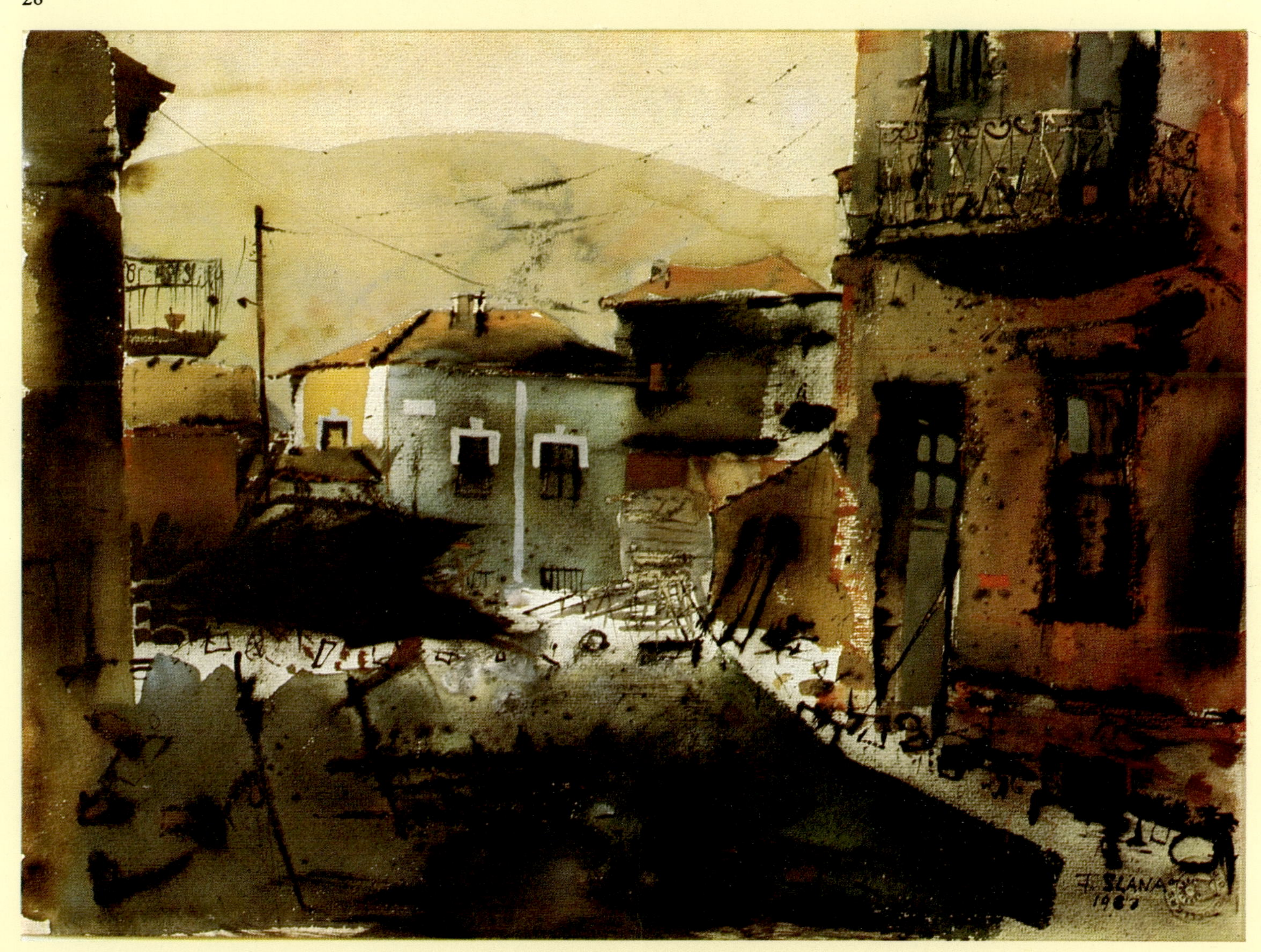

29

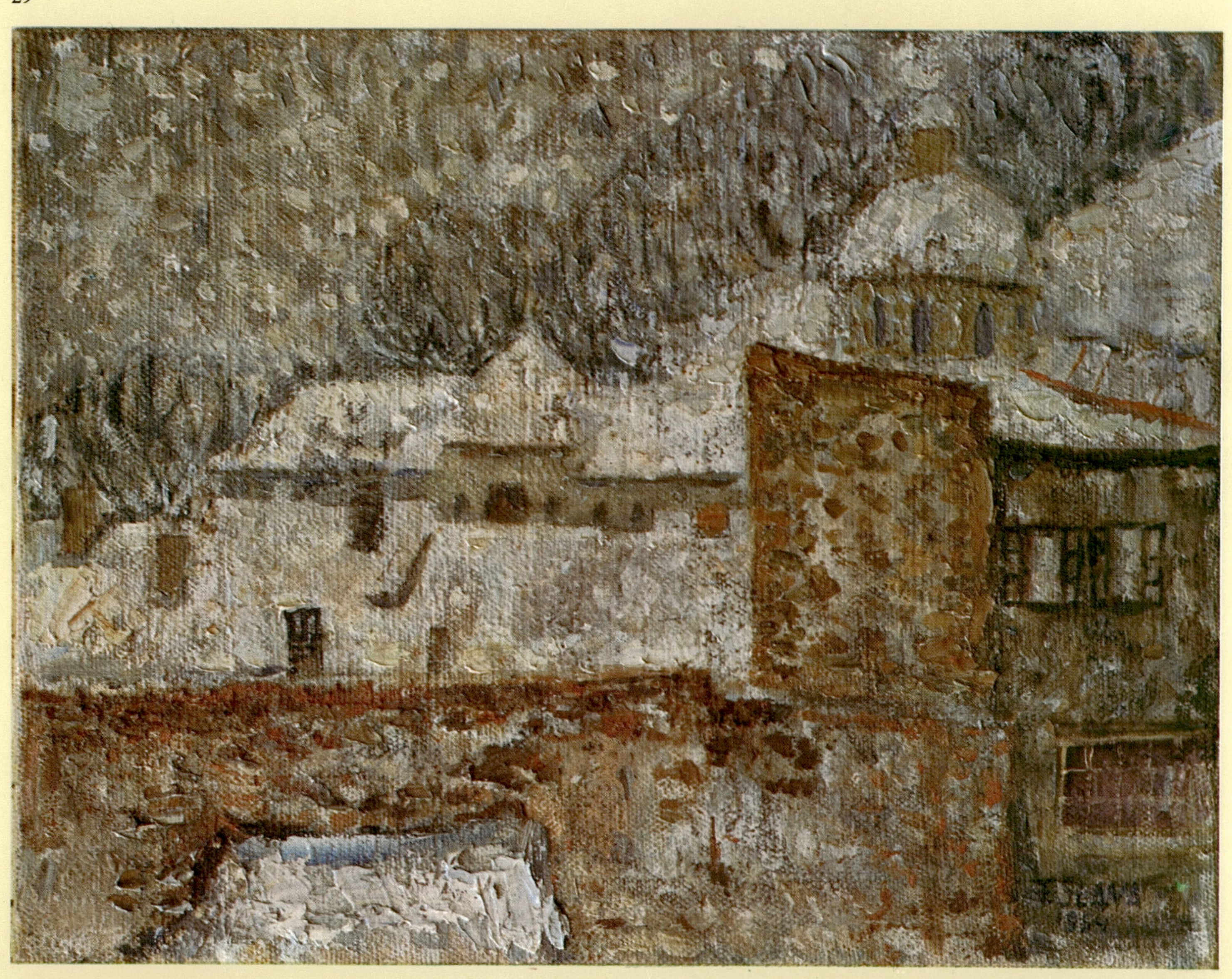

30

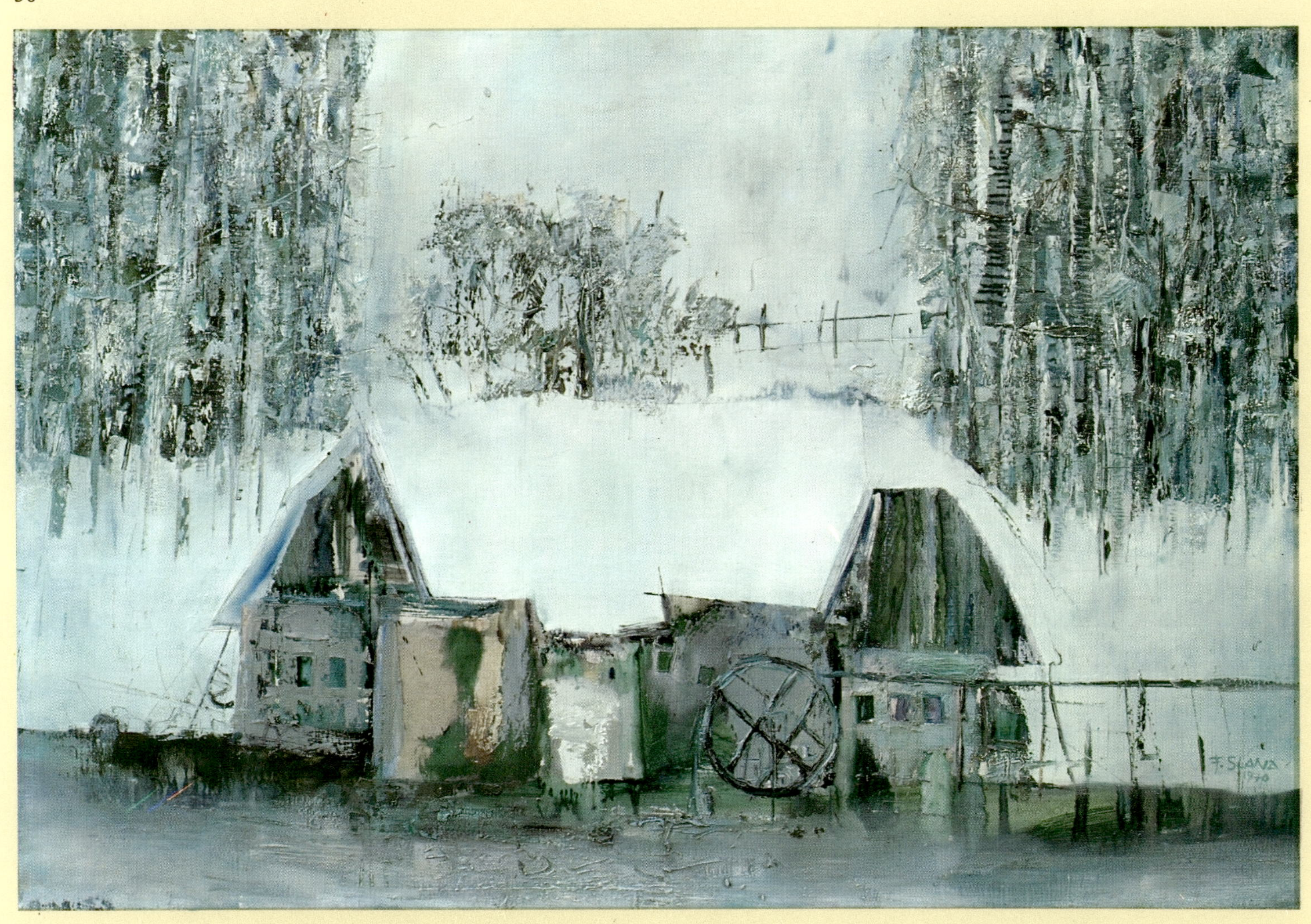

31

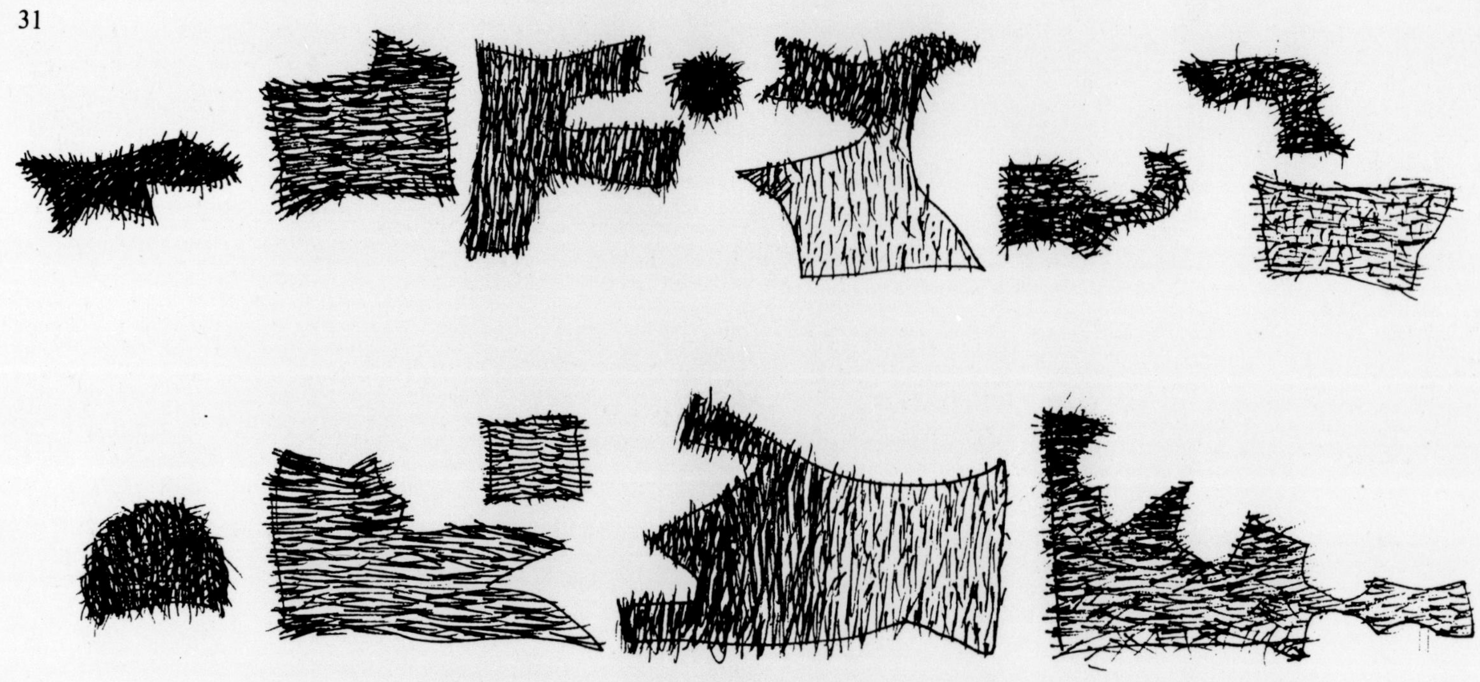

32

33

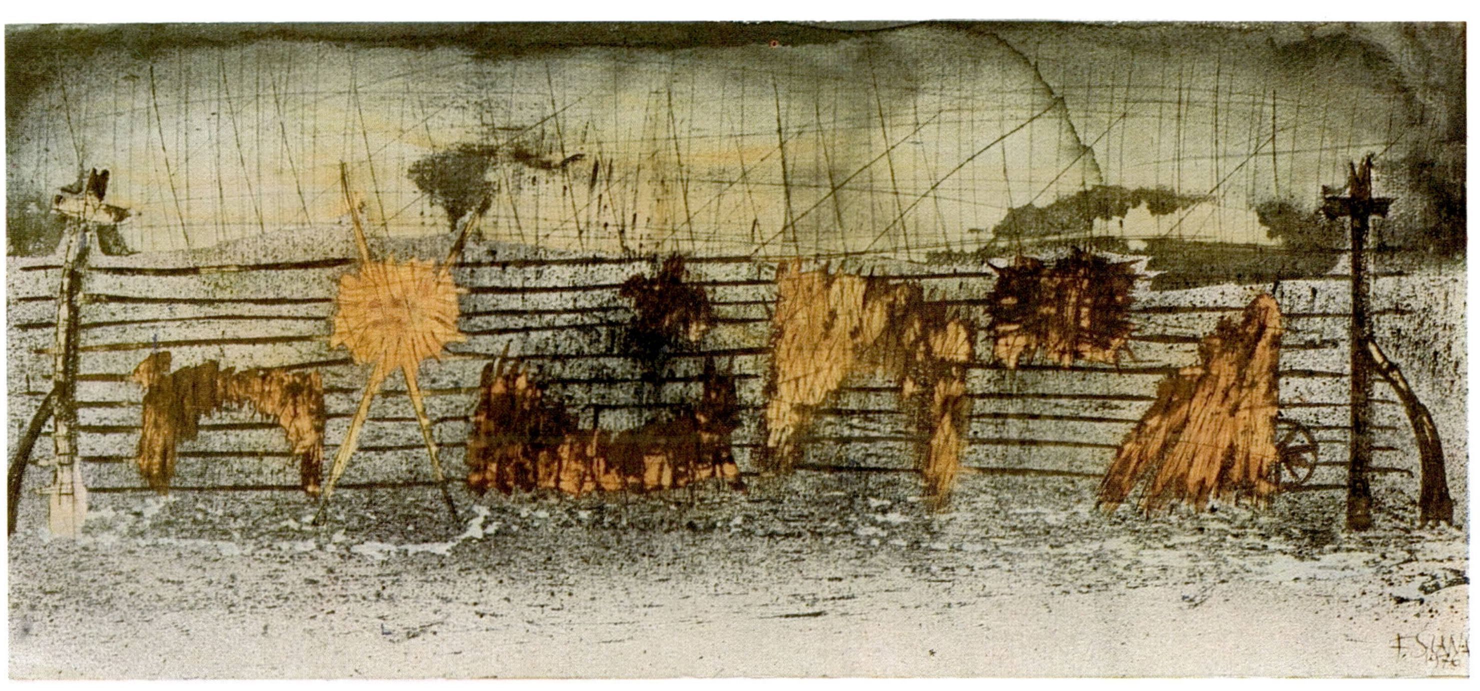

34

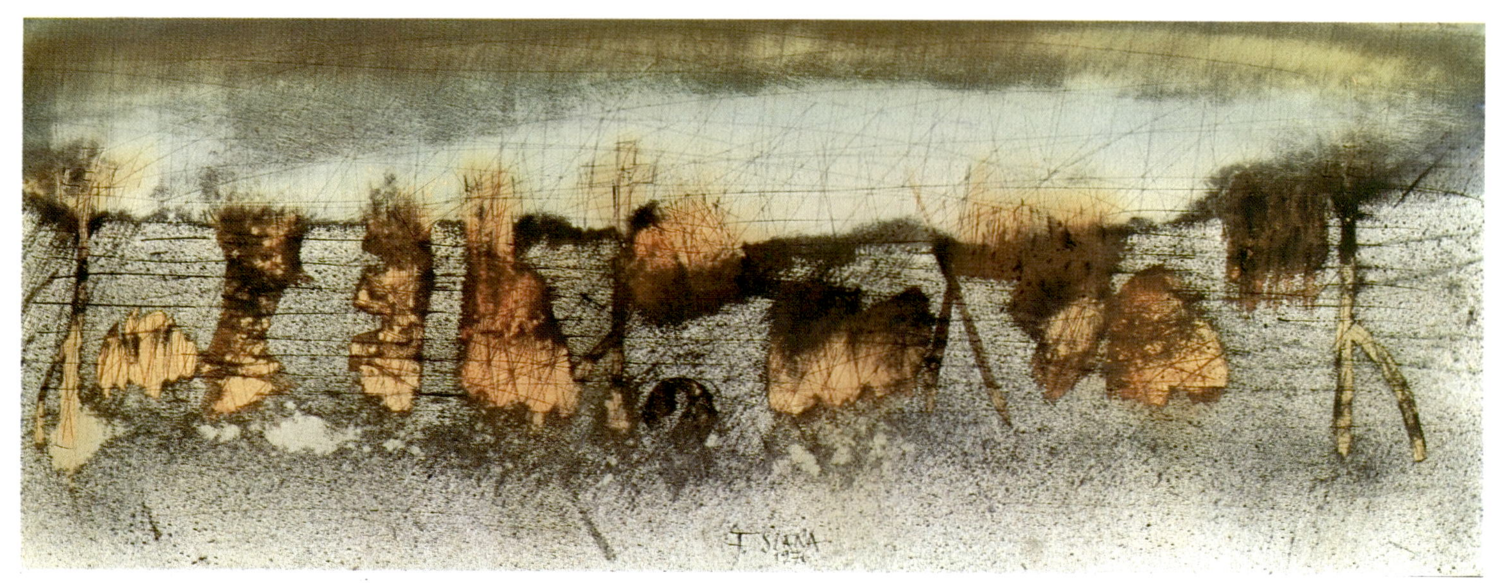

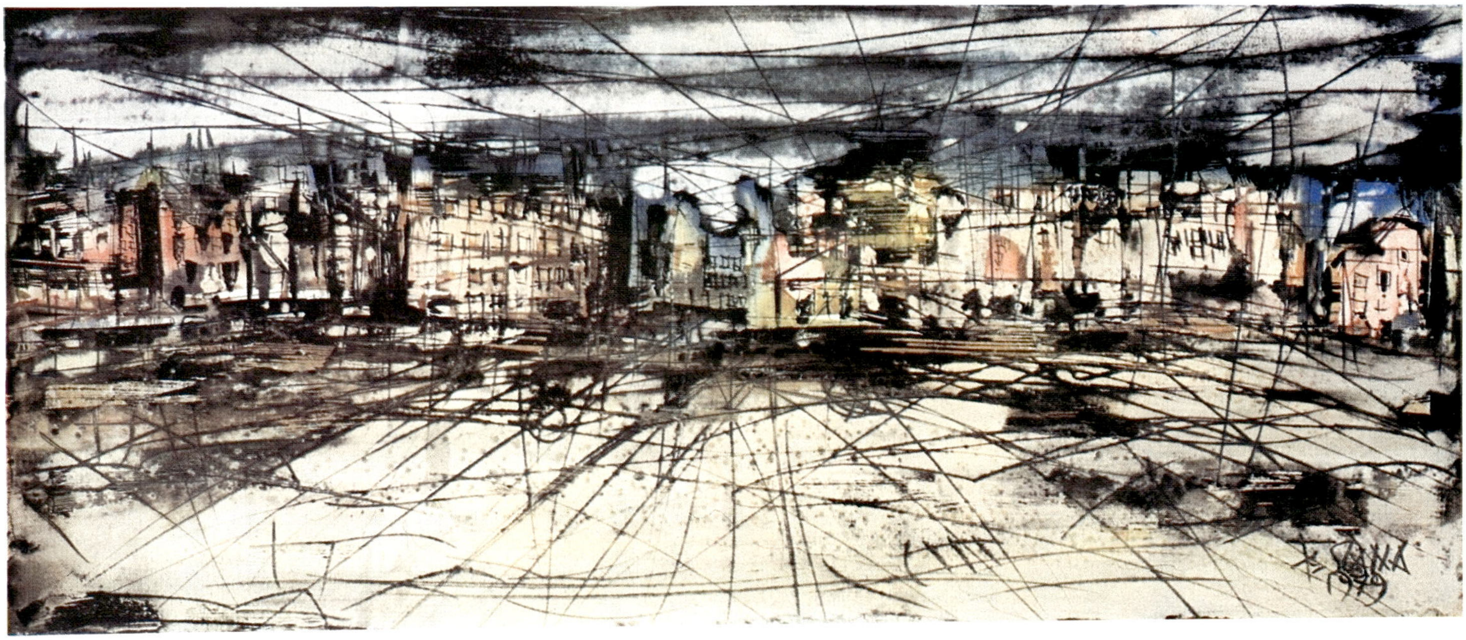

35

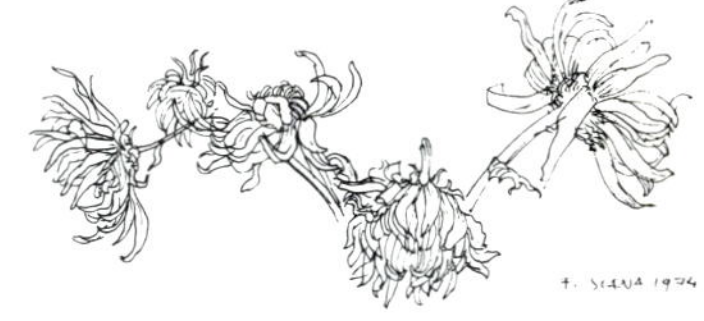

36

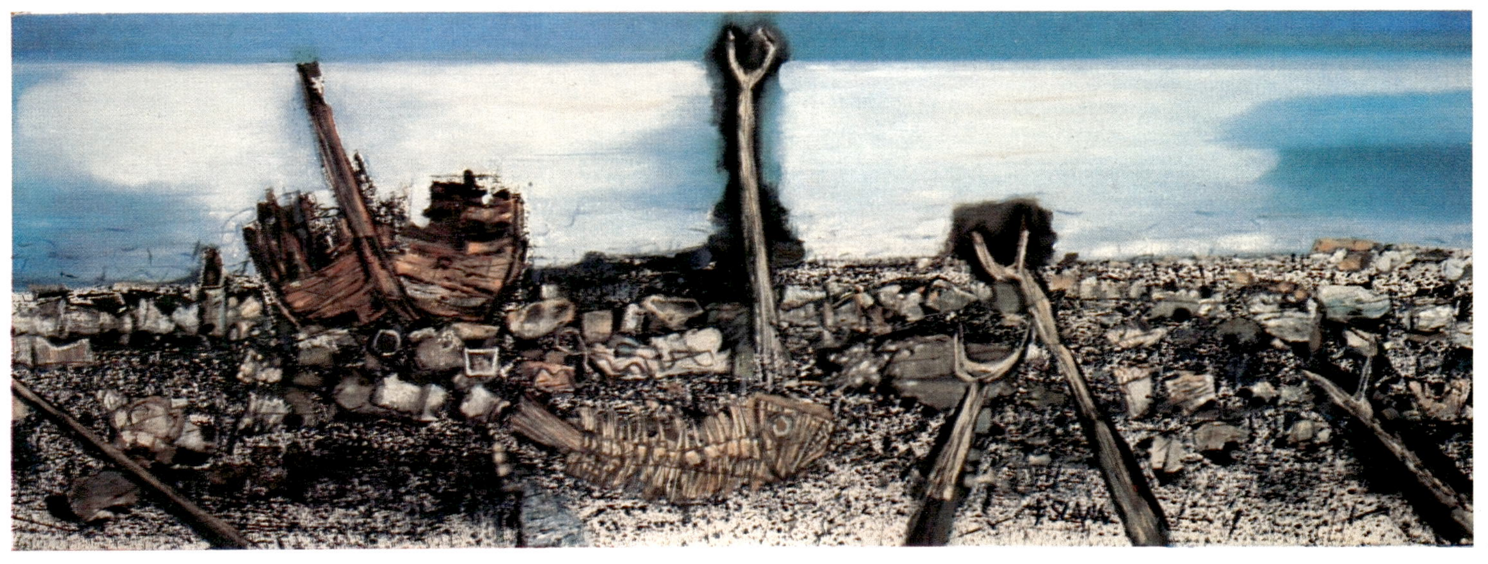

37

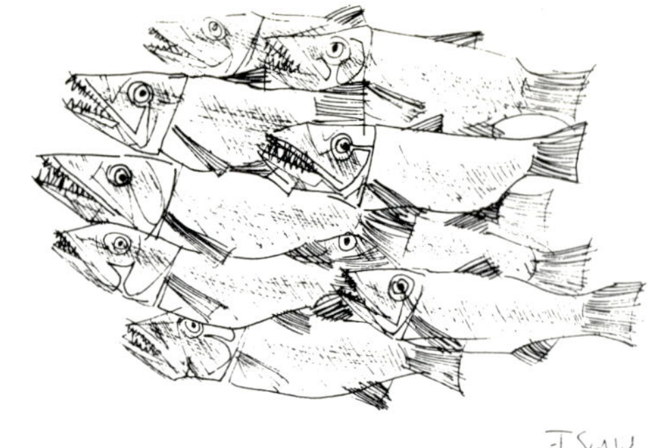

38

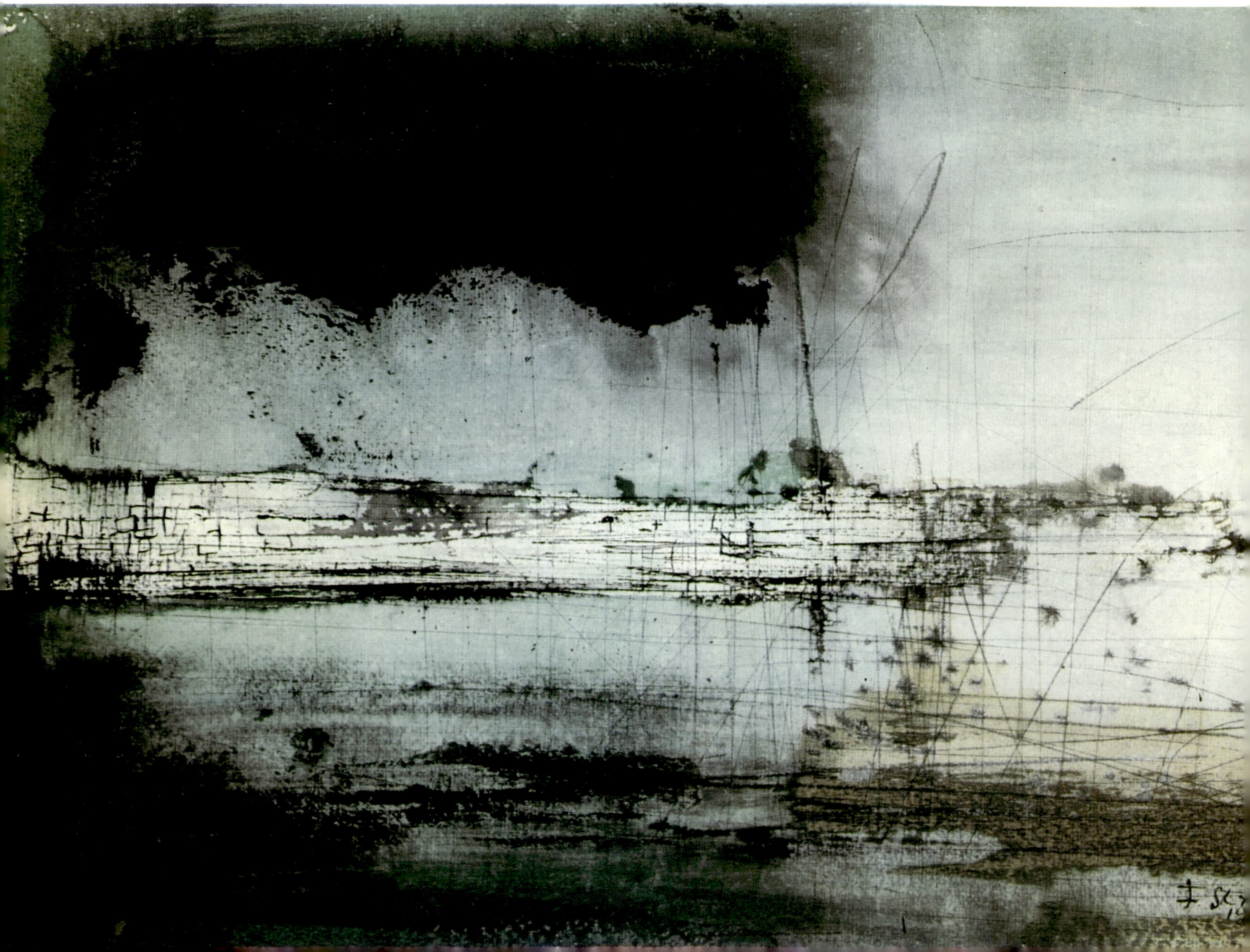

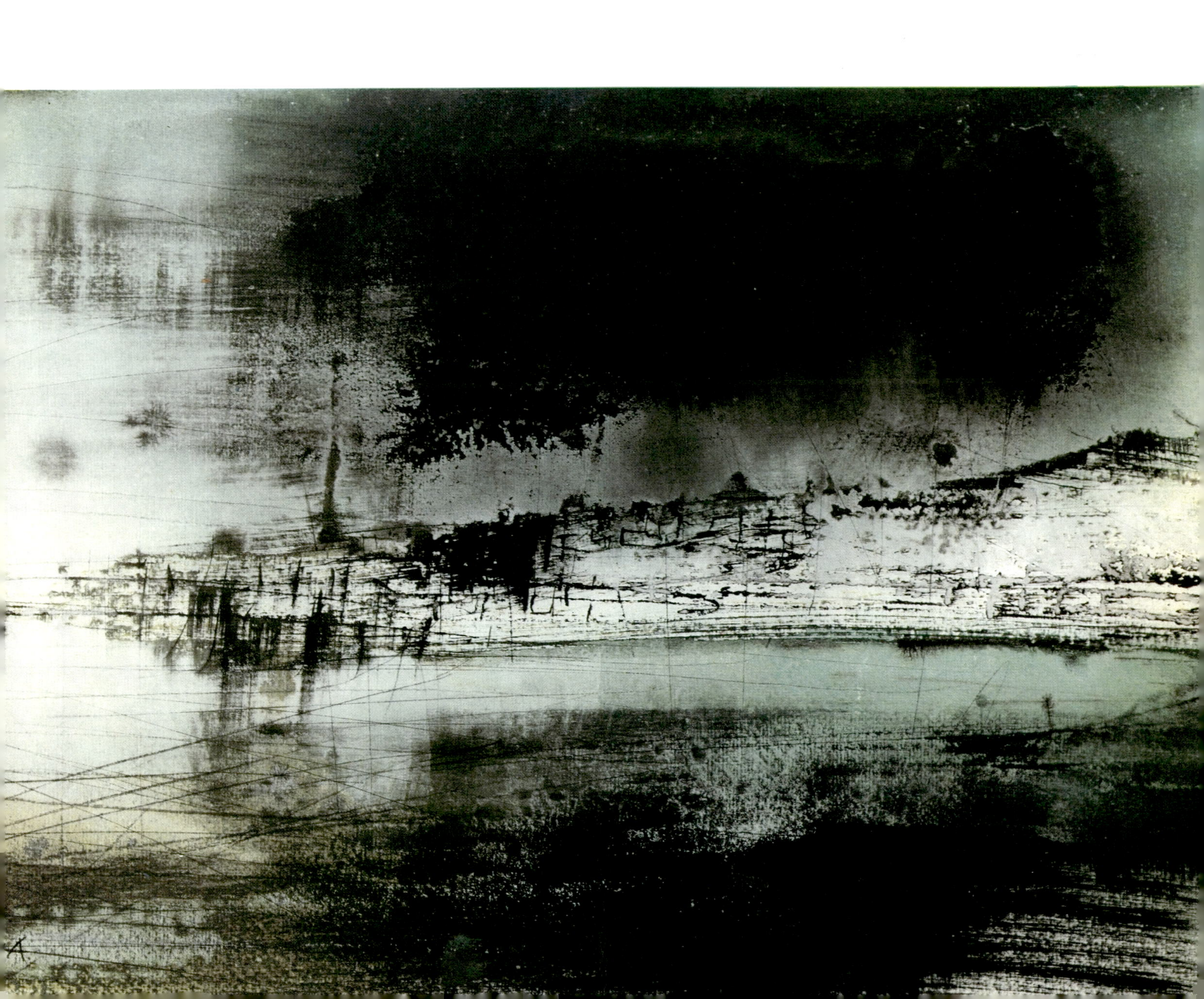

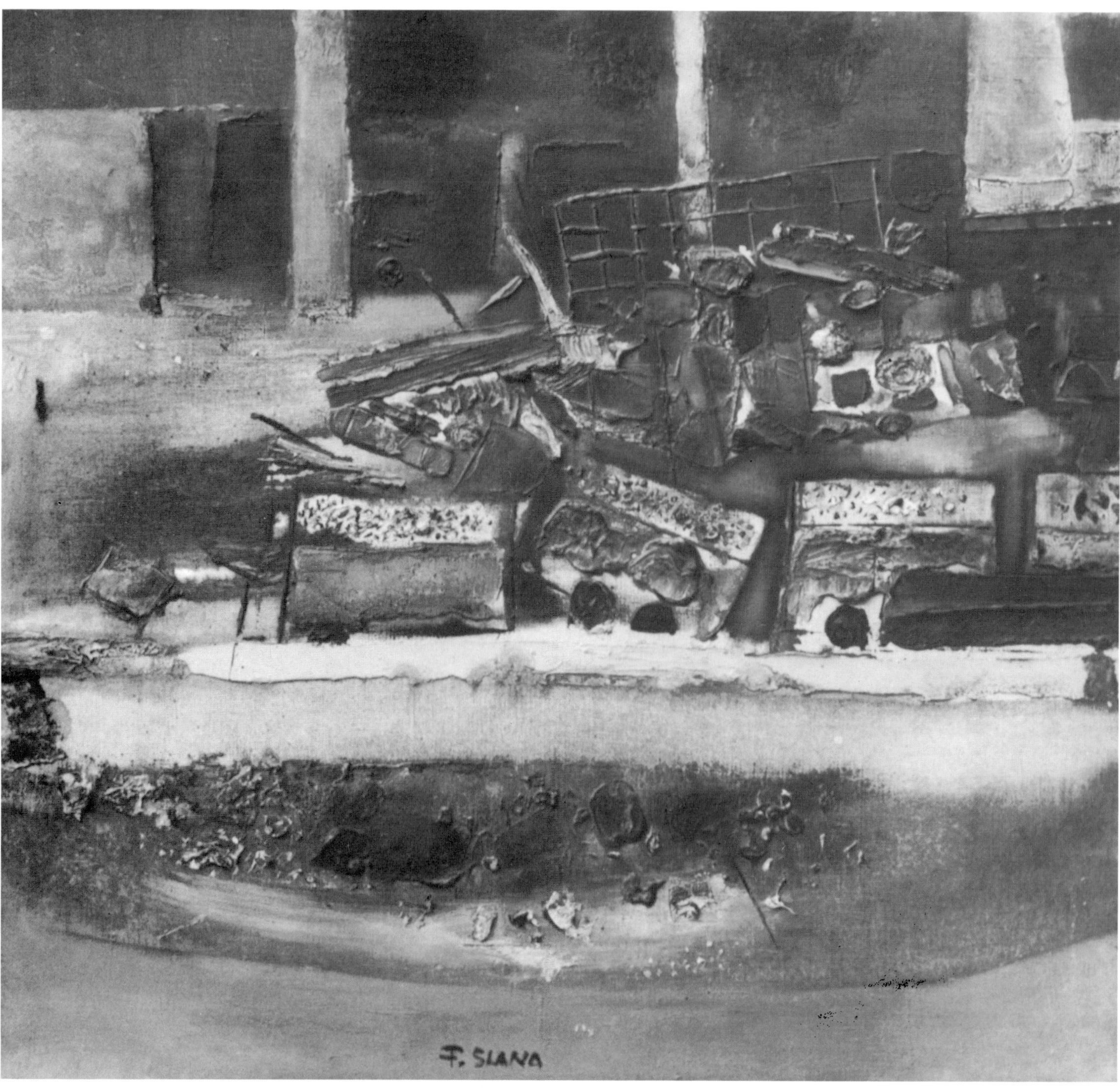
F. SIANA

40

41

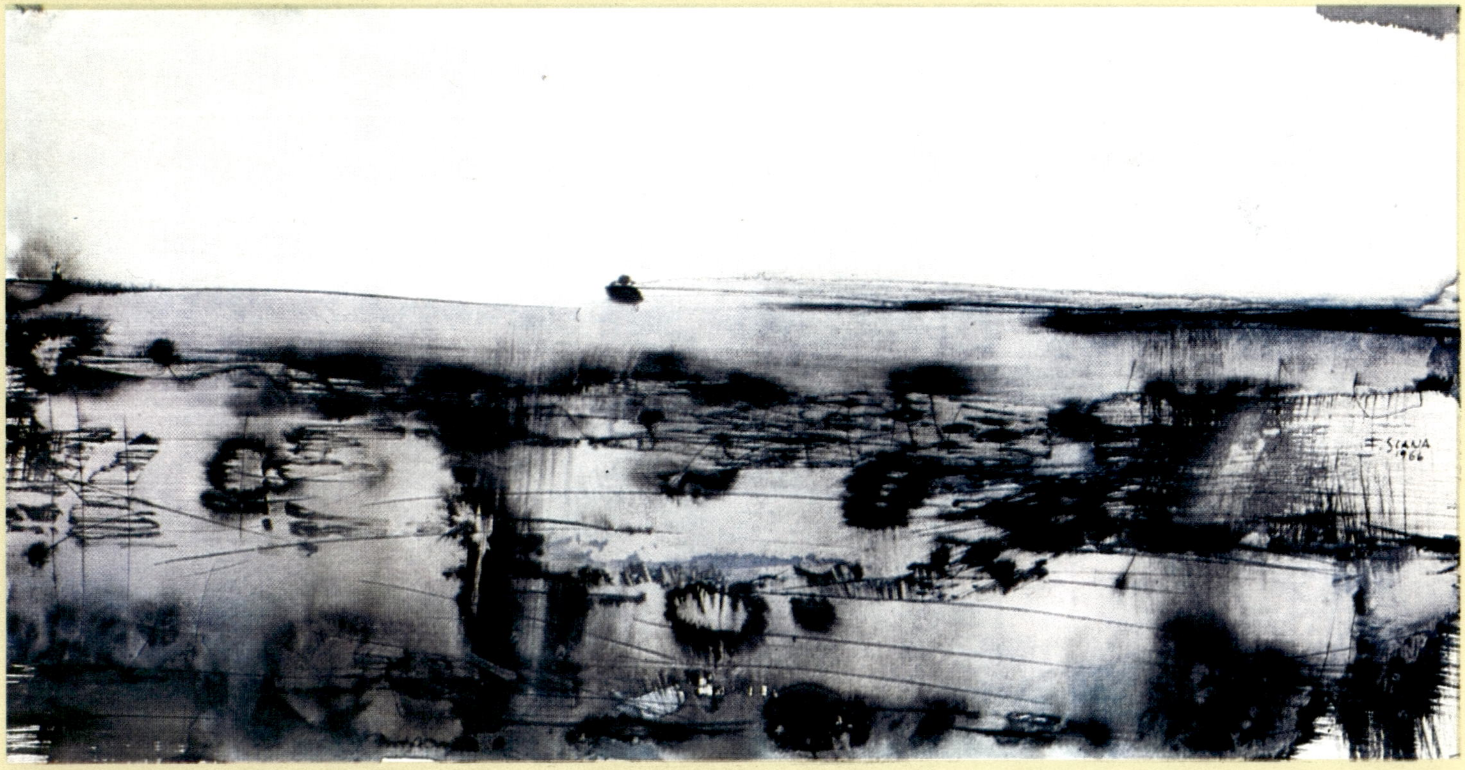

42

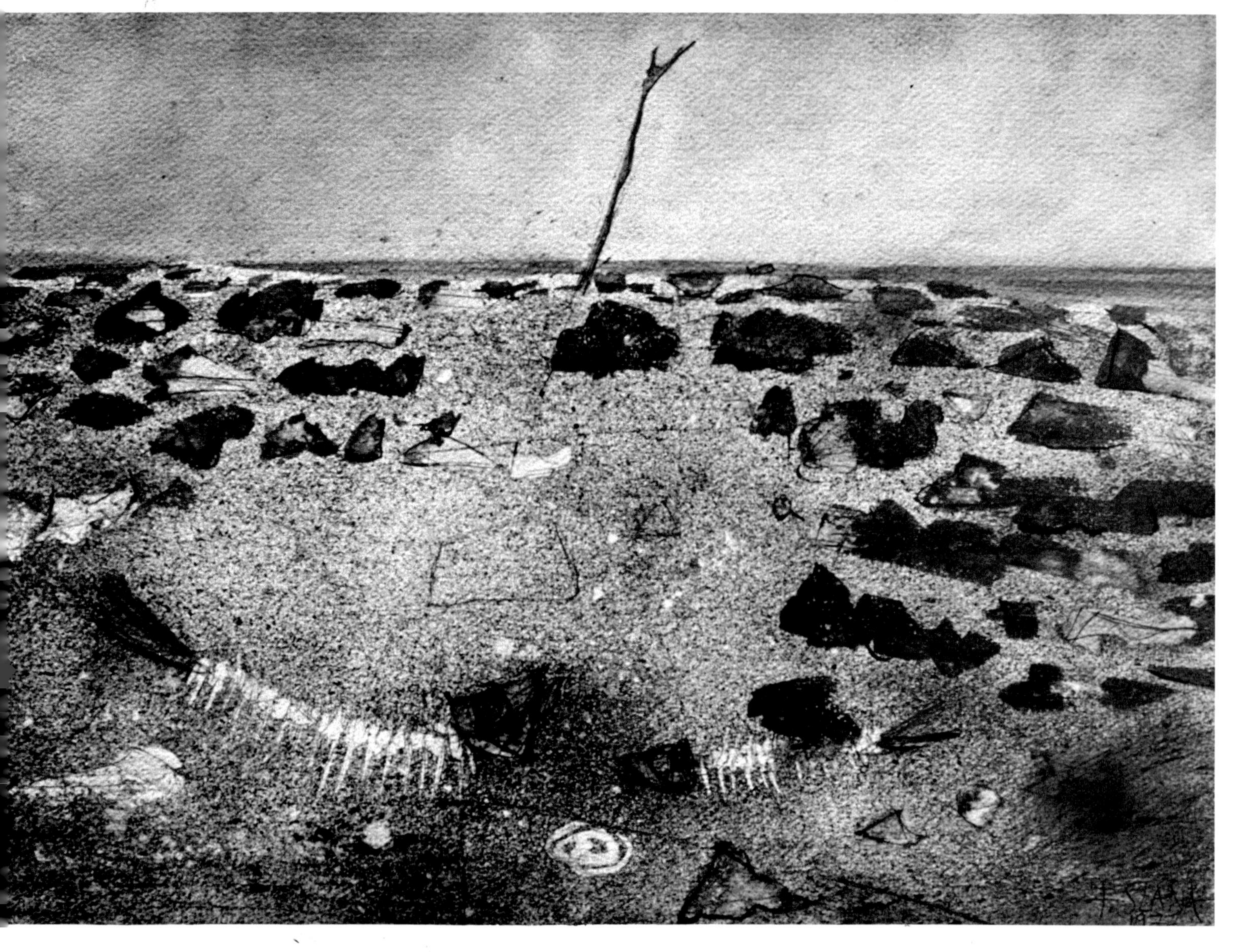

43

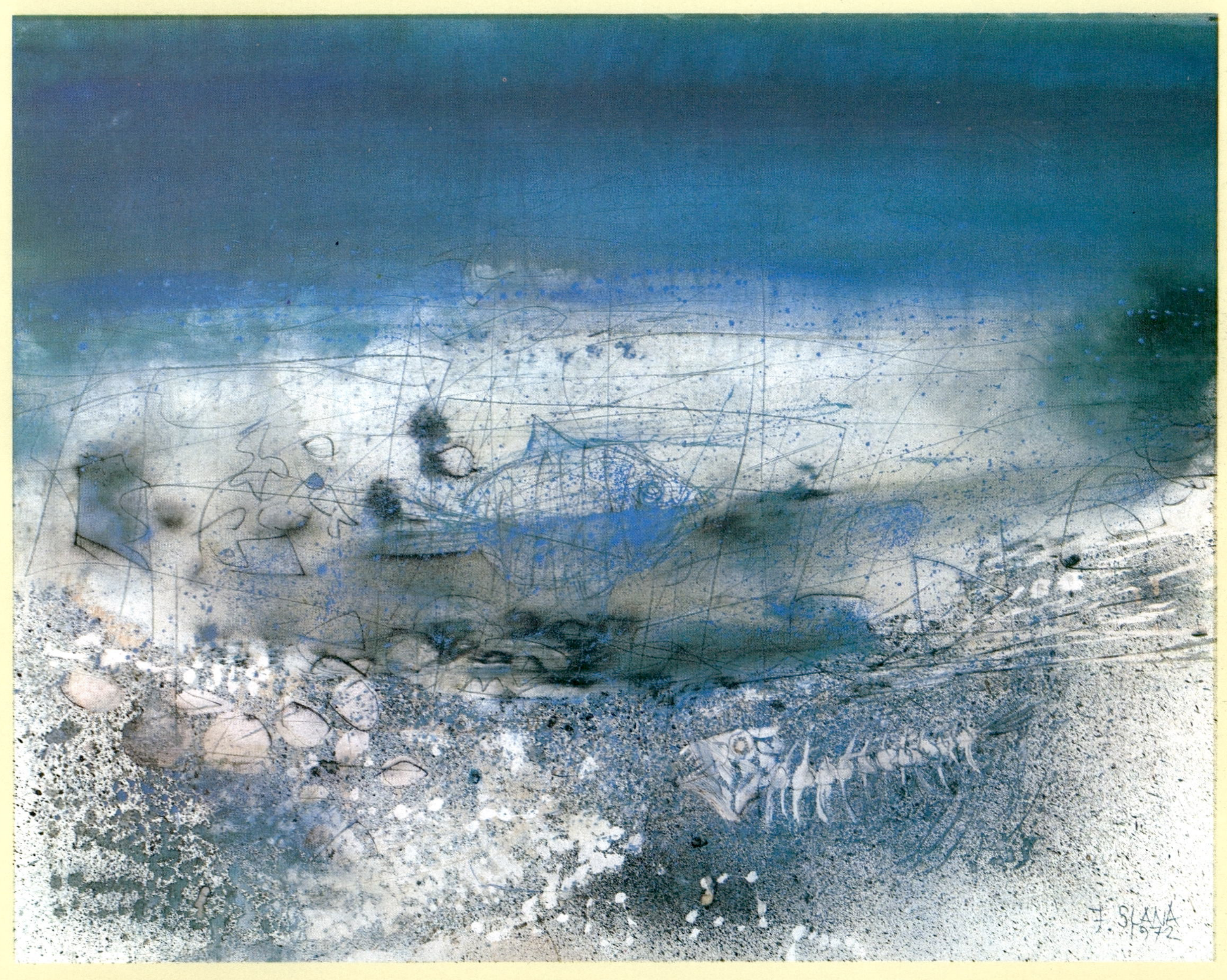

44

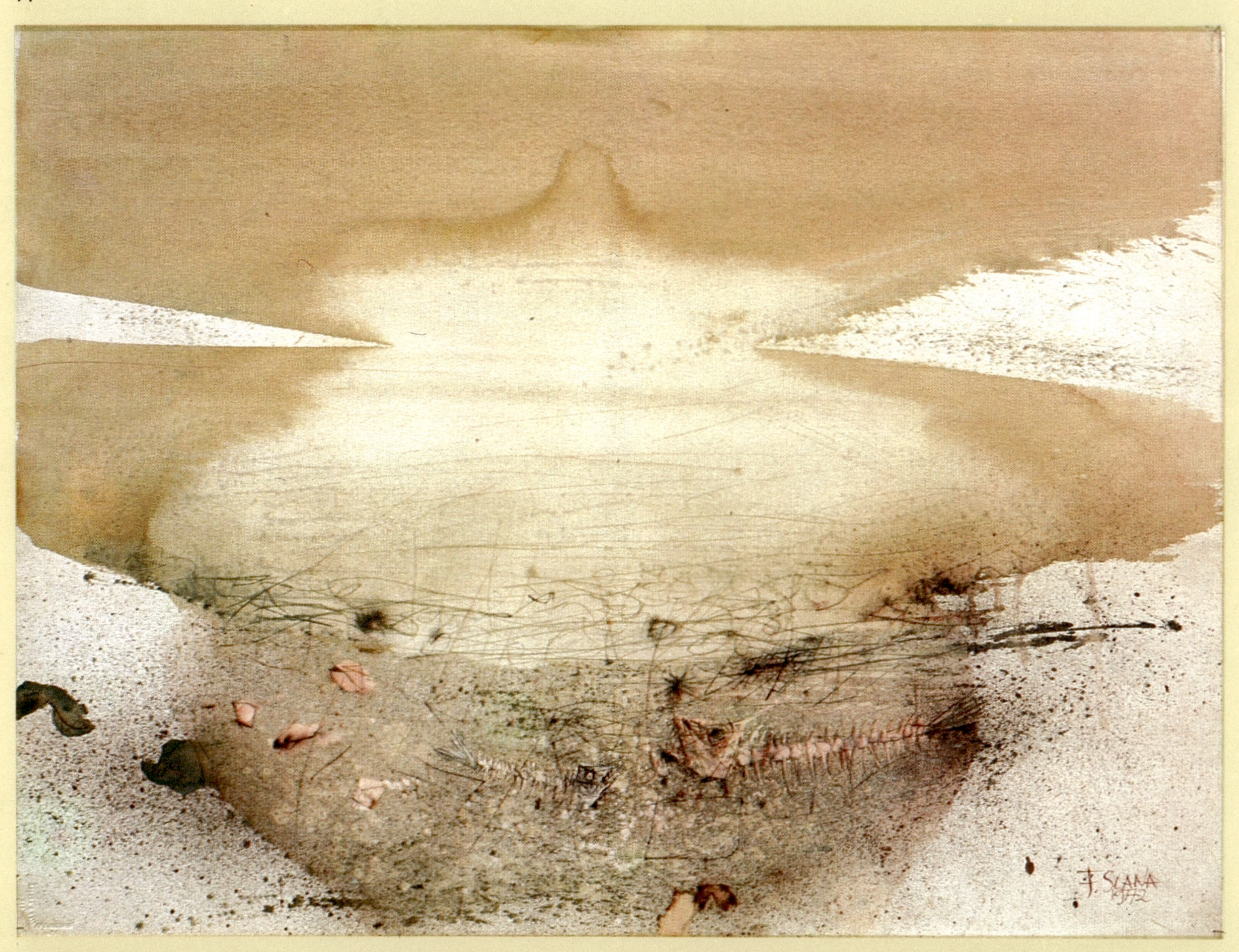

45

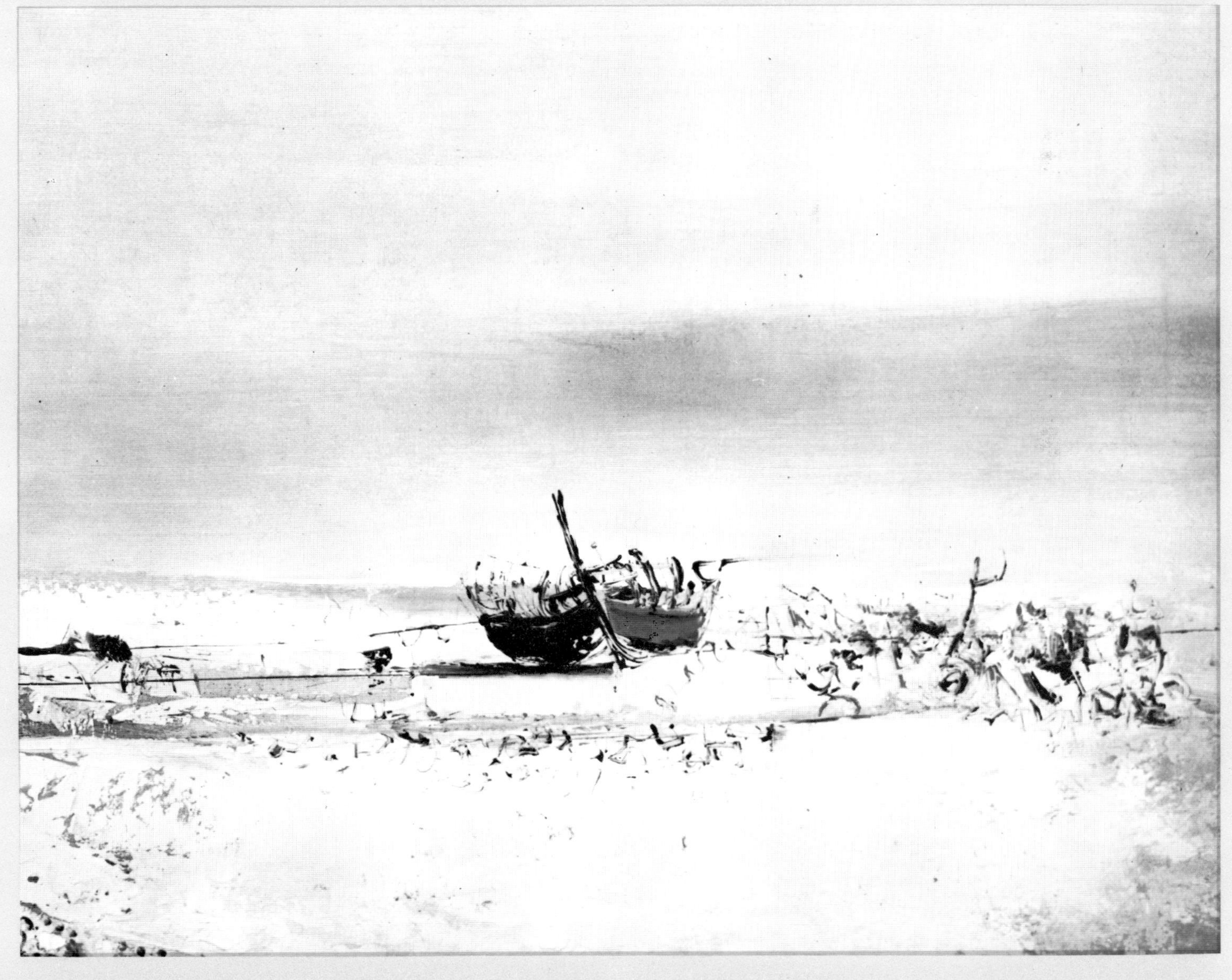

46

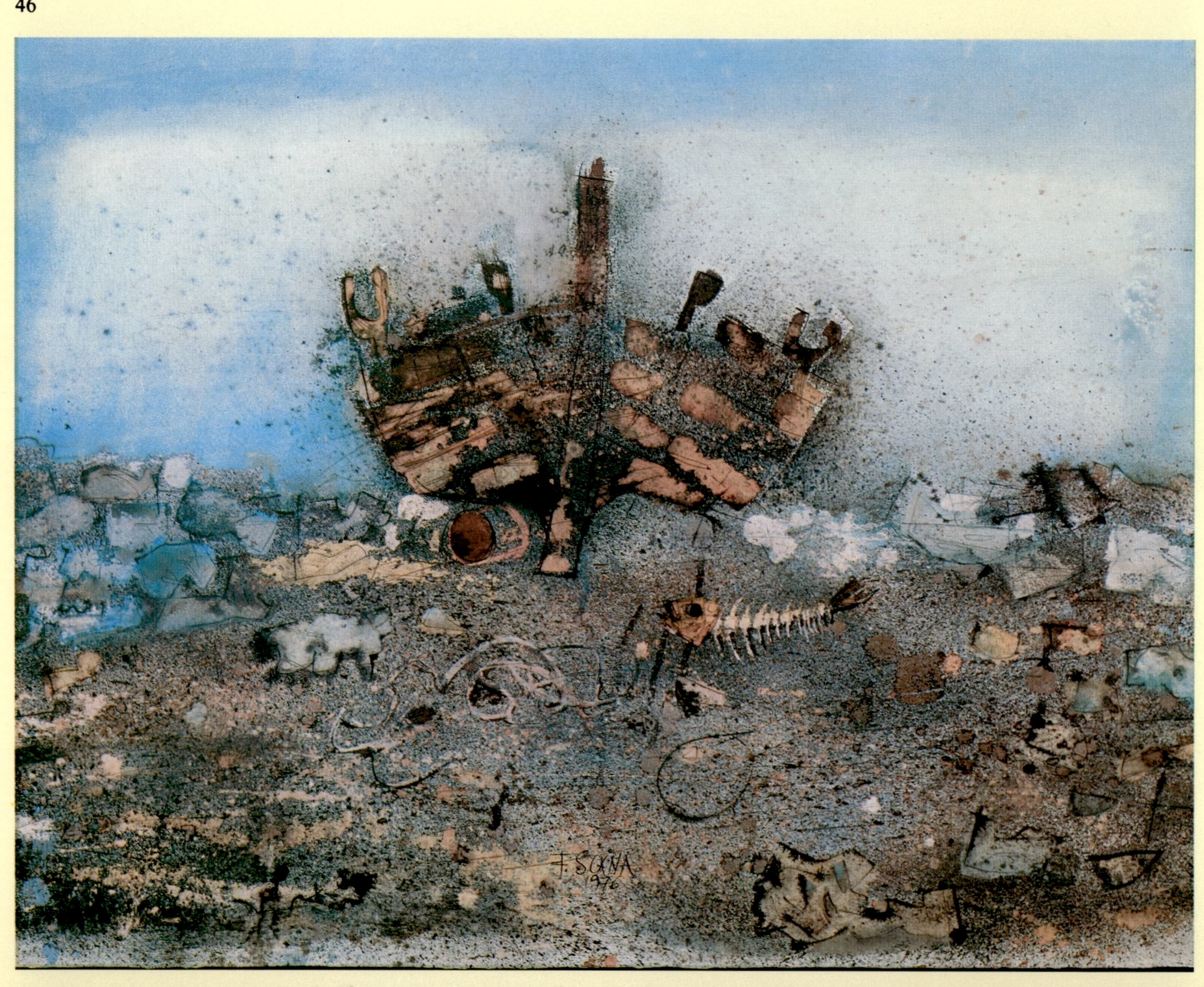

47

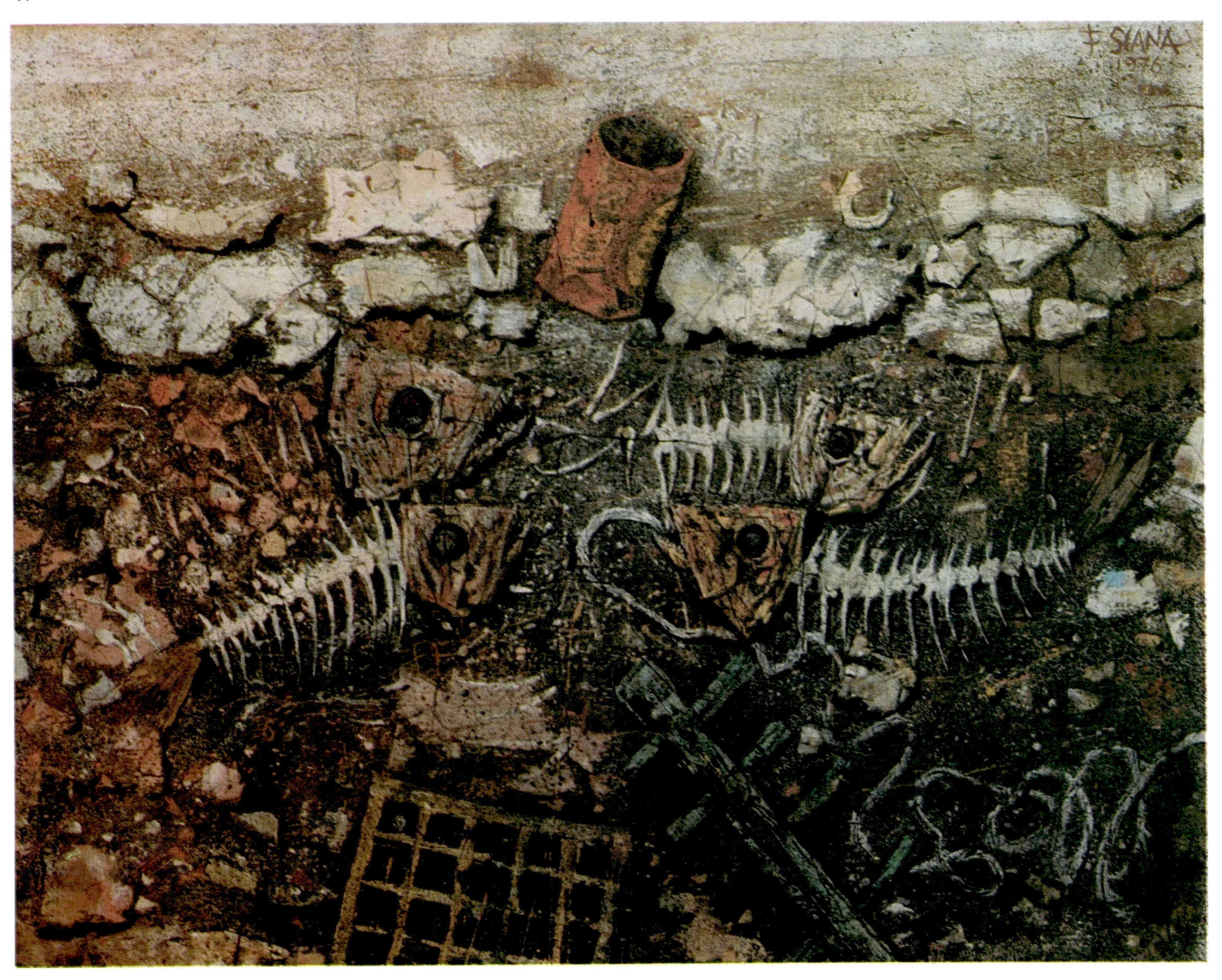

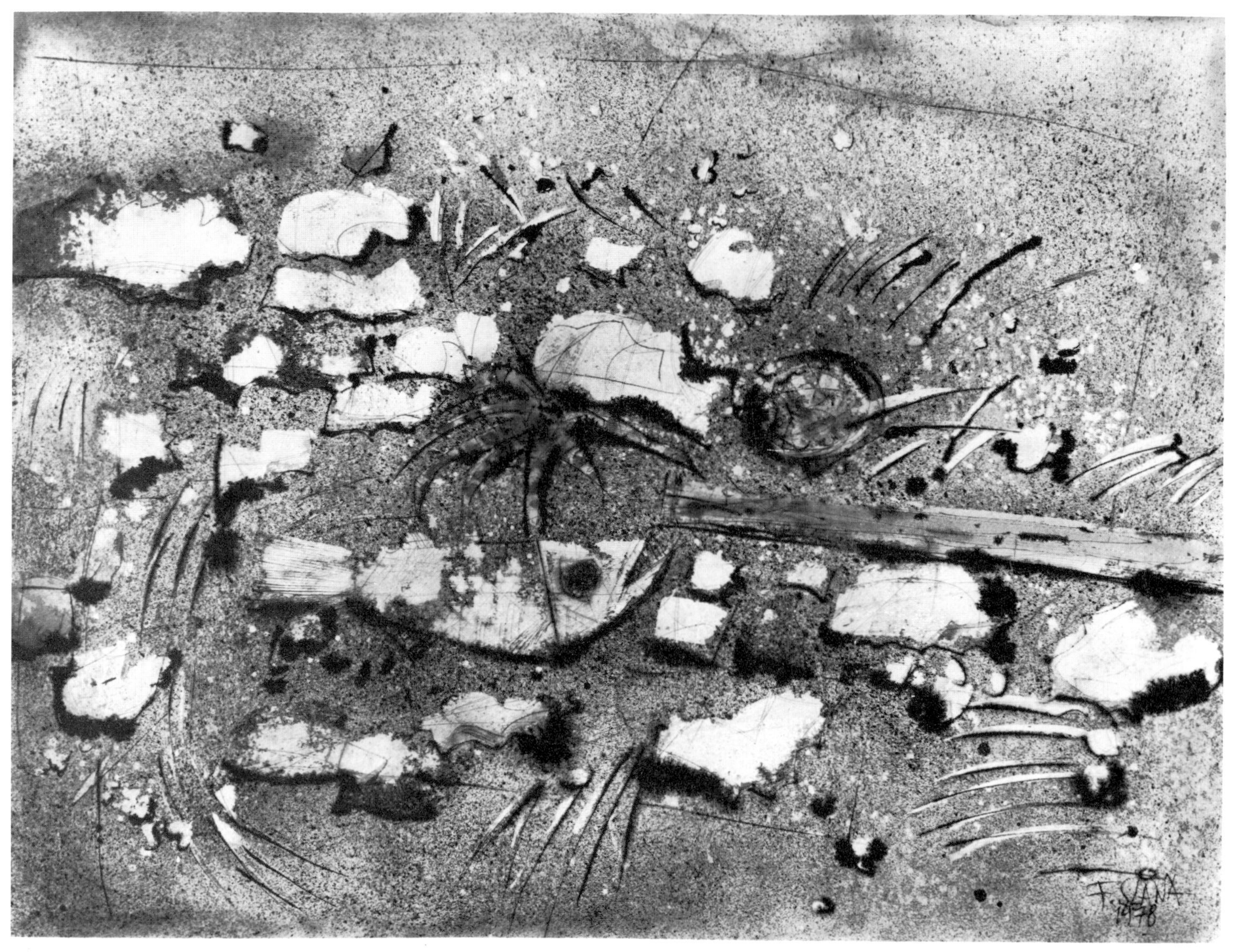

49

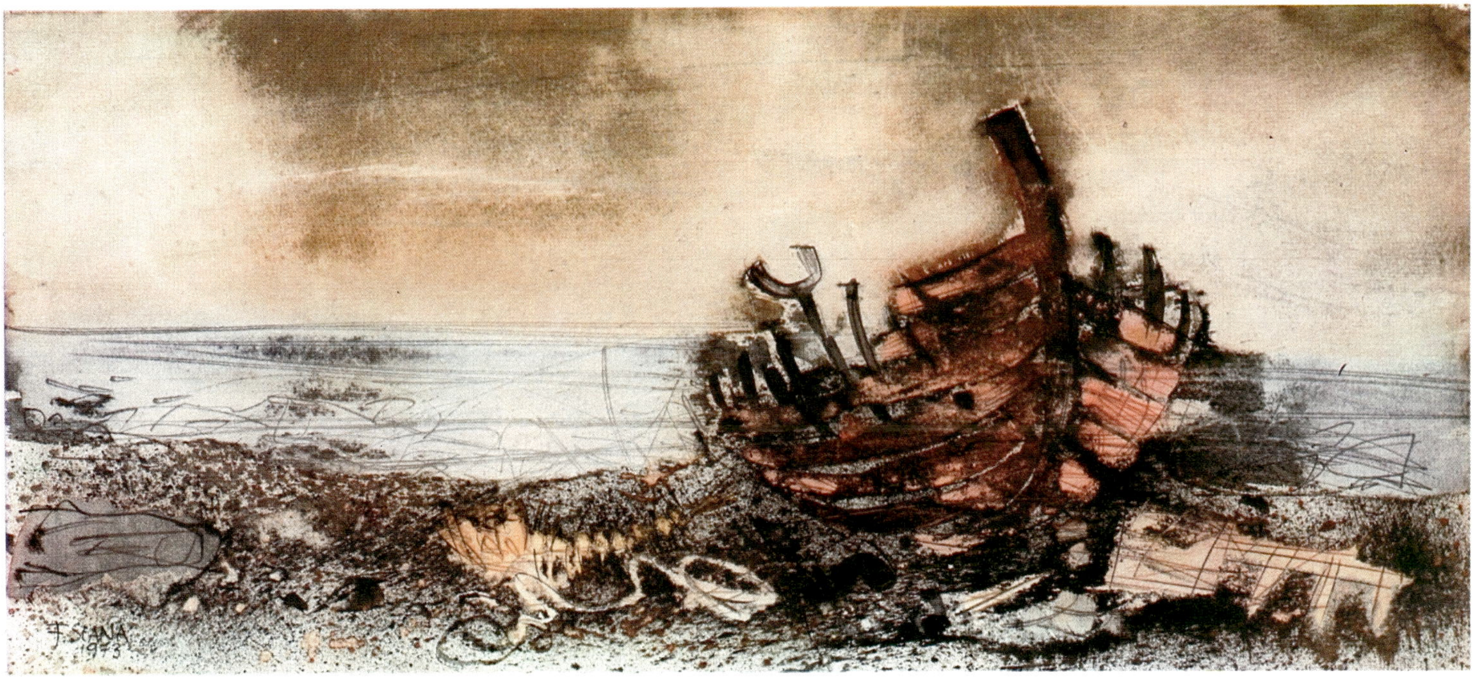

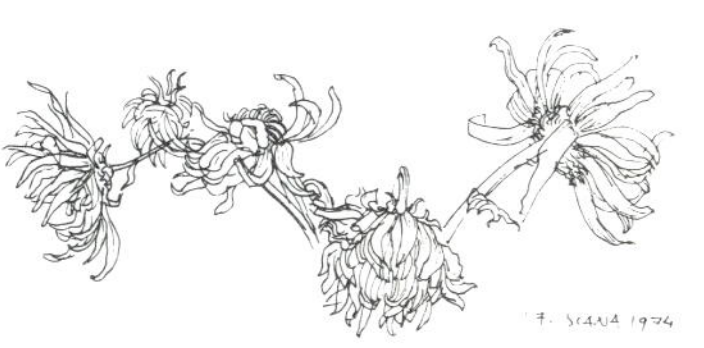

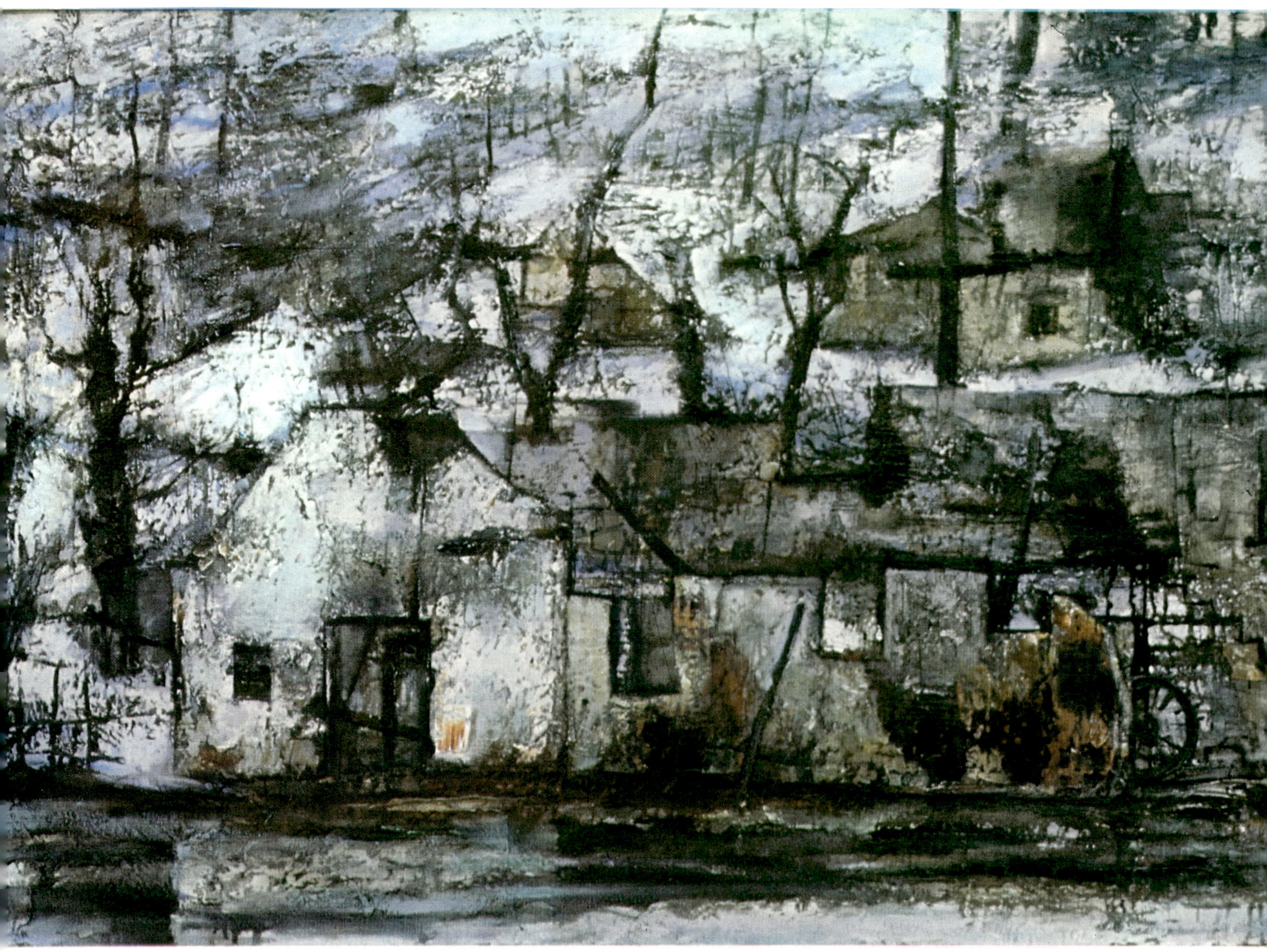

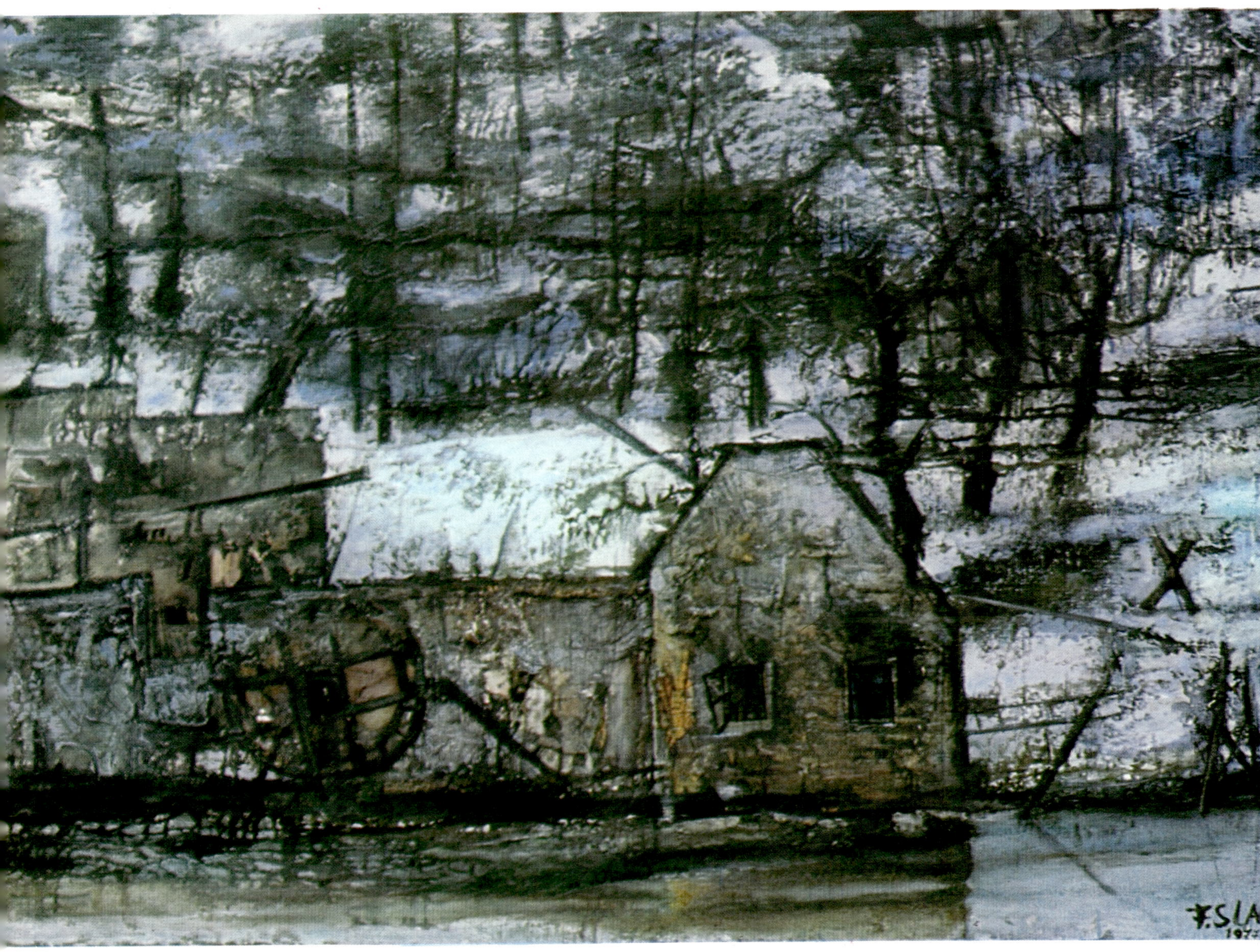

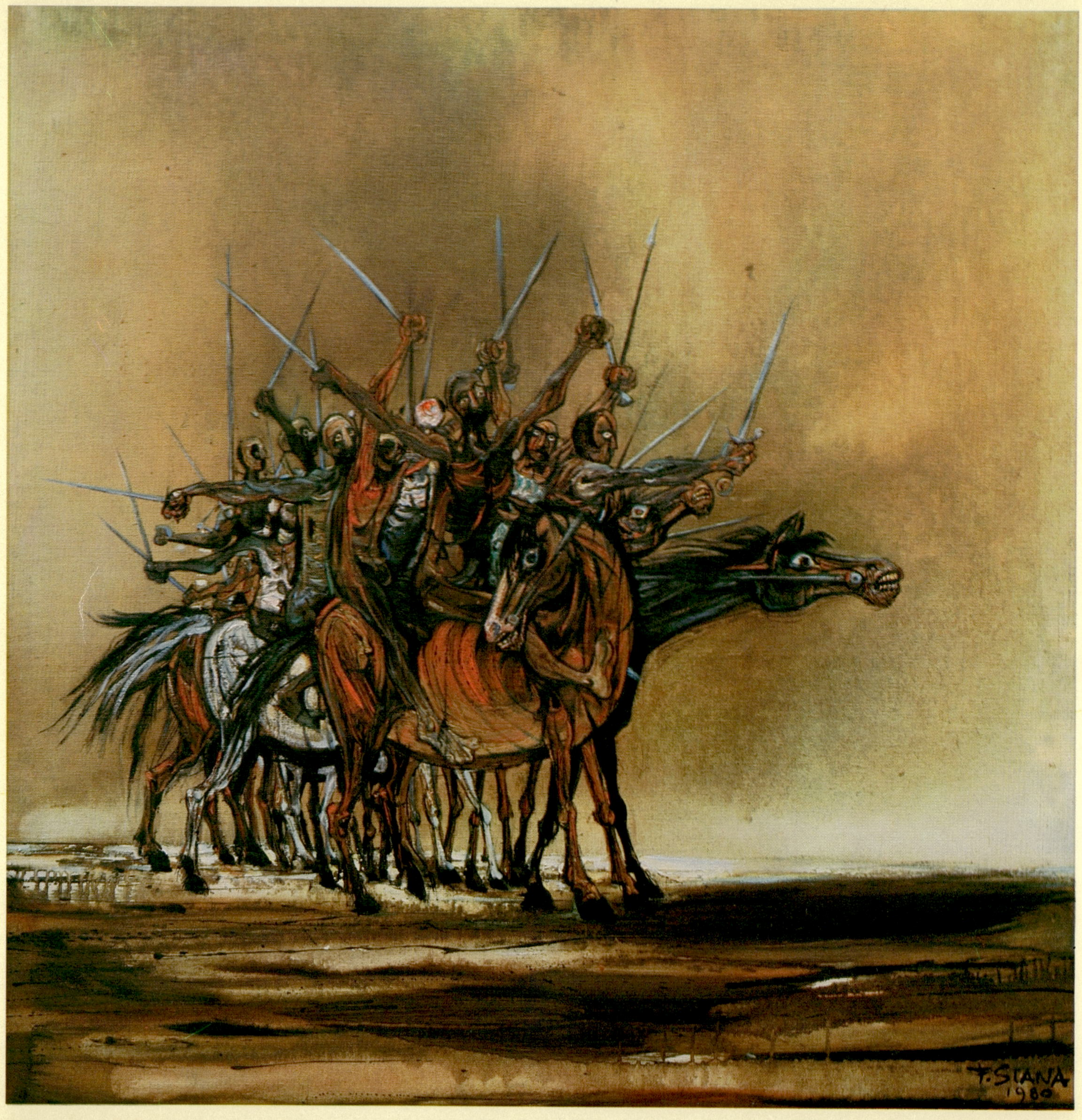

52

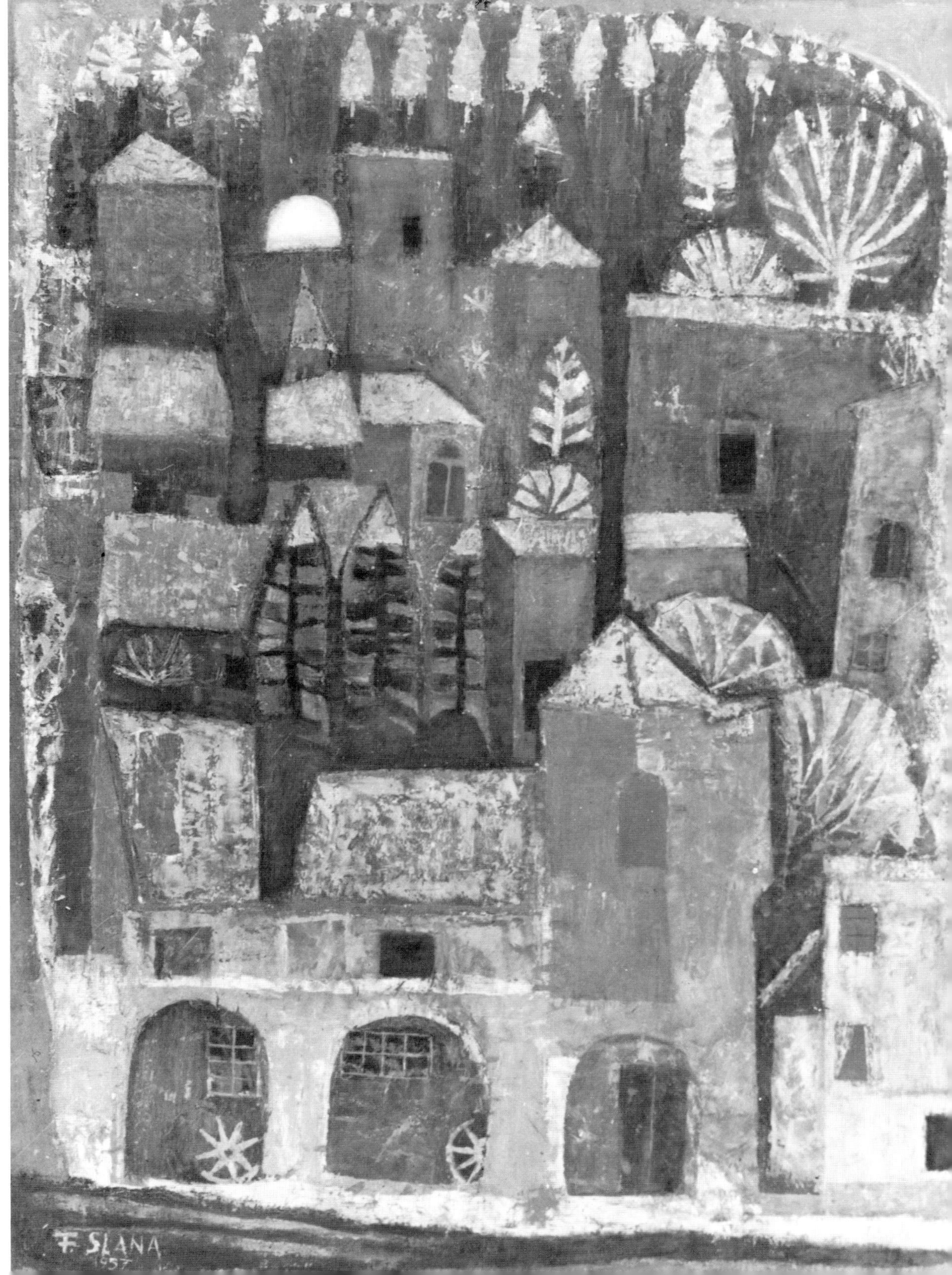

53

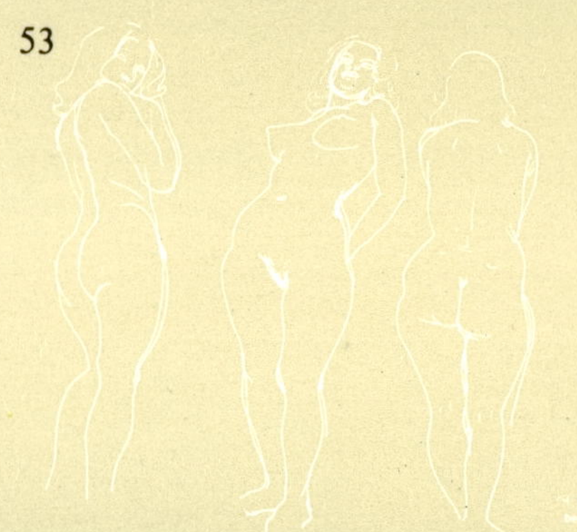

54

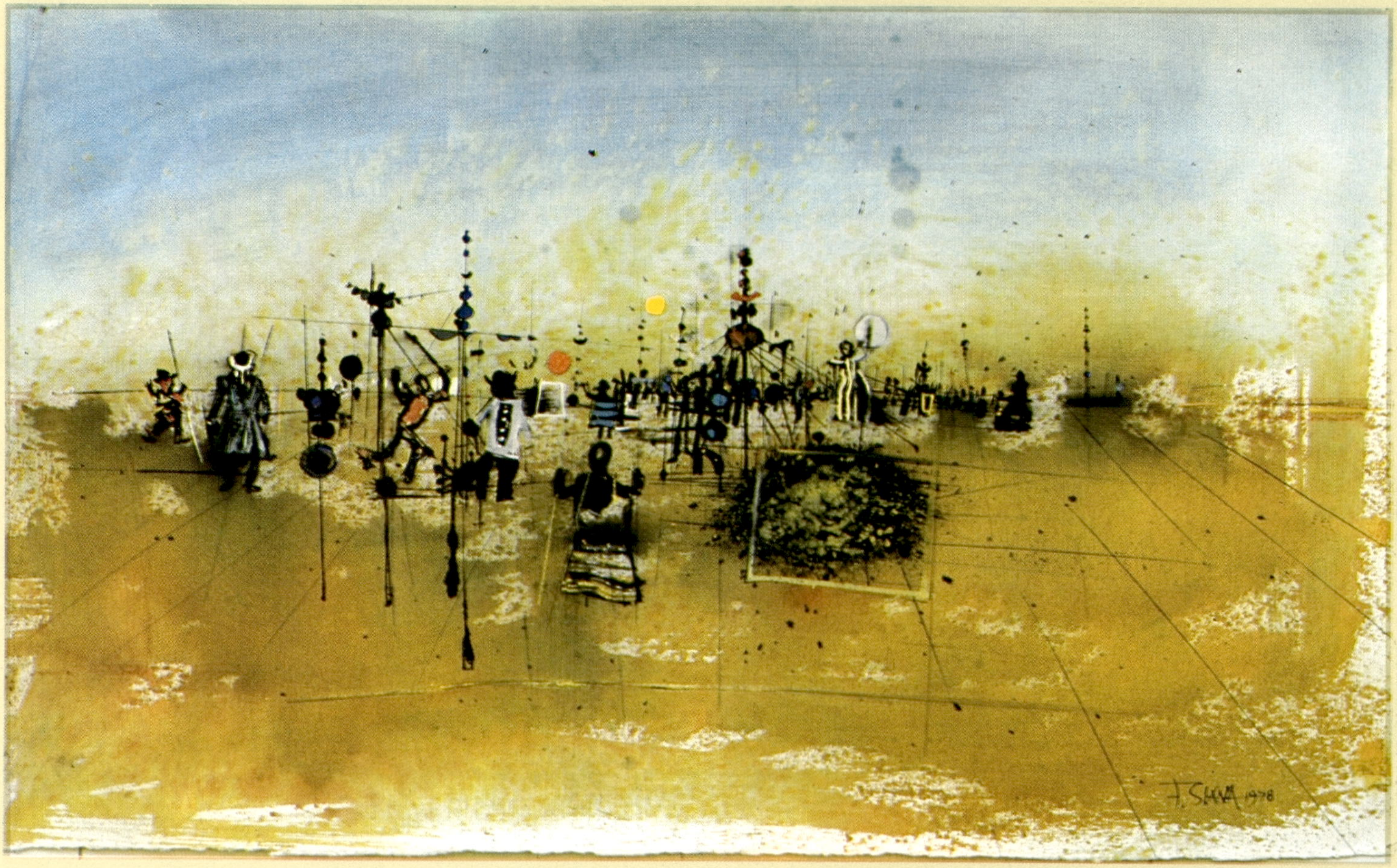

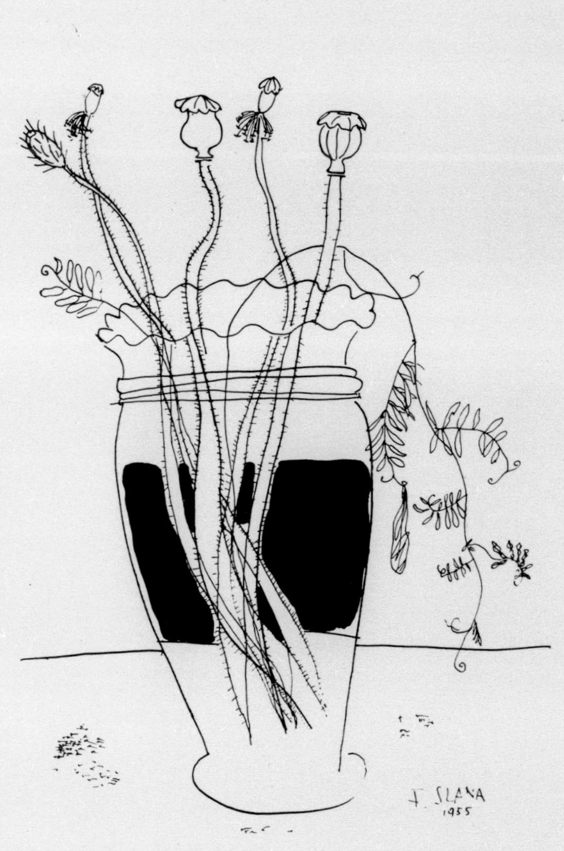

55

56

57

58

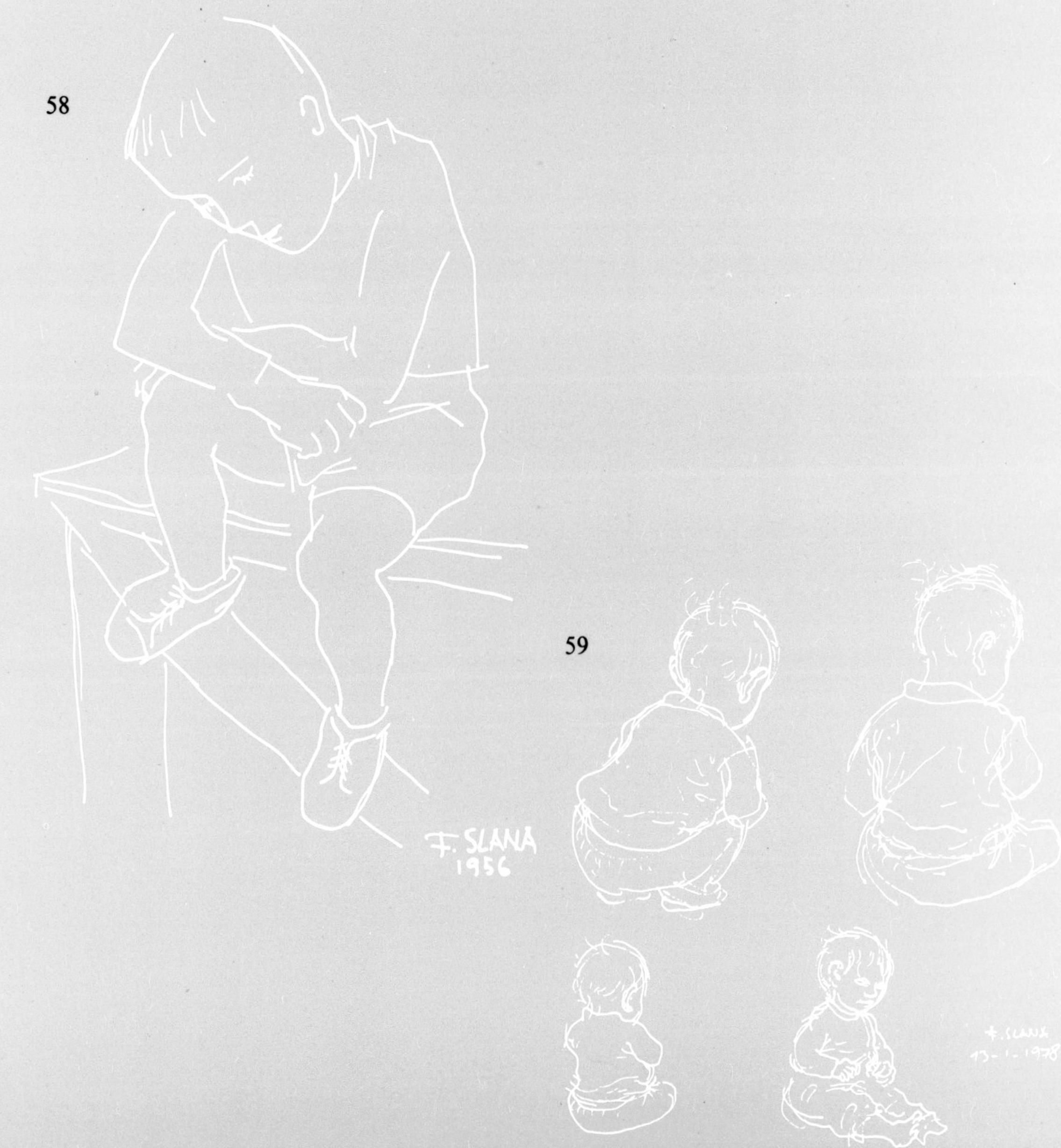

59

F. SLANA
31.9.1980

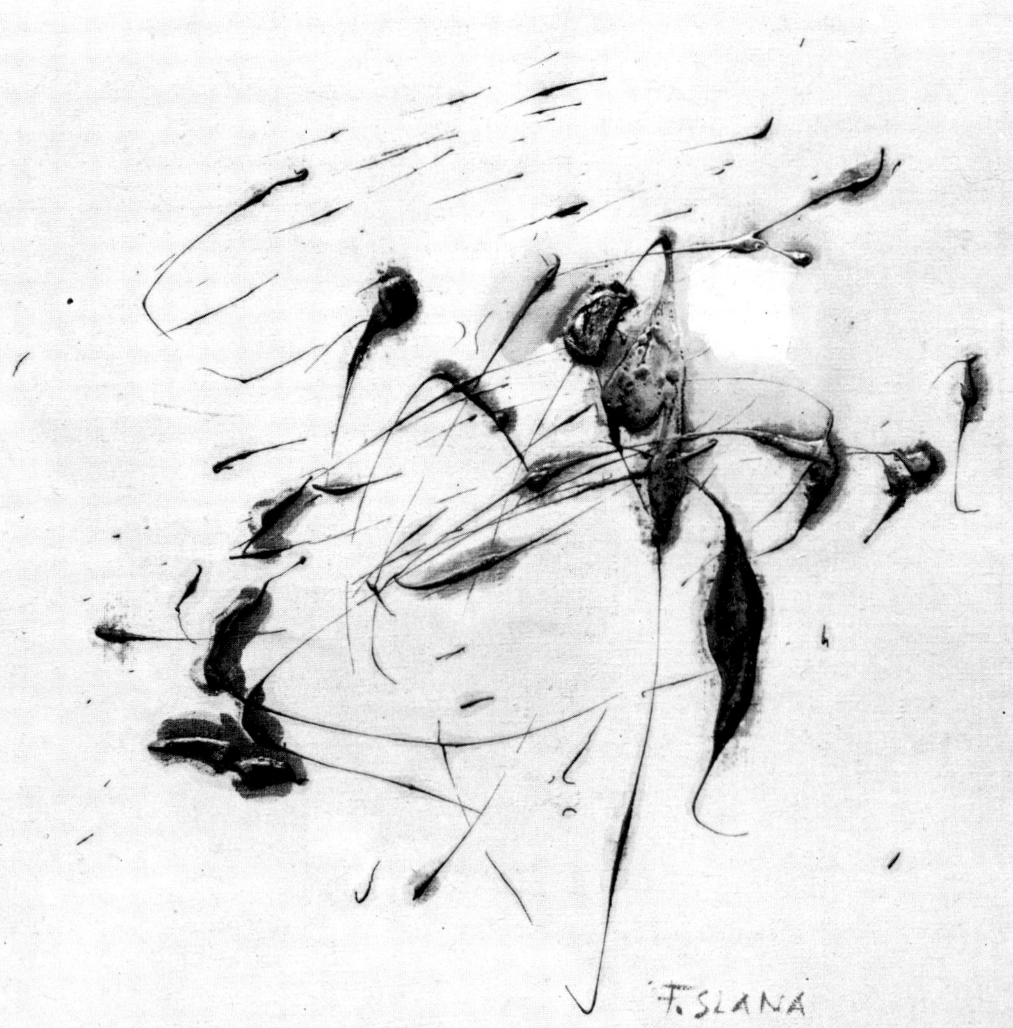
F. SLANA

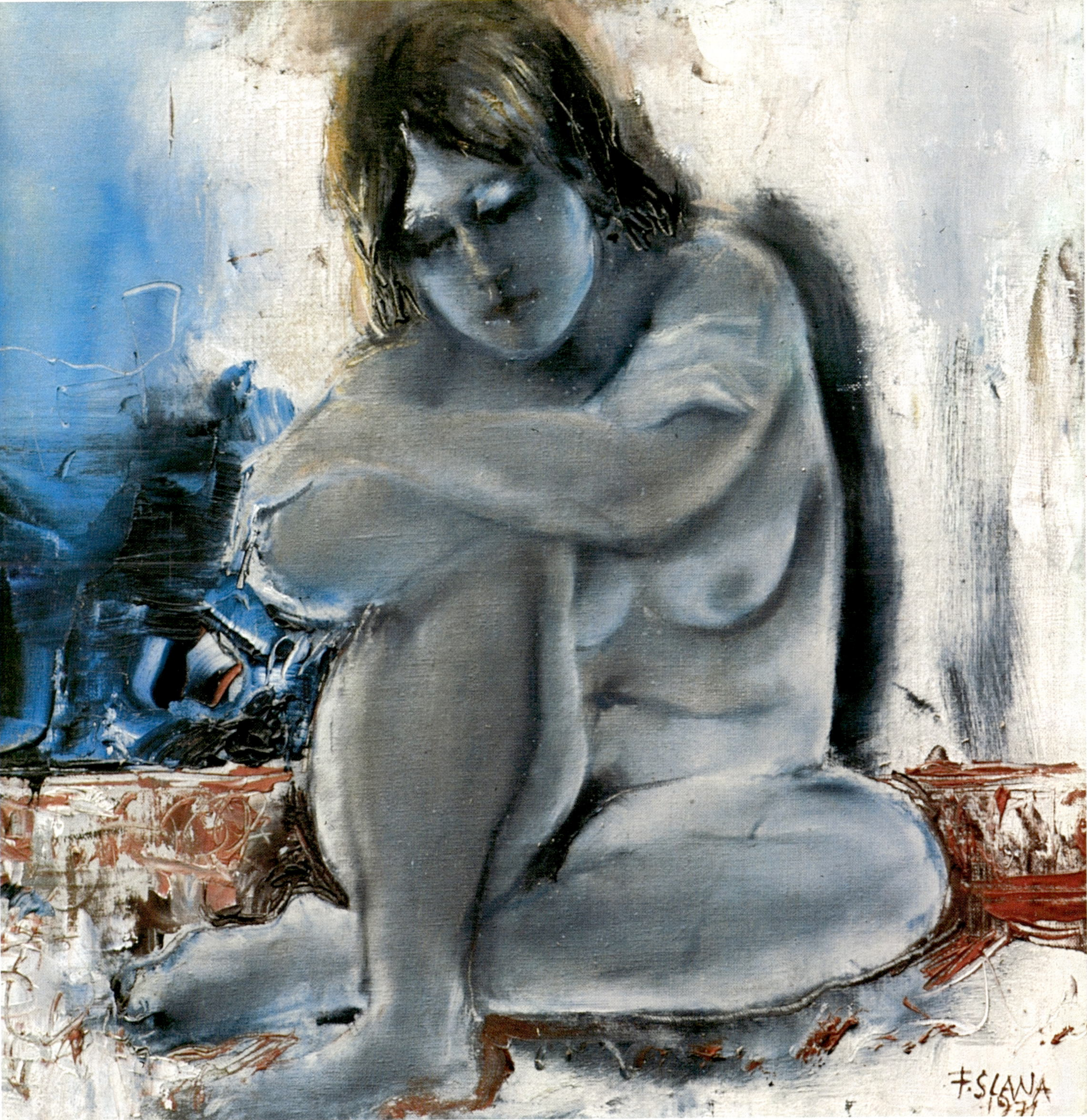
F.SLANA
1971

63

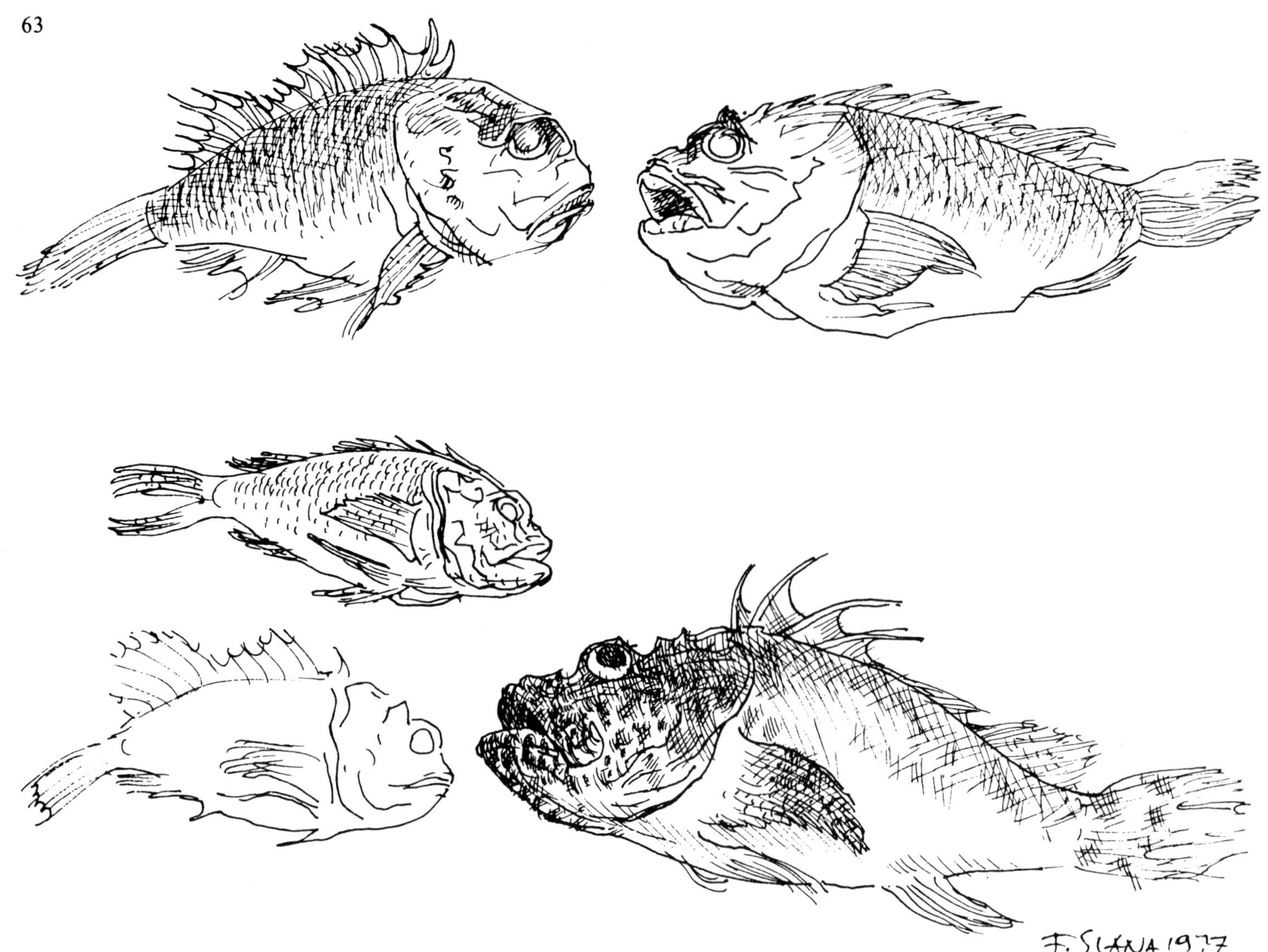

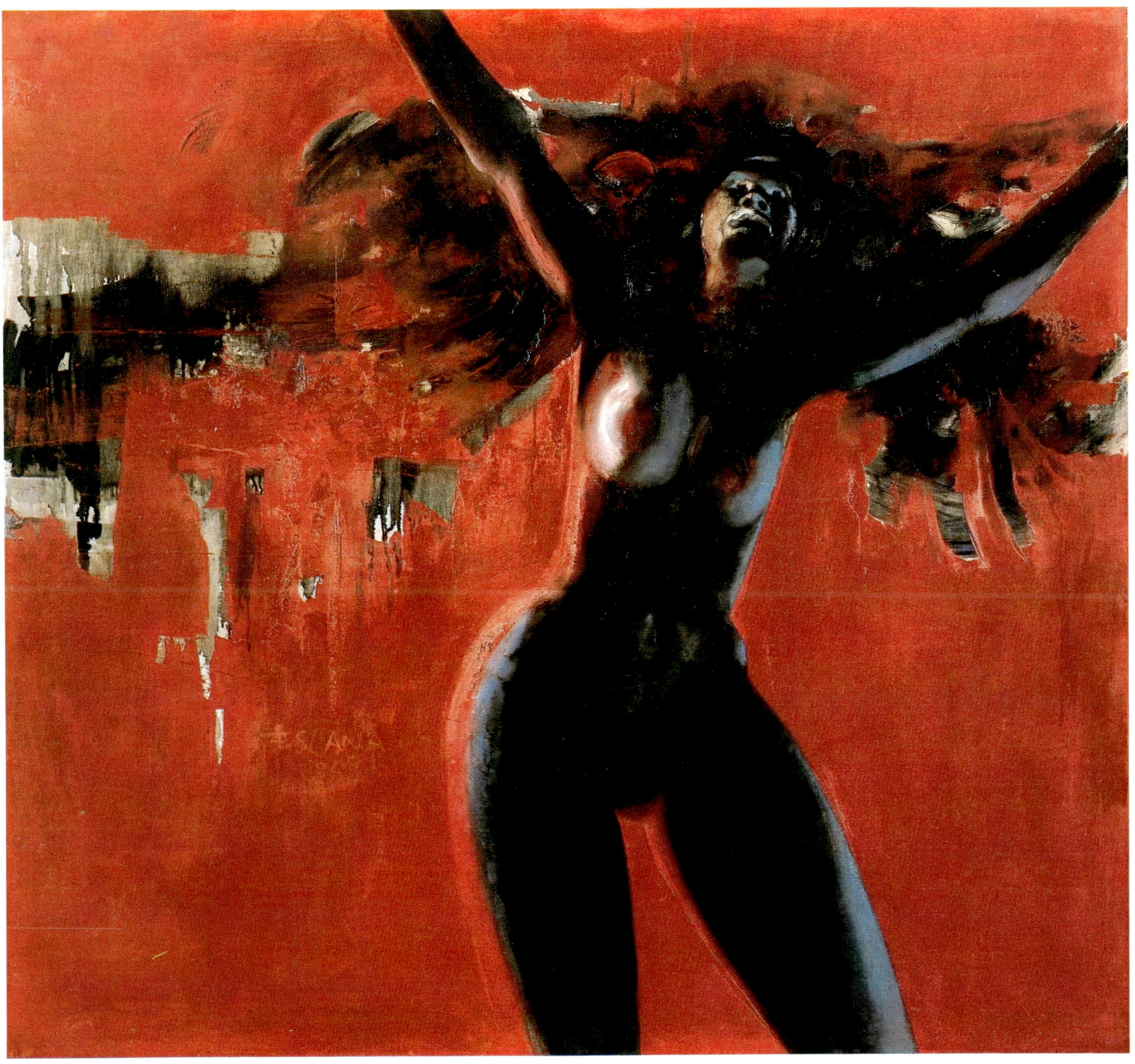

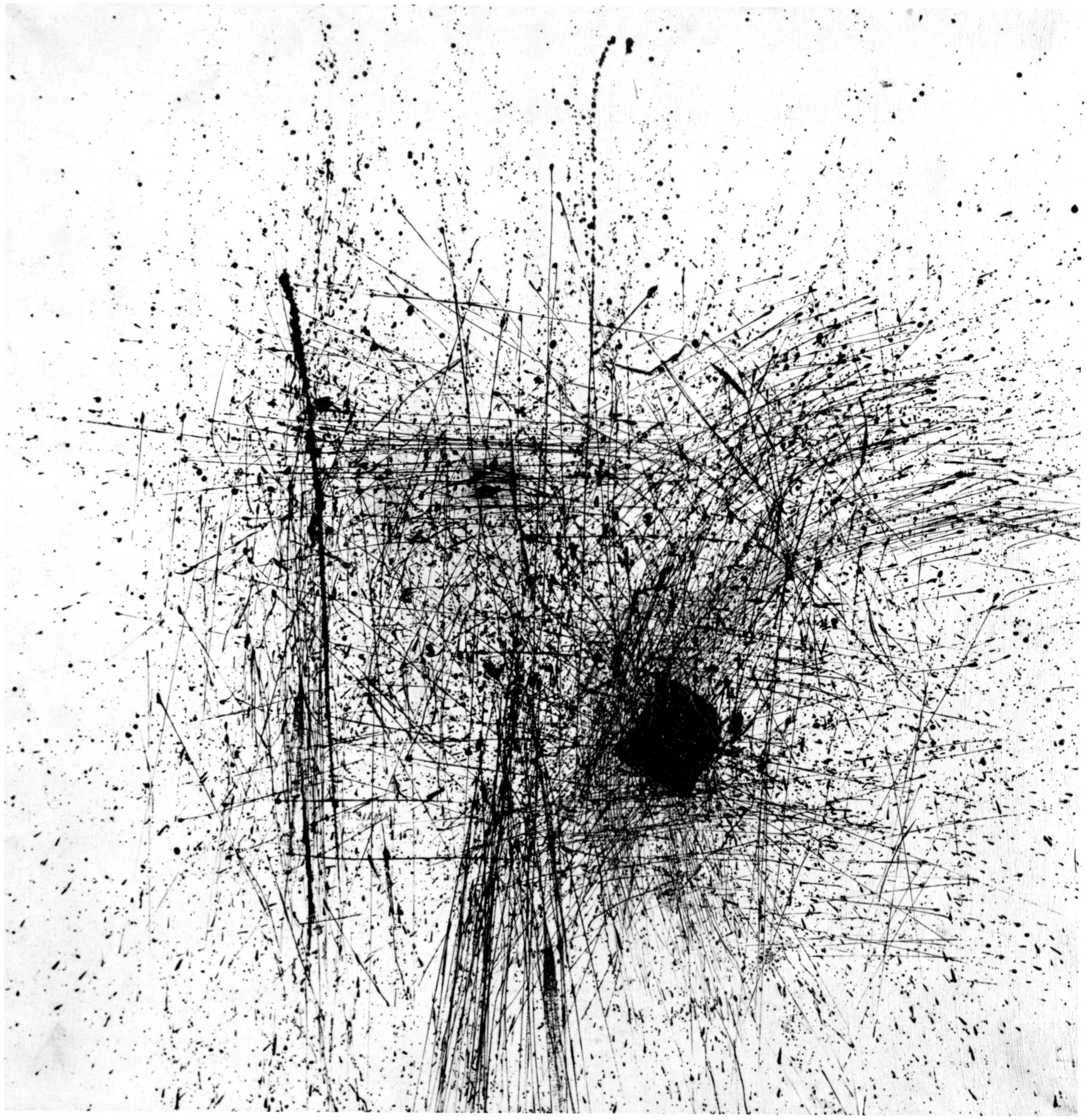

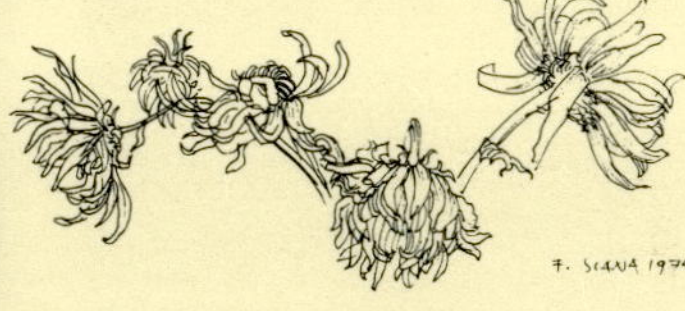
F. SCANA 1974

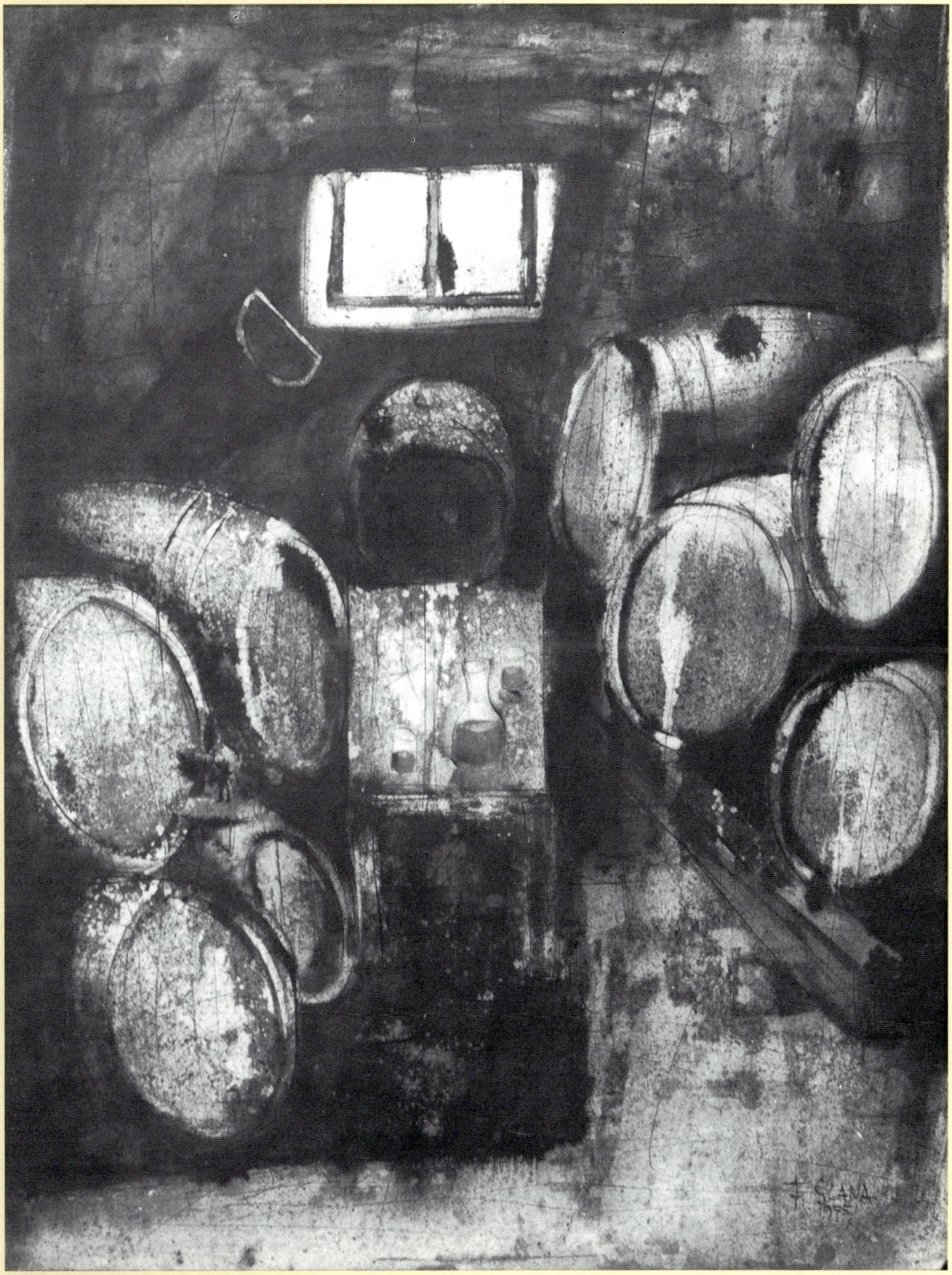

67

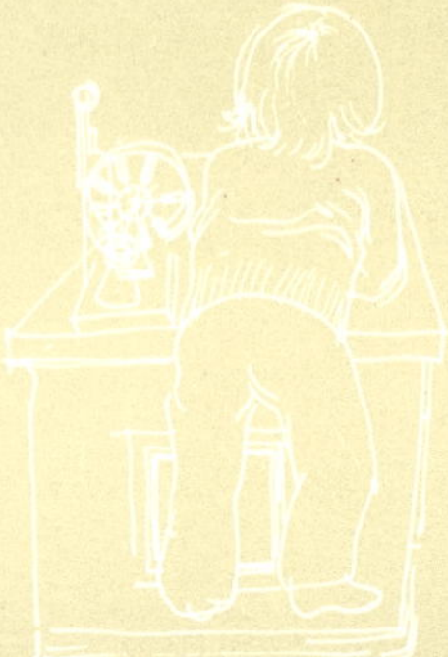

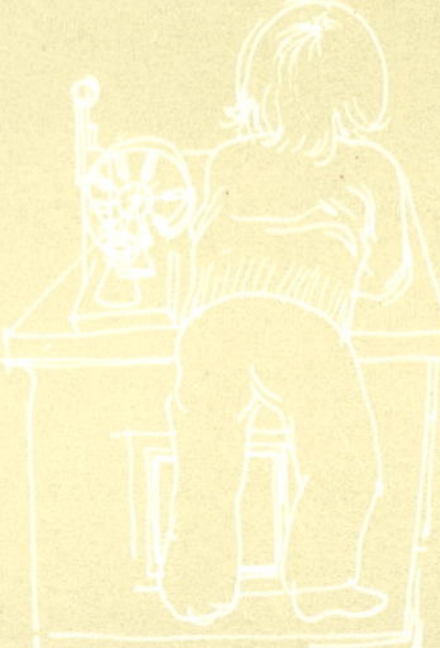

68

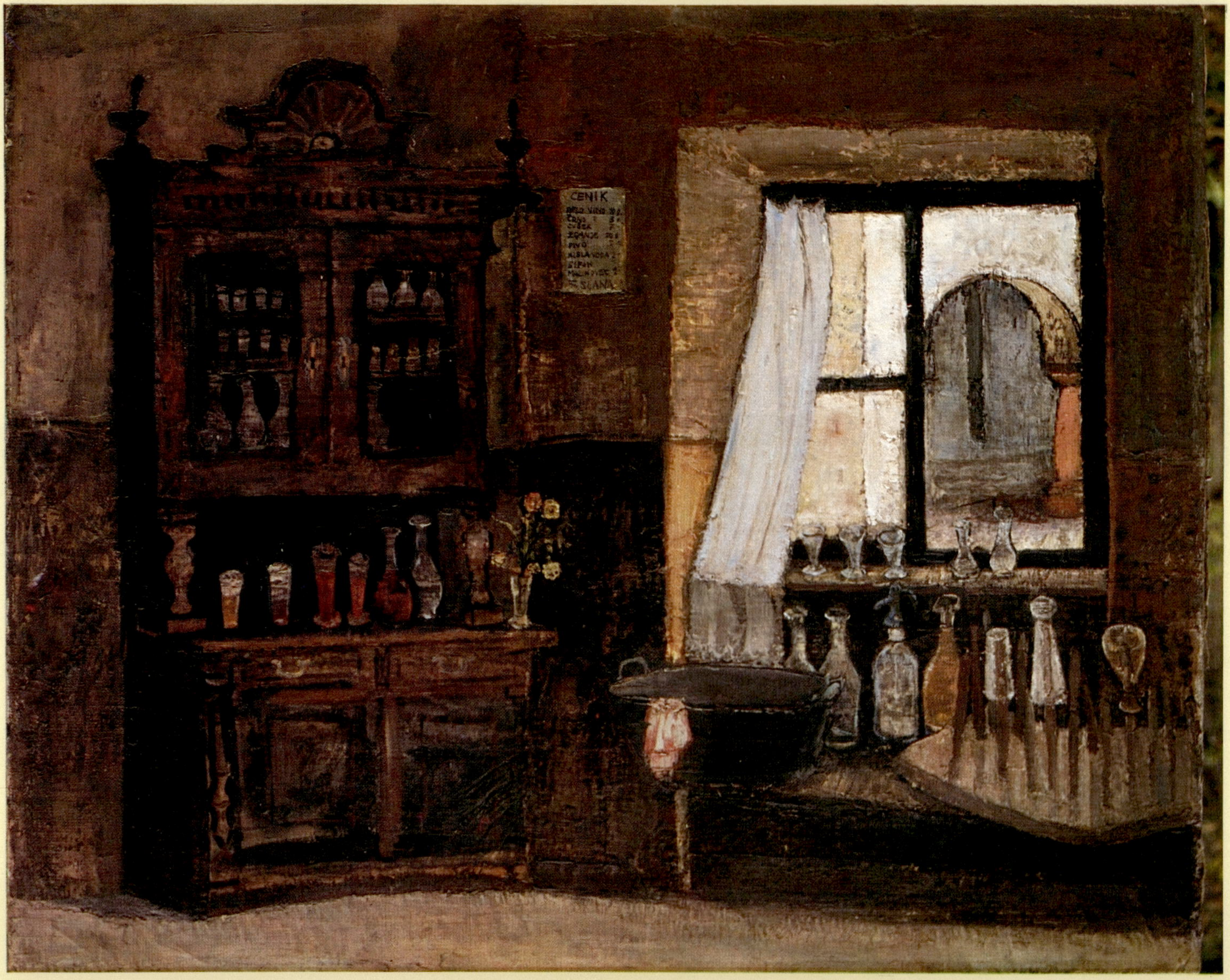

69

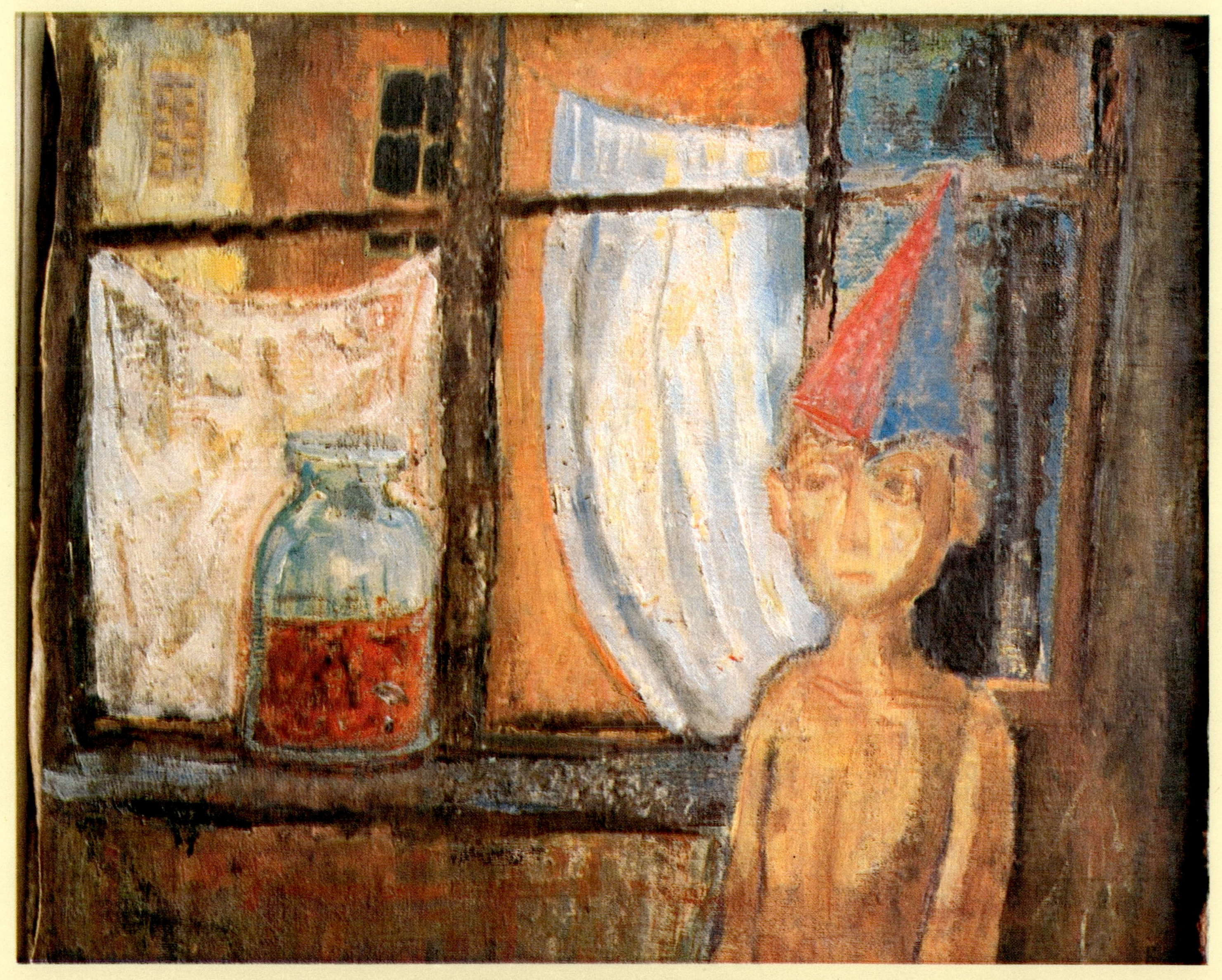

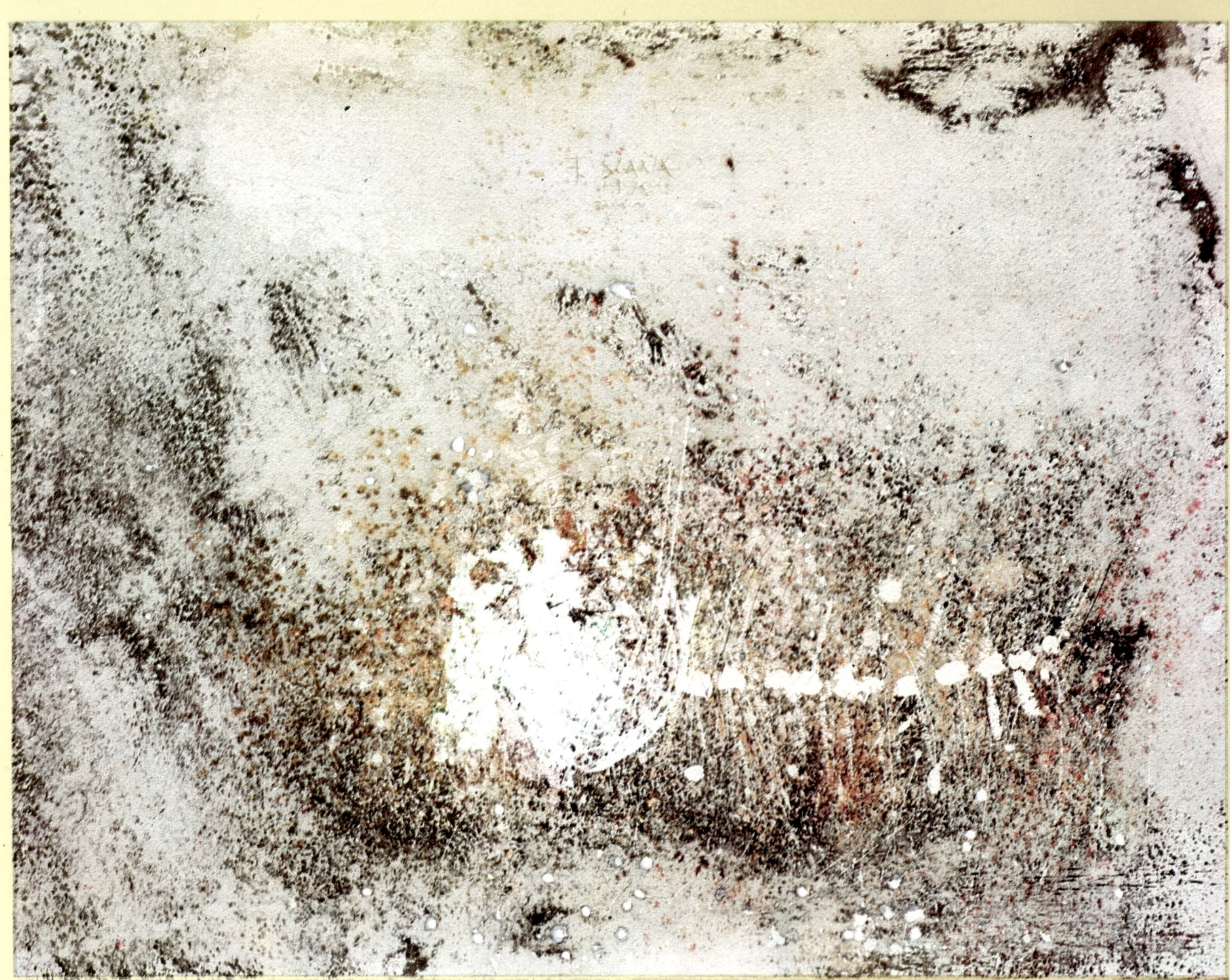

70

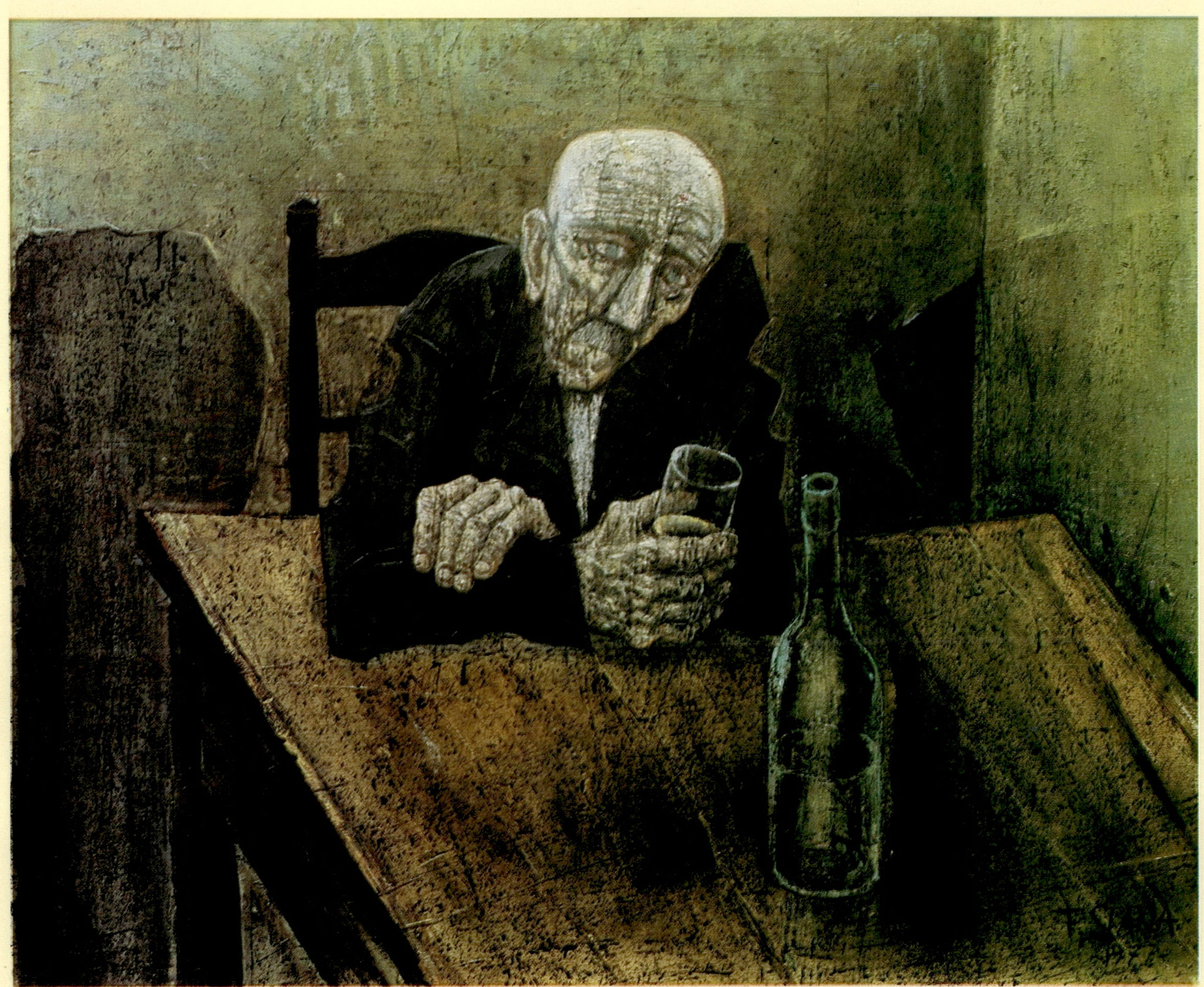

71

72

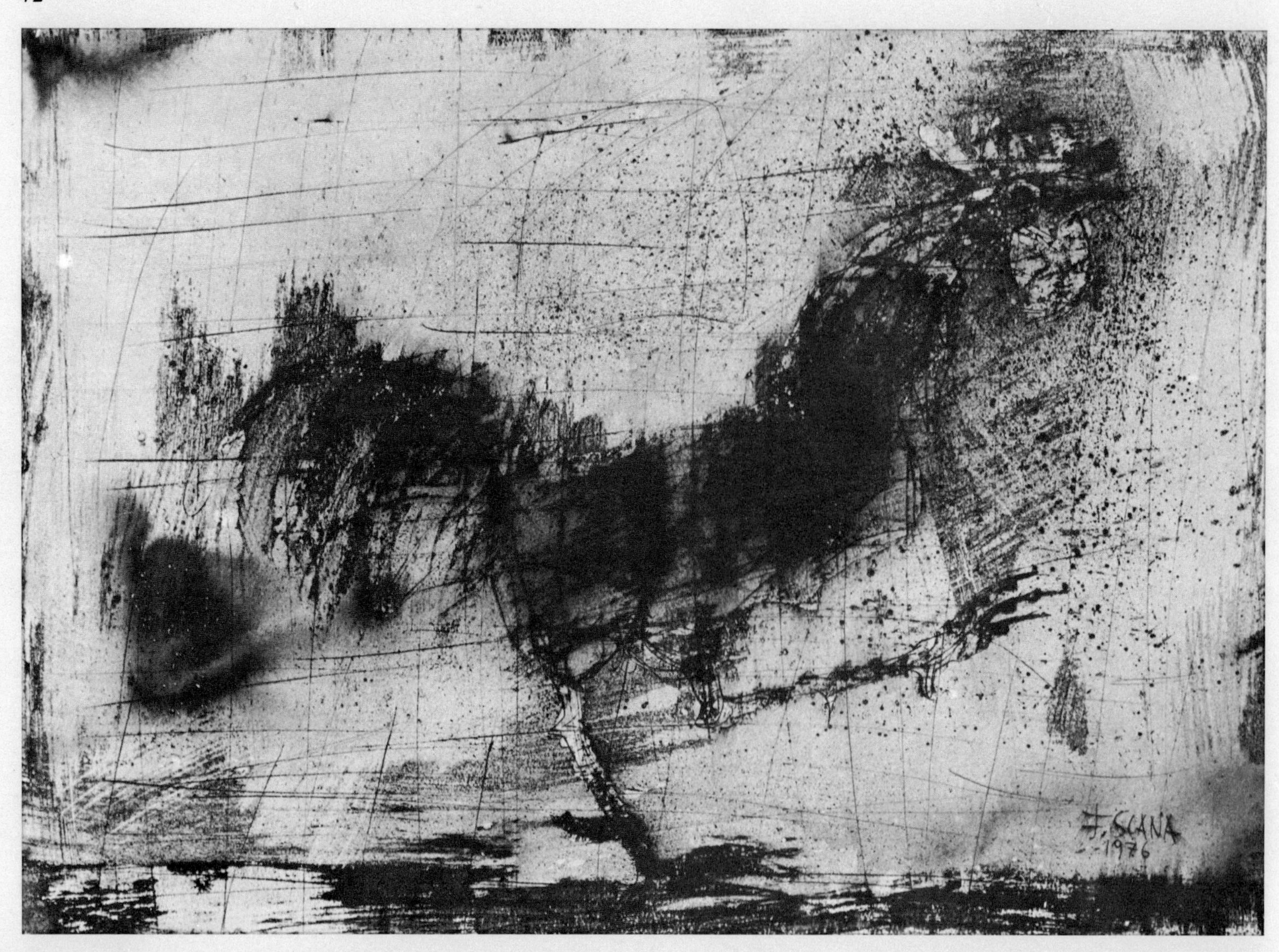

73

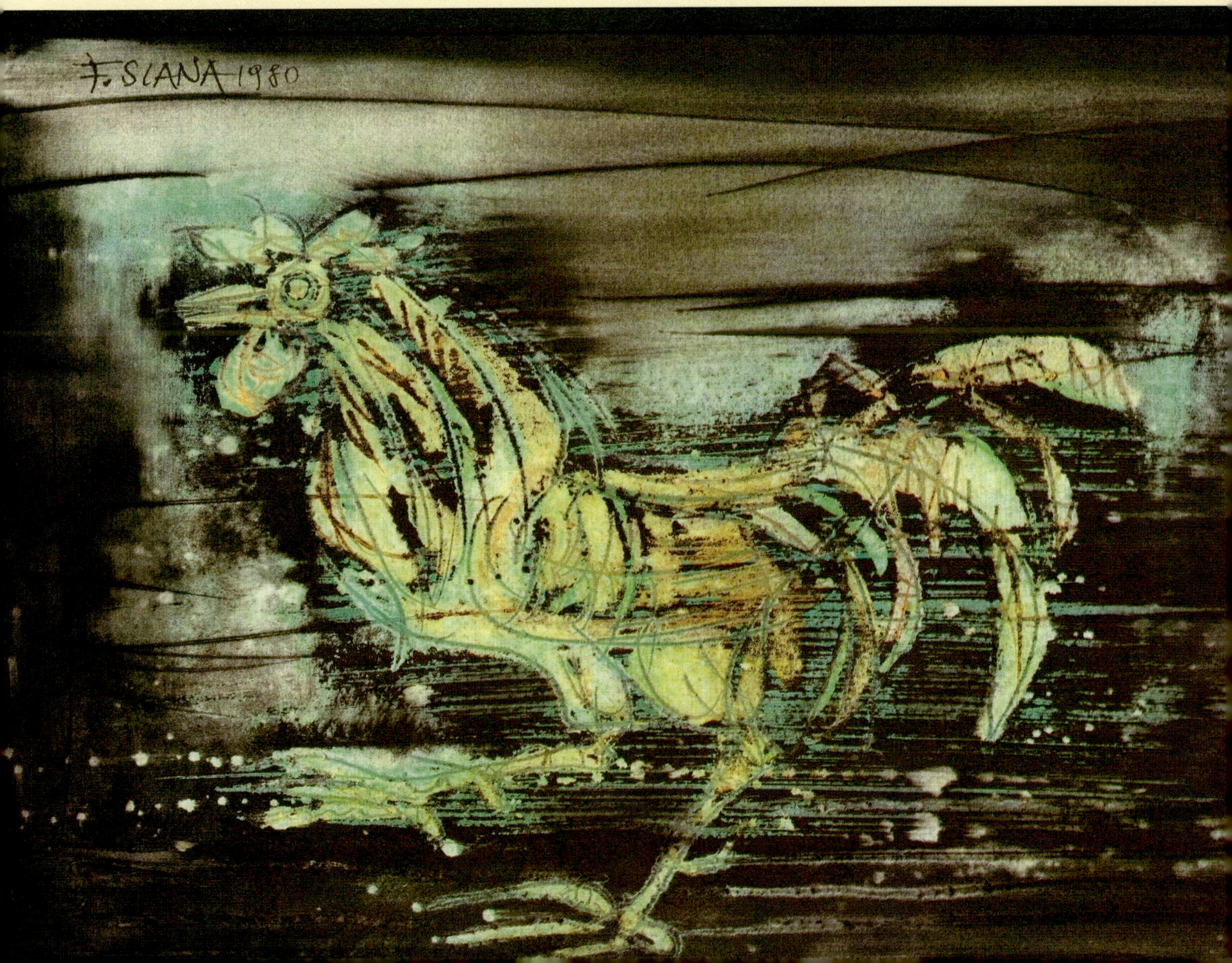

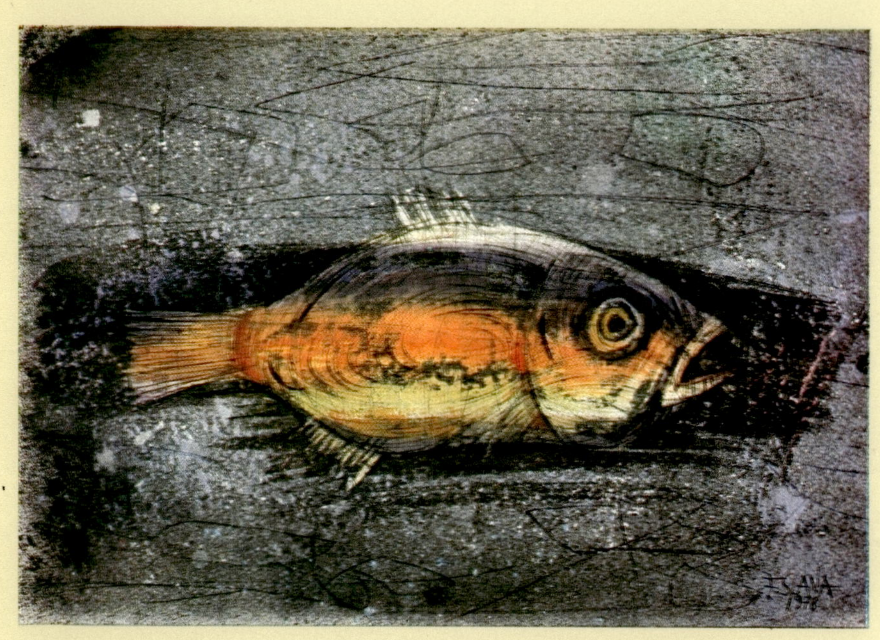

75

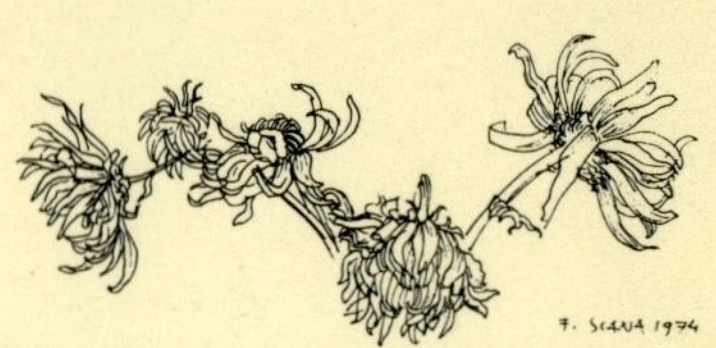

74

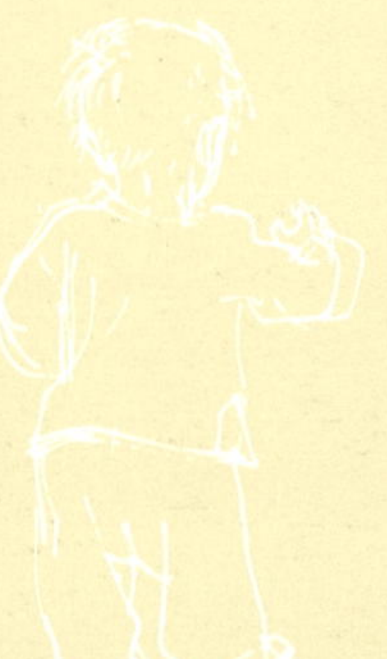

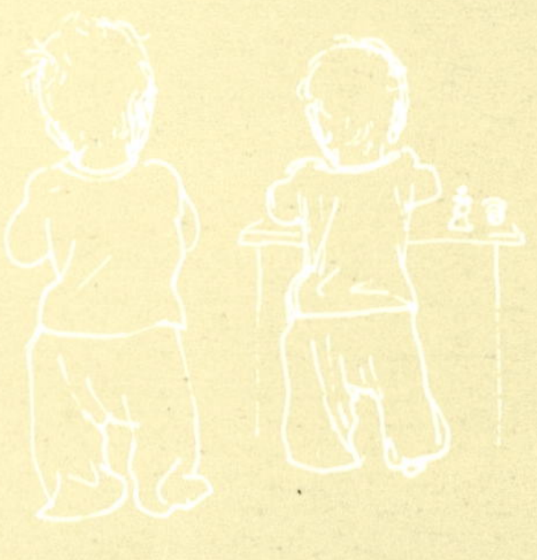

76

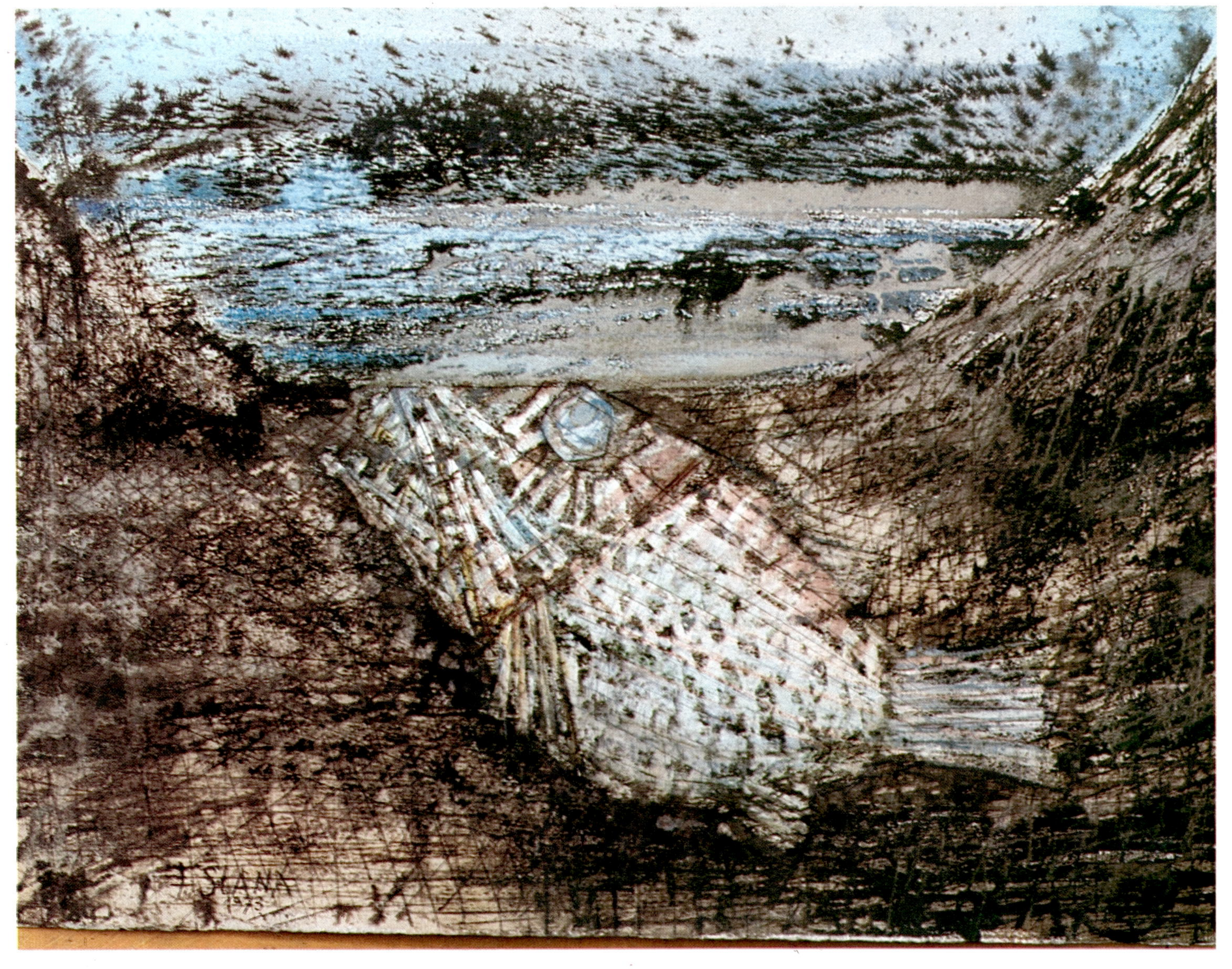

21 FEBRUAR 1978
F. SLANA
21 FEBRUAR 1978
F. SLANA
12·8·1977
KRAPANJ
F. SLANA
KRAPANJ
1980
F. SLANA

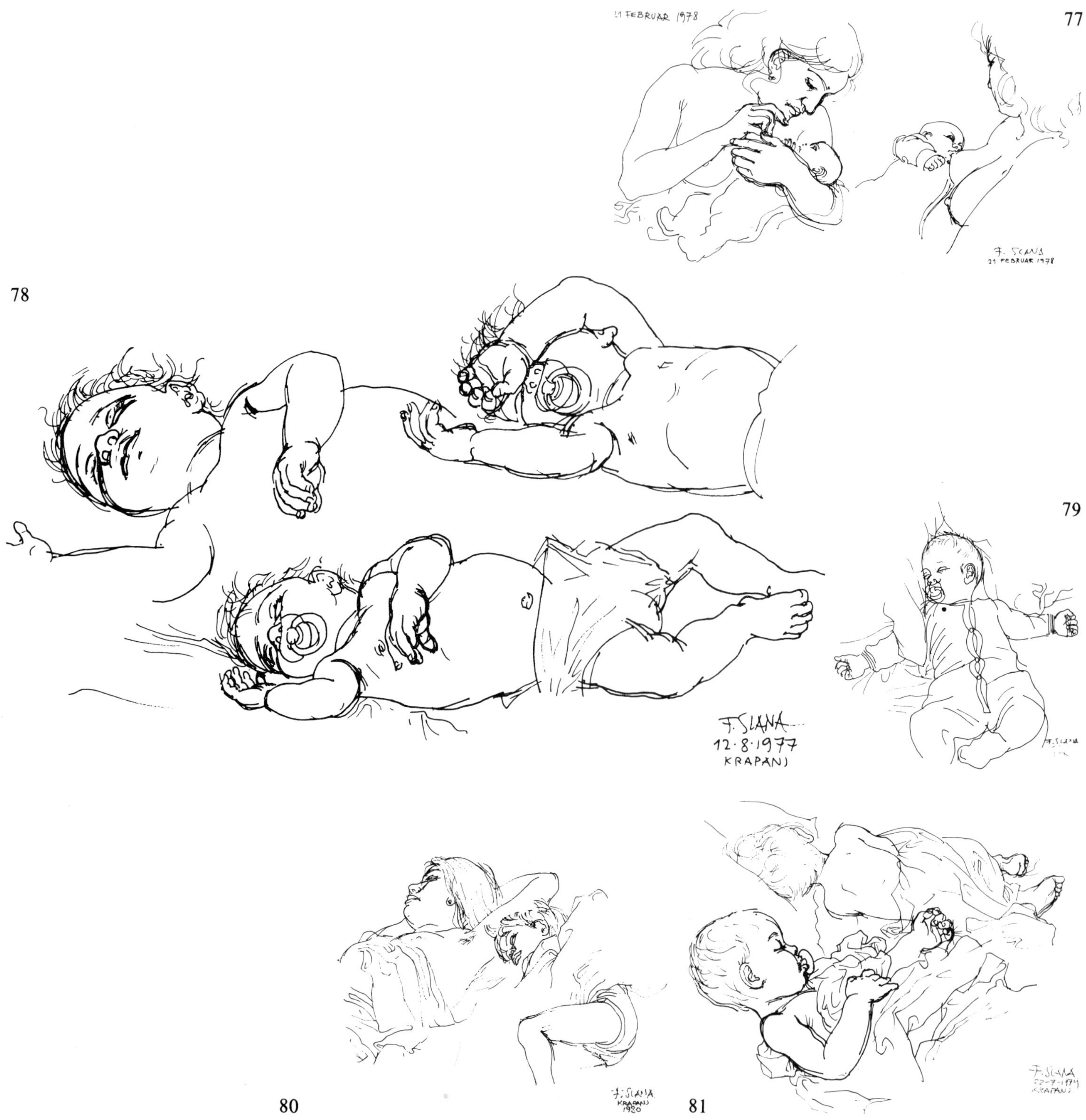

77

78

79

80

81

82

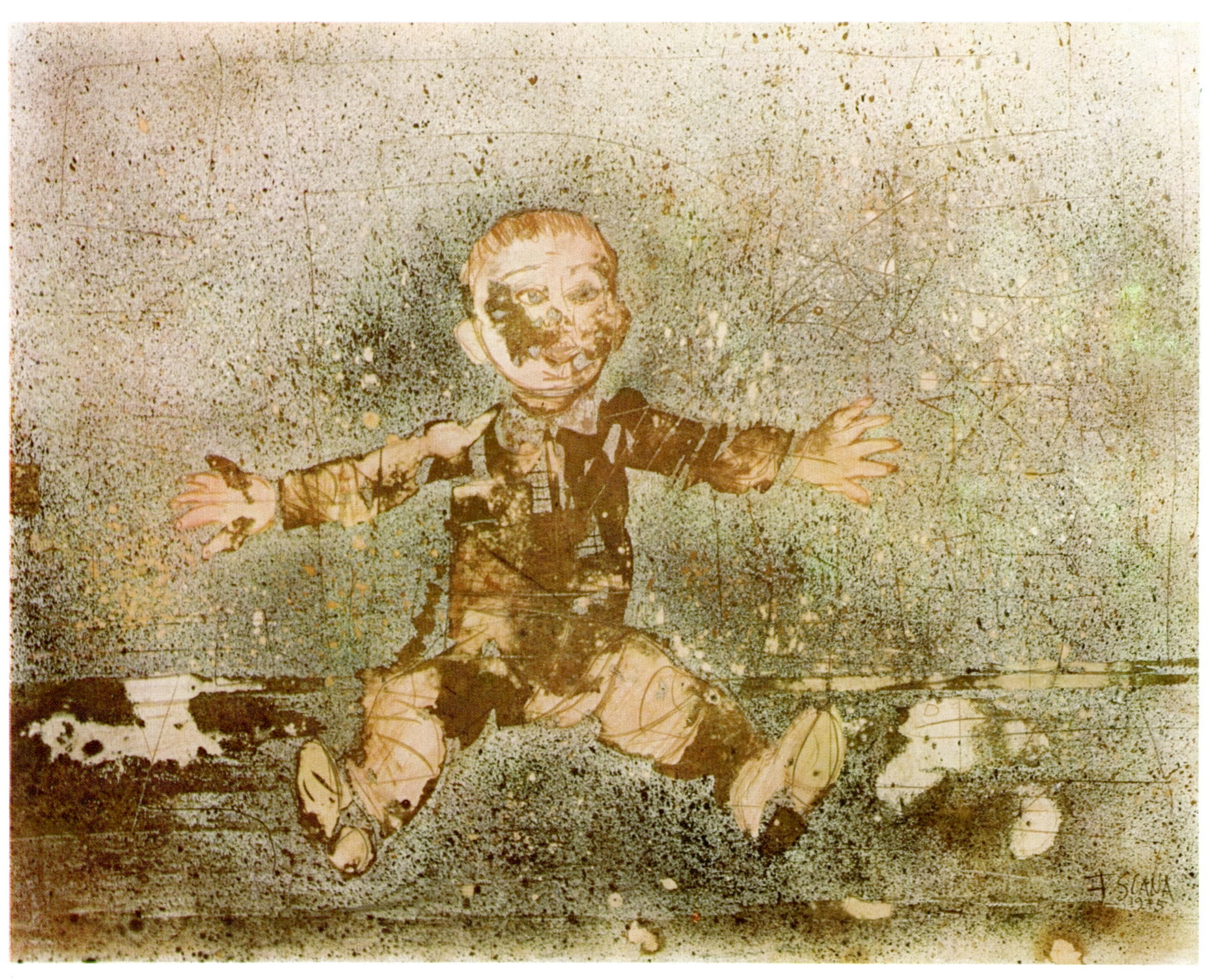

83

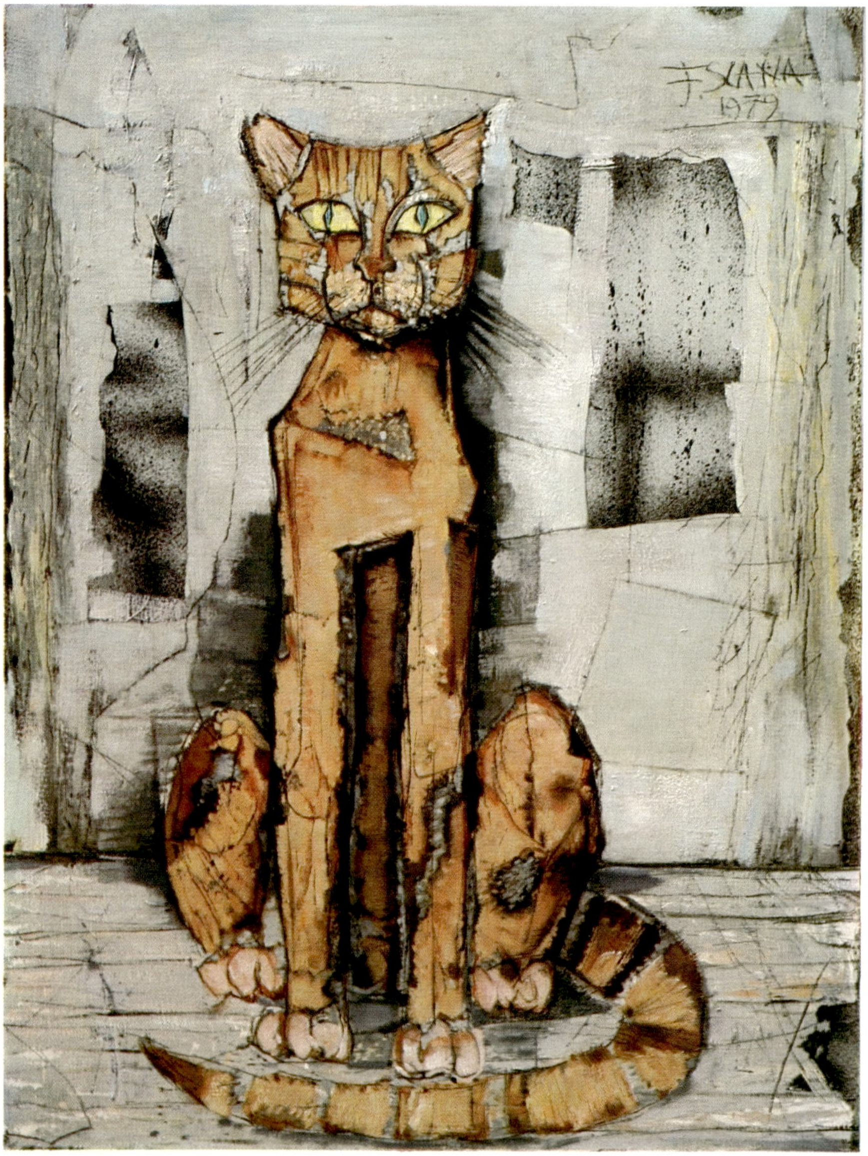

84

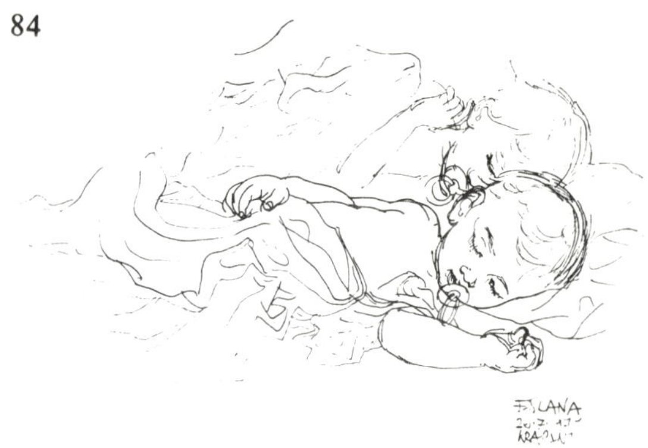

85

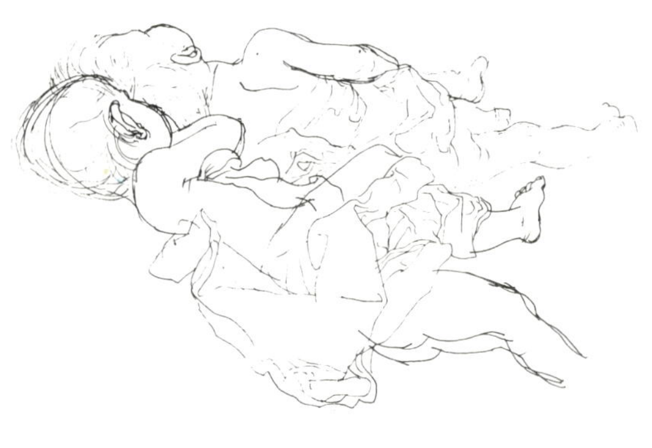

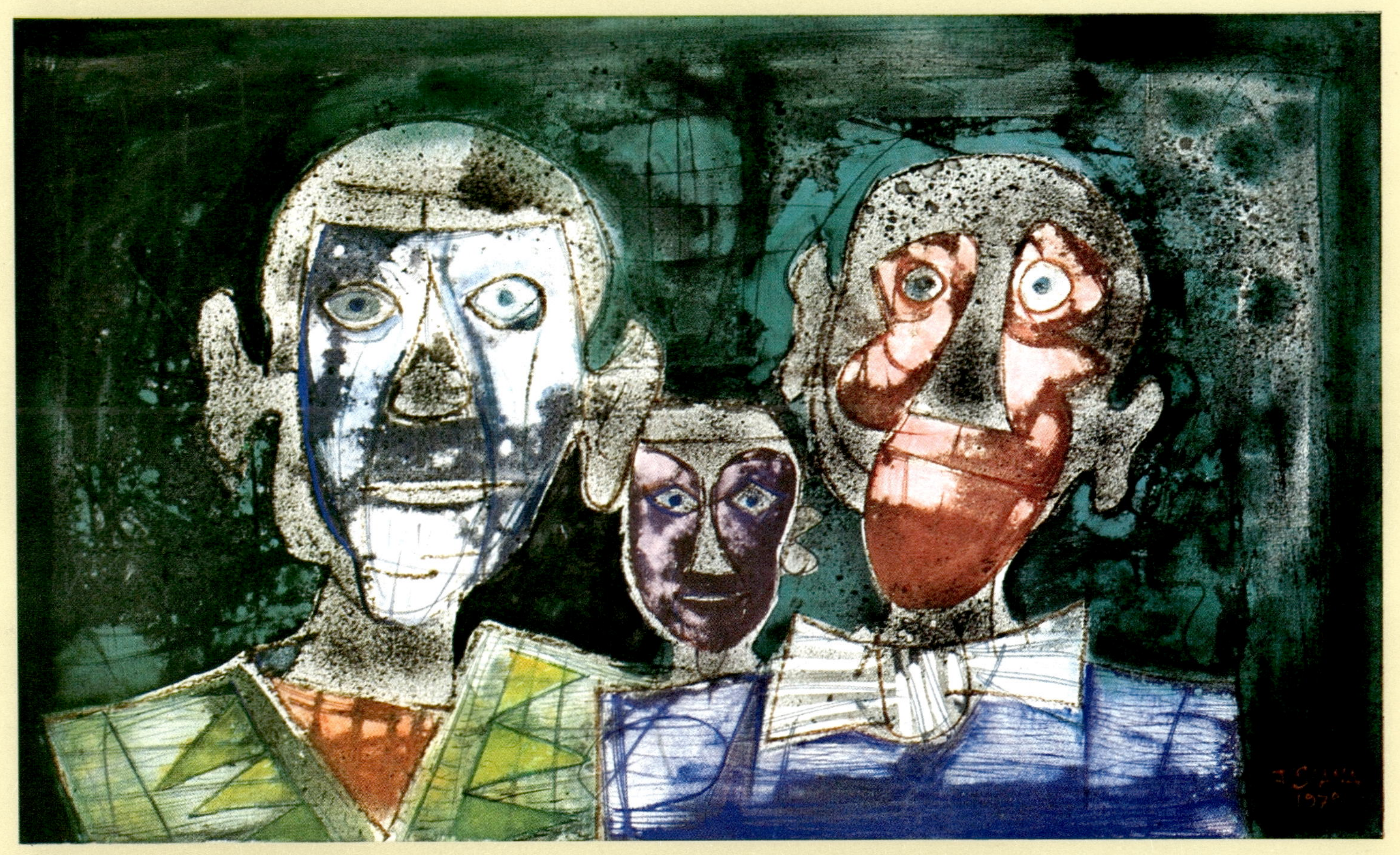

87

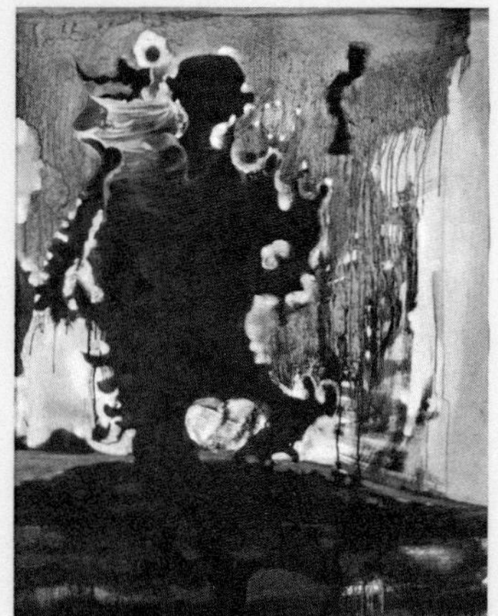

88

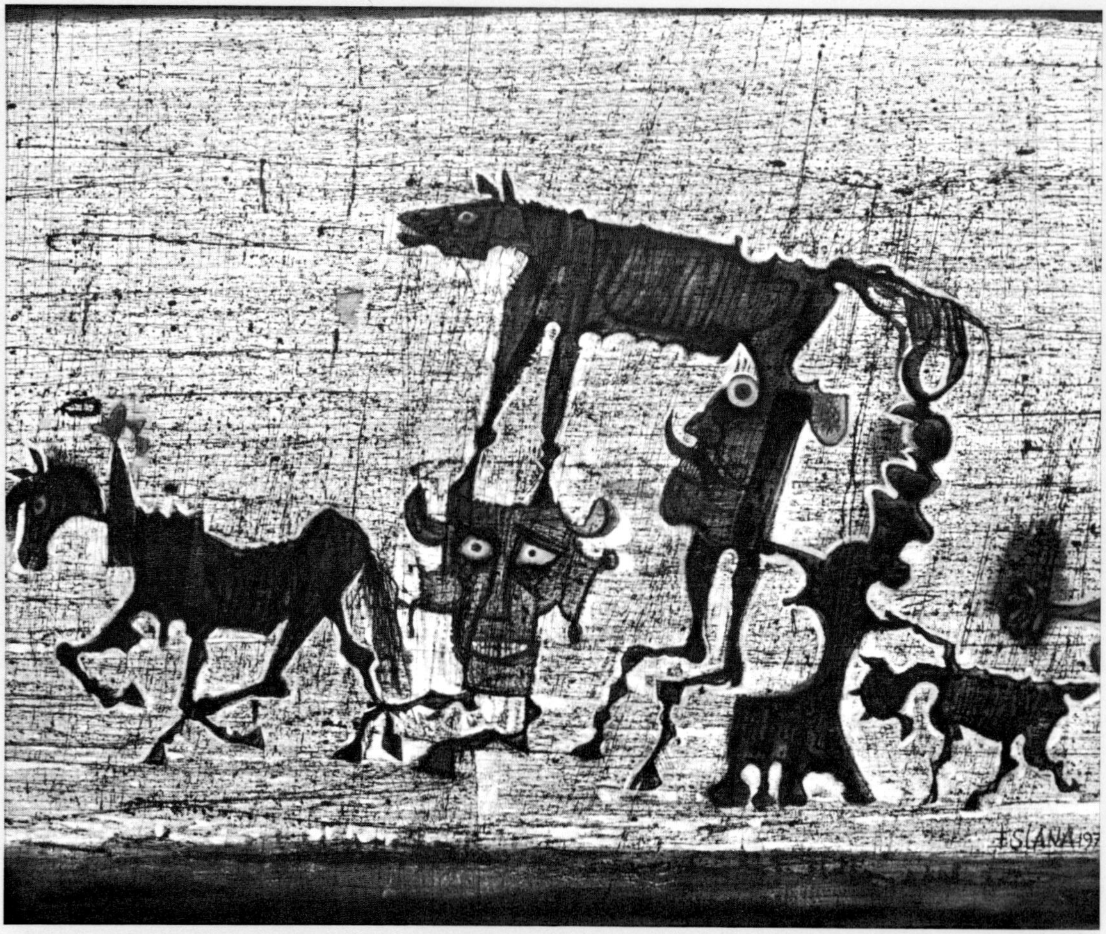

89

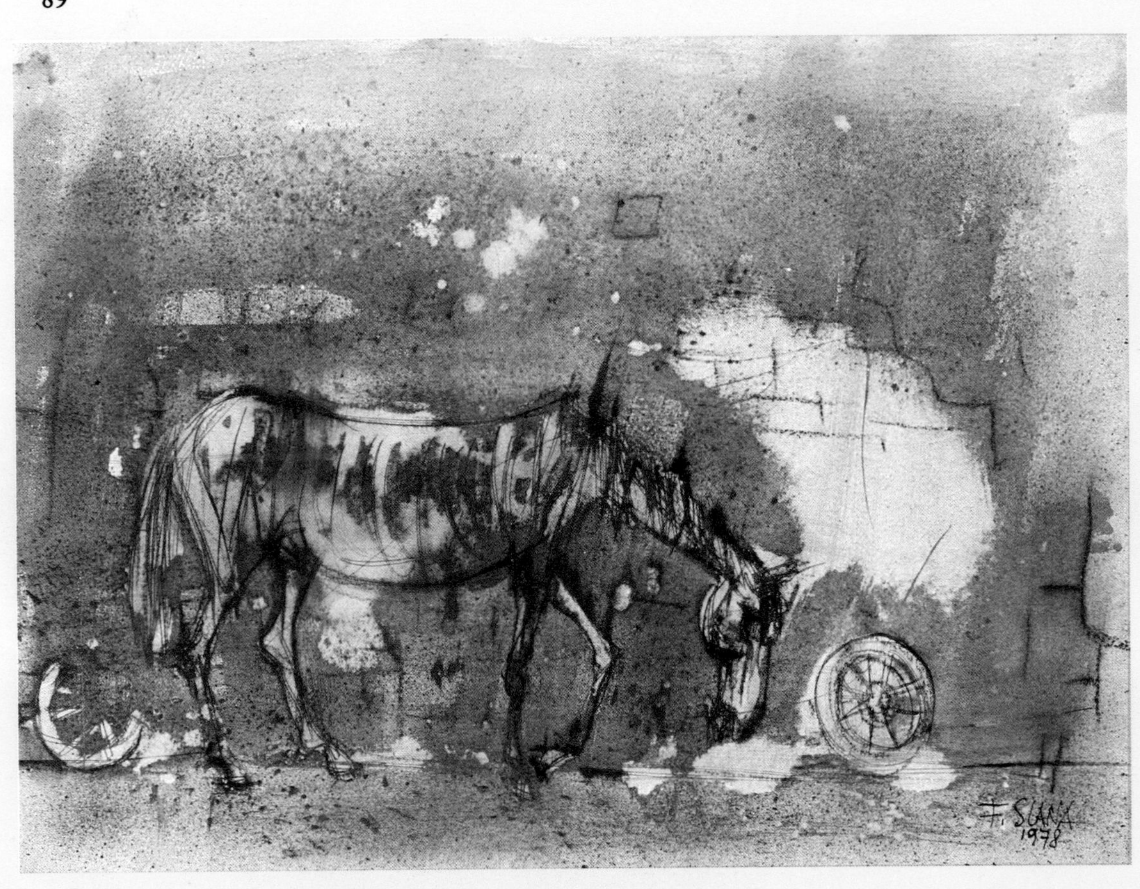

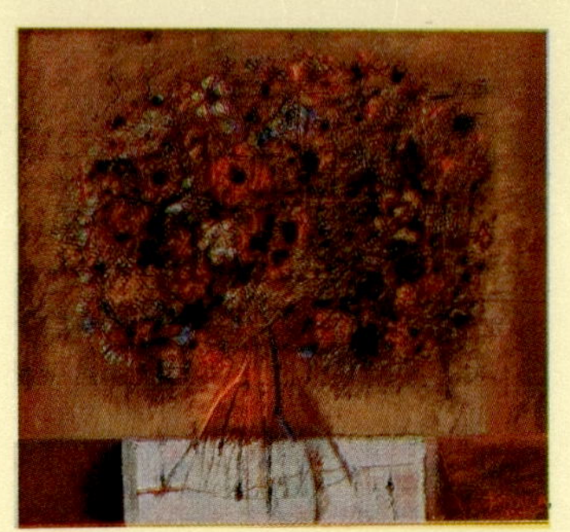

90

91

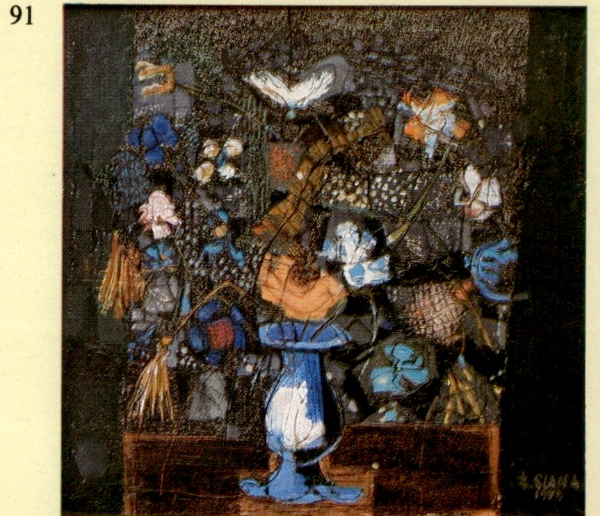

92

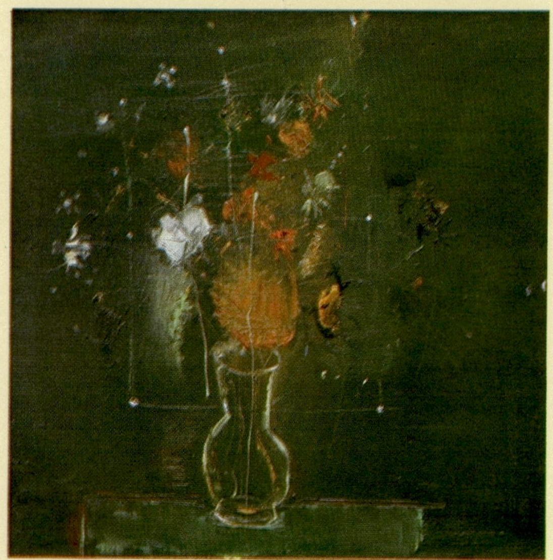

93

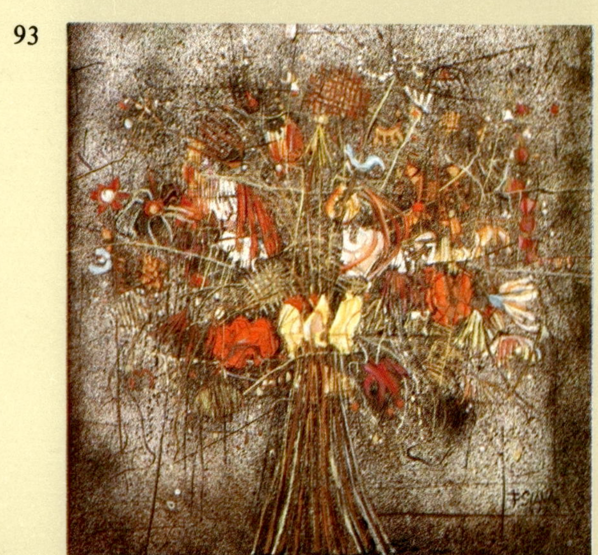

94

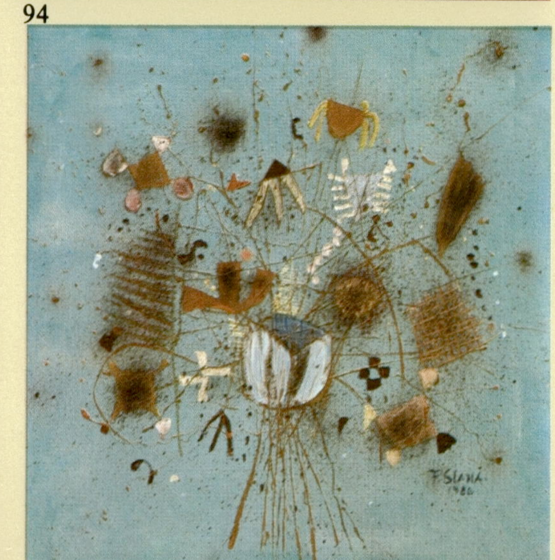

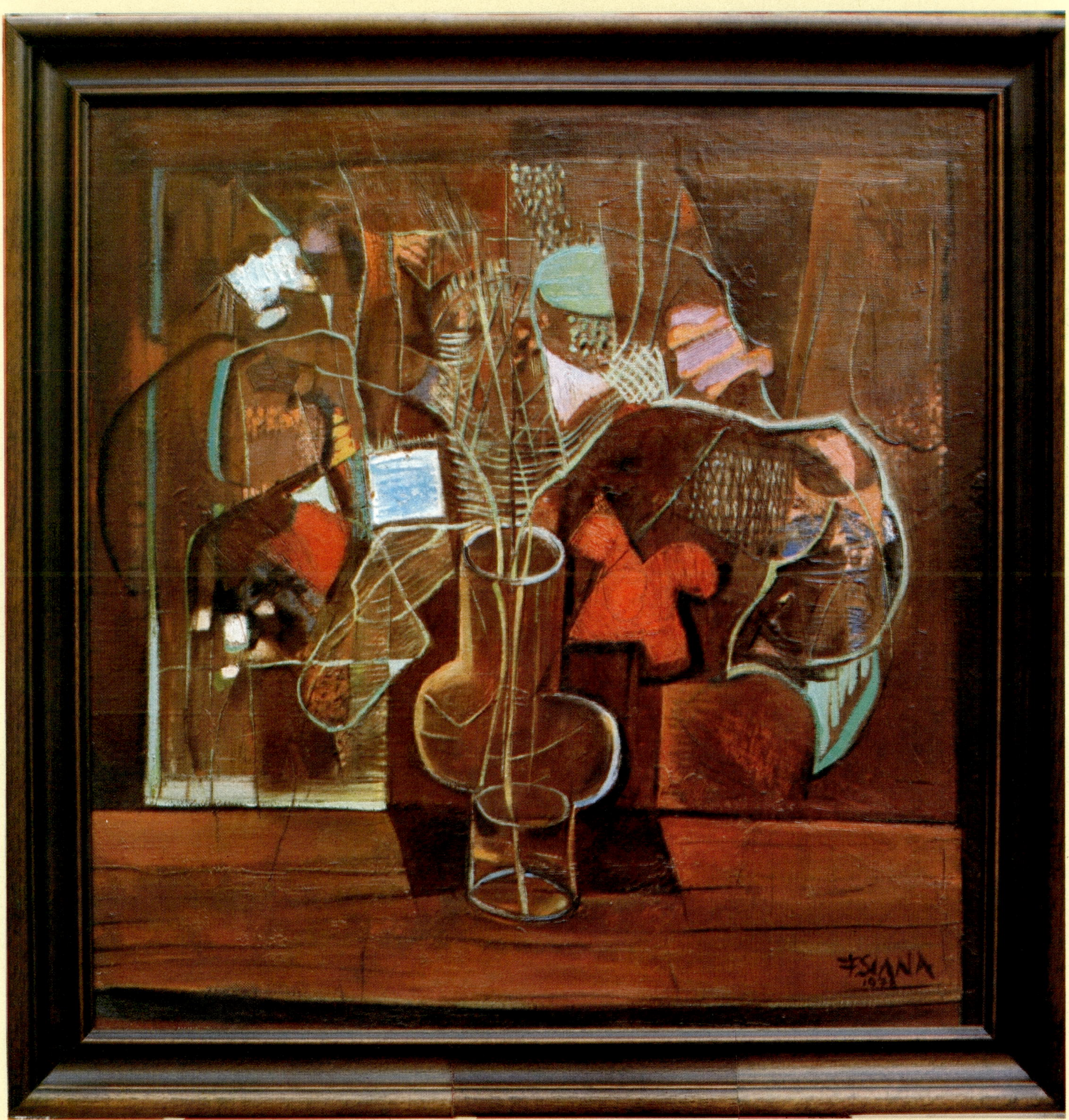

96

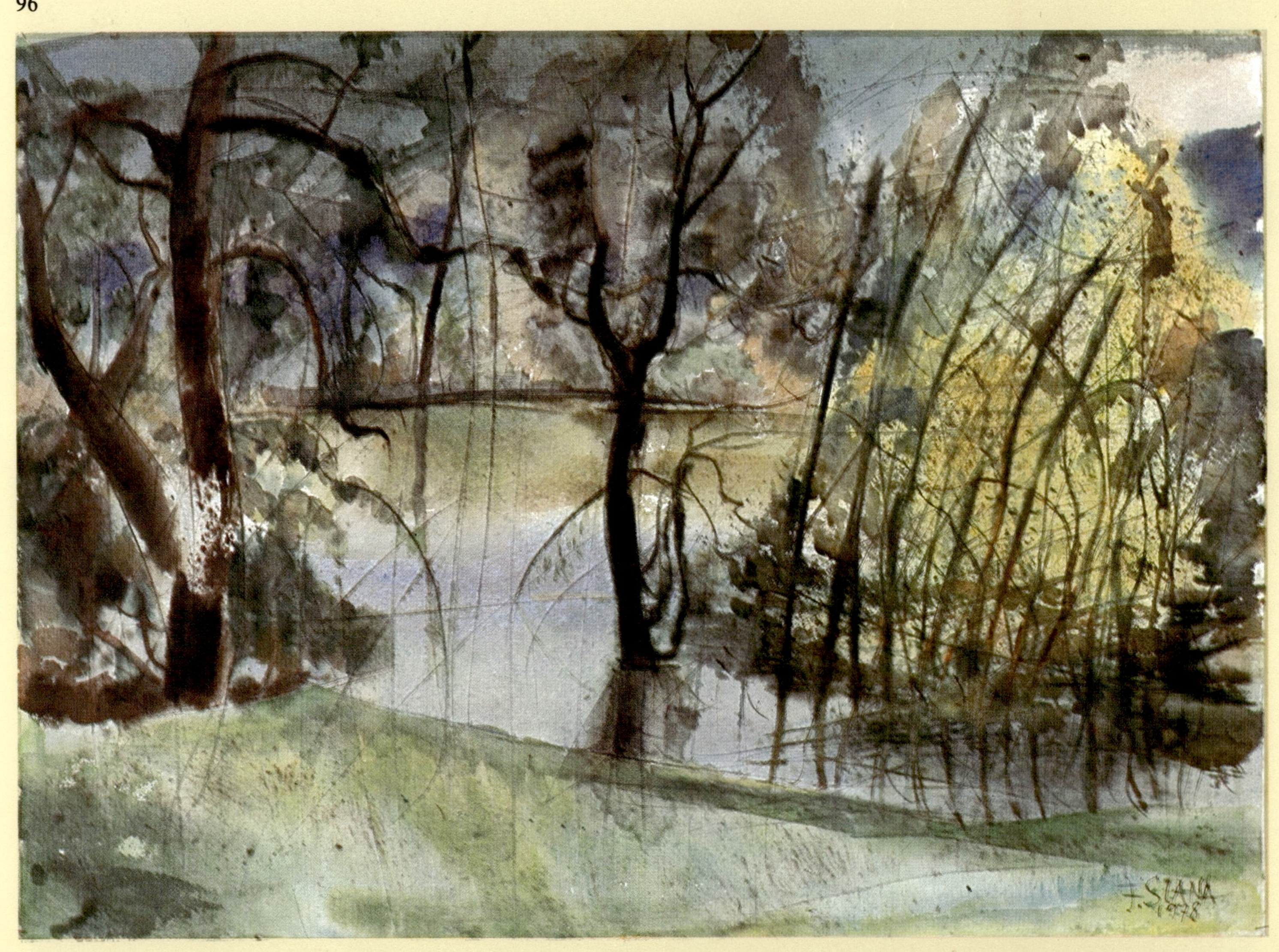

97

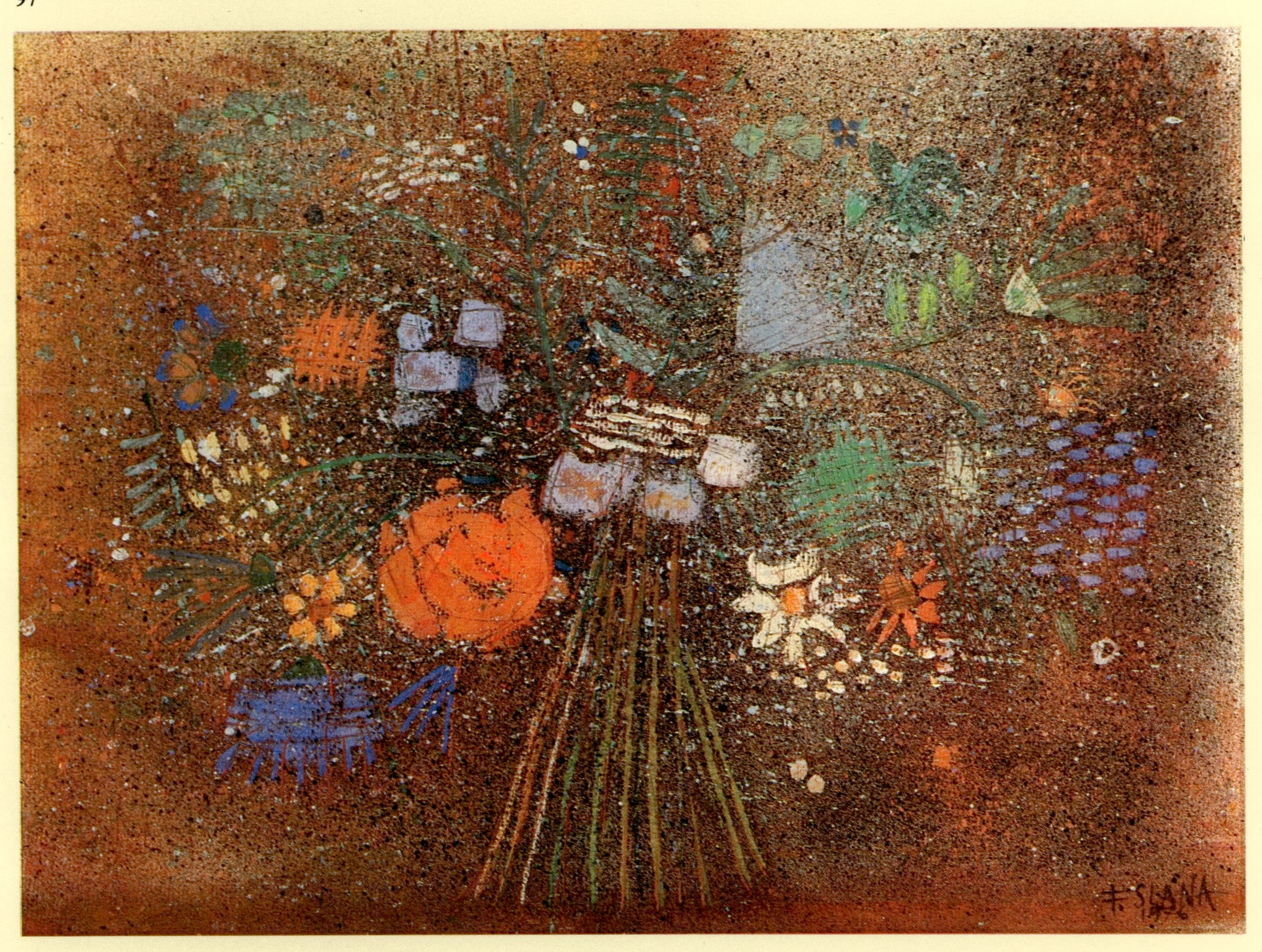

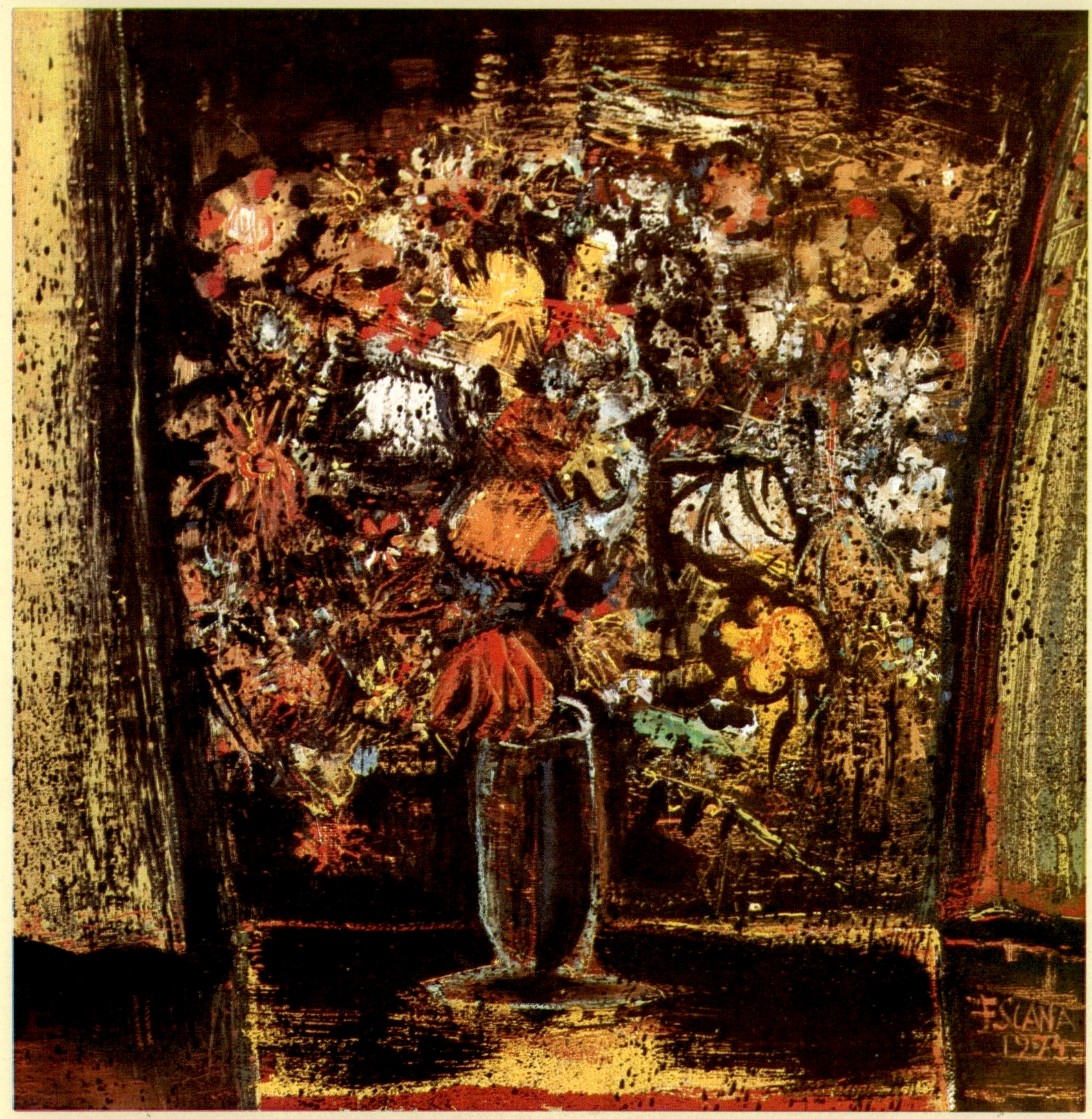

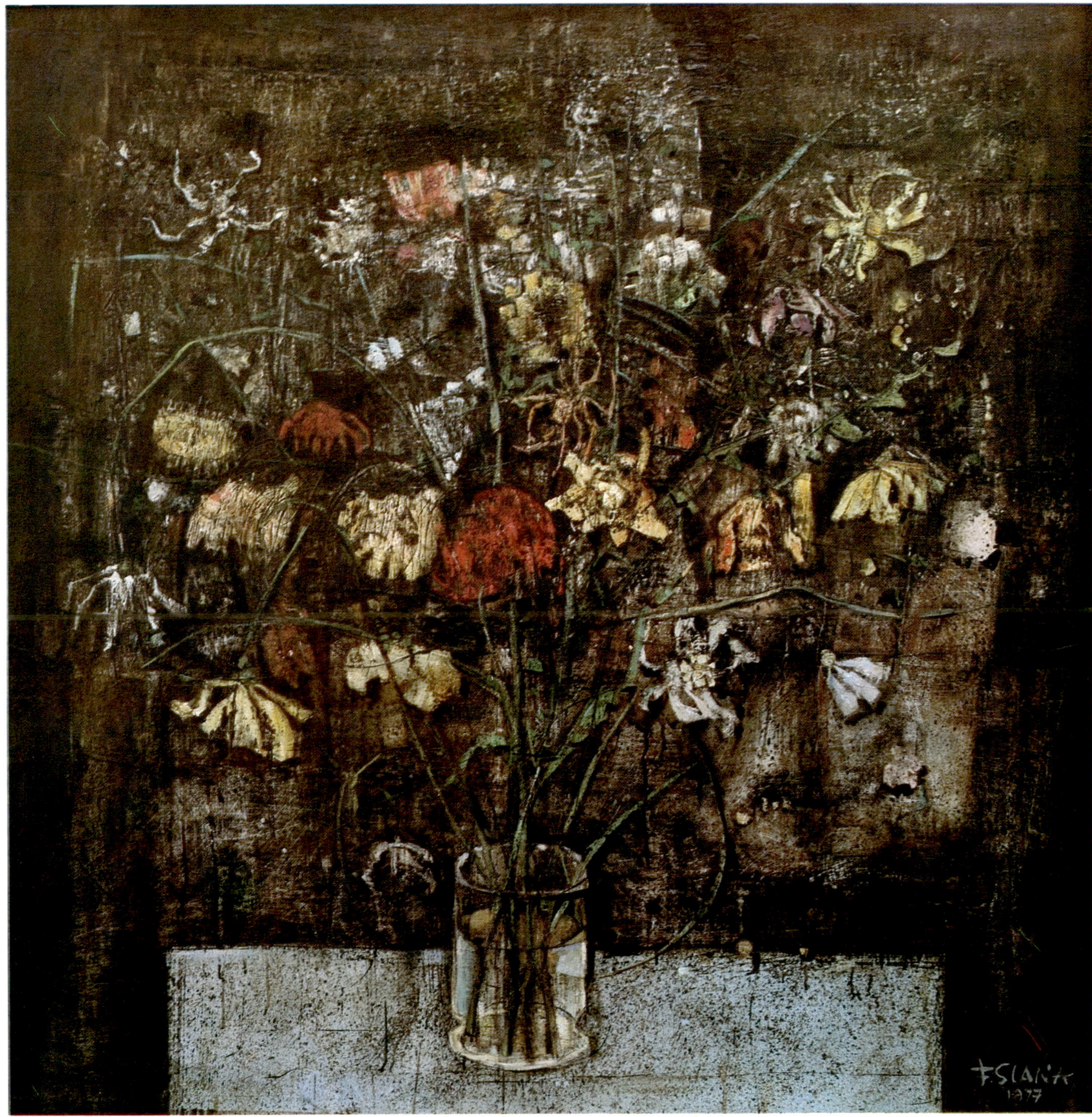
F.SLANIK
1977

100

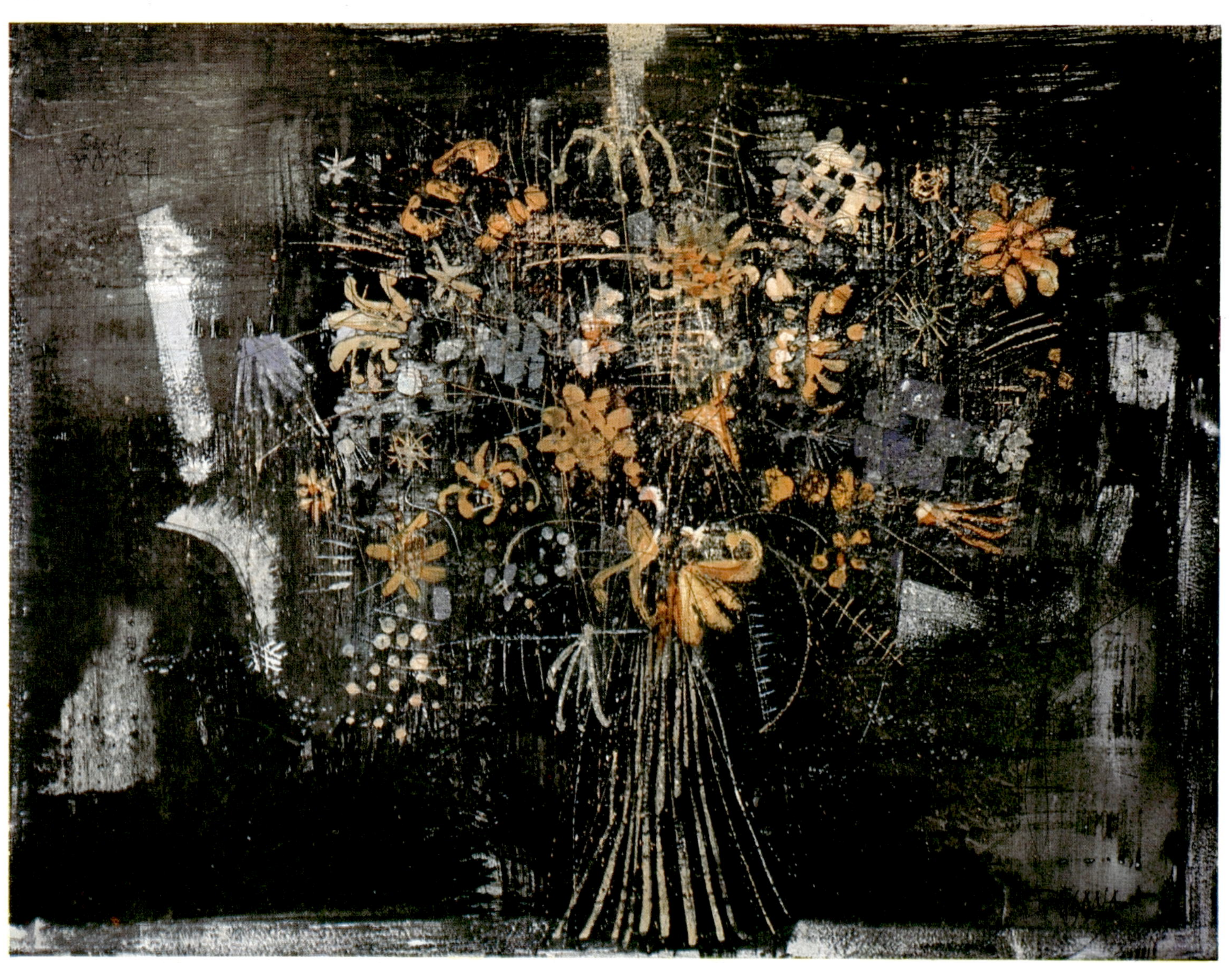

101

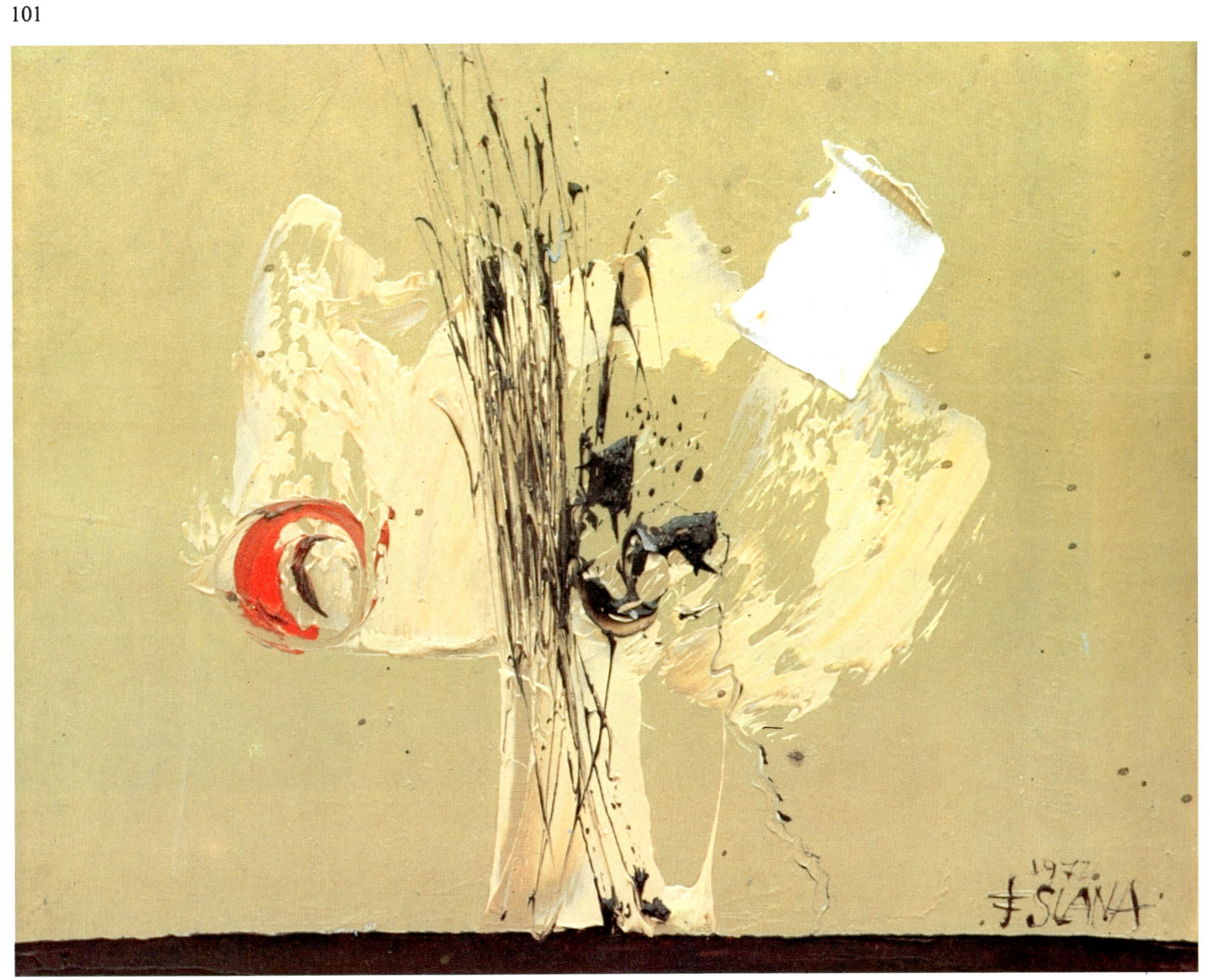

102

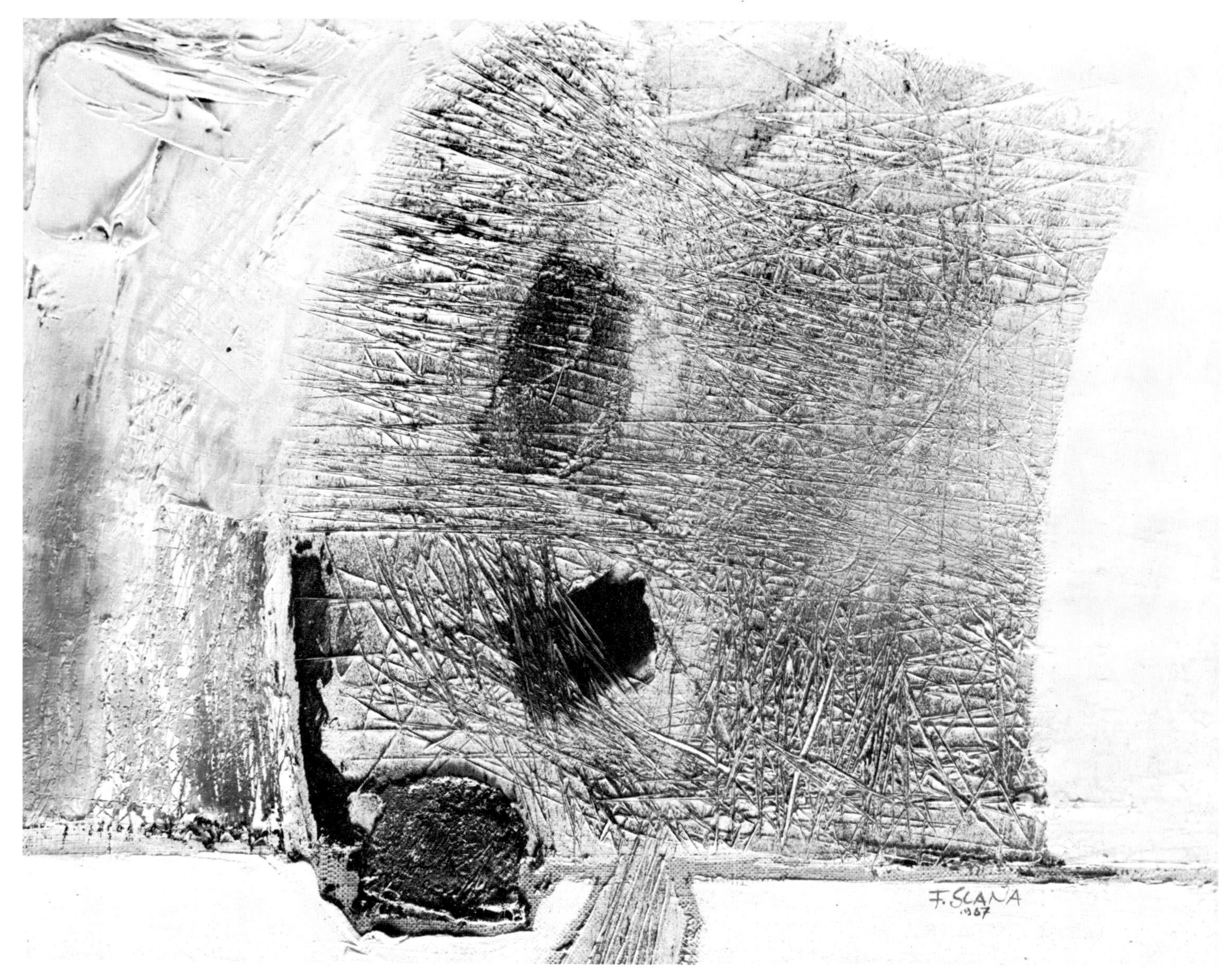

103

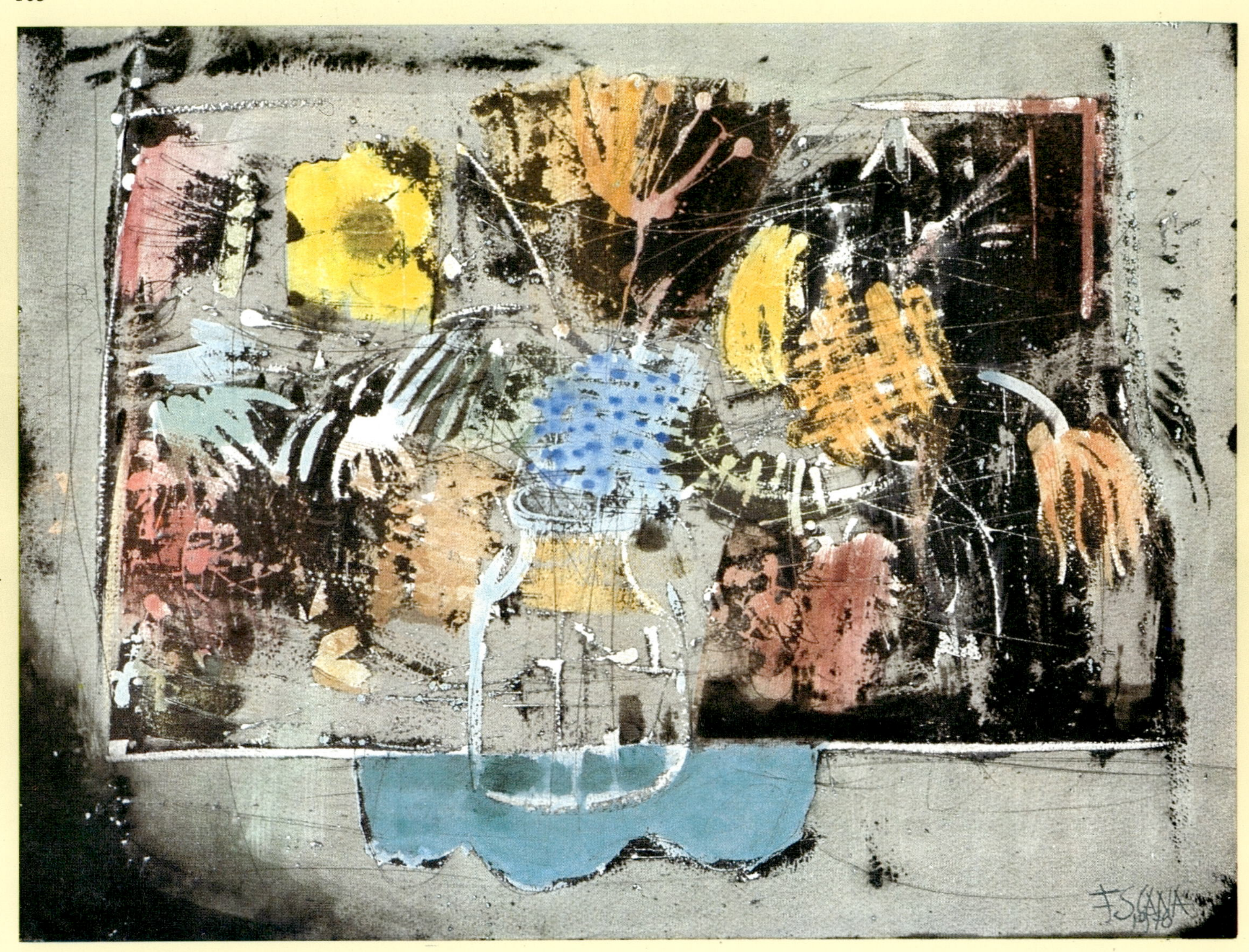

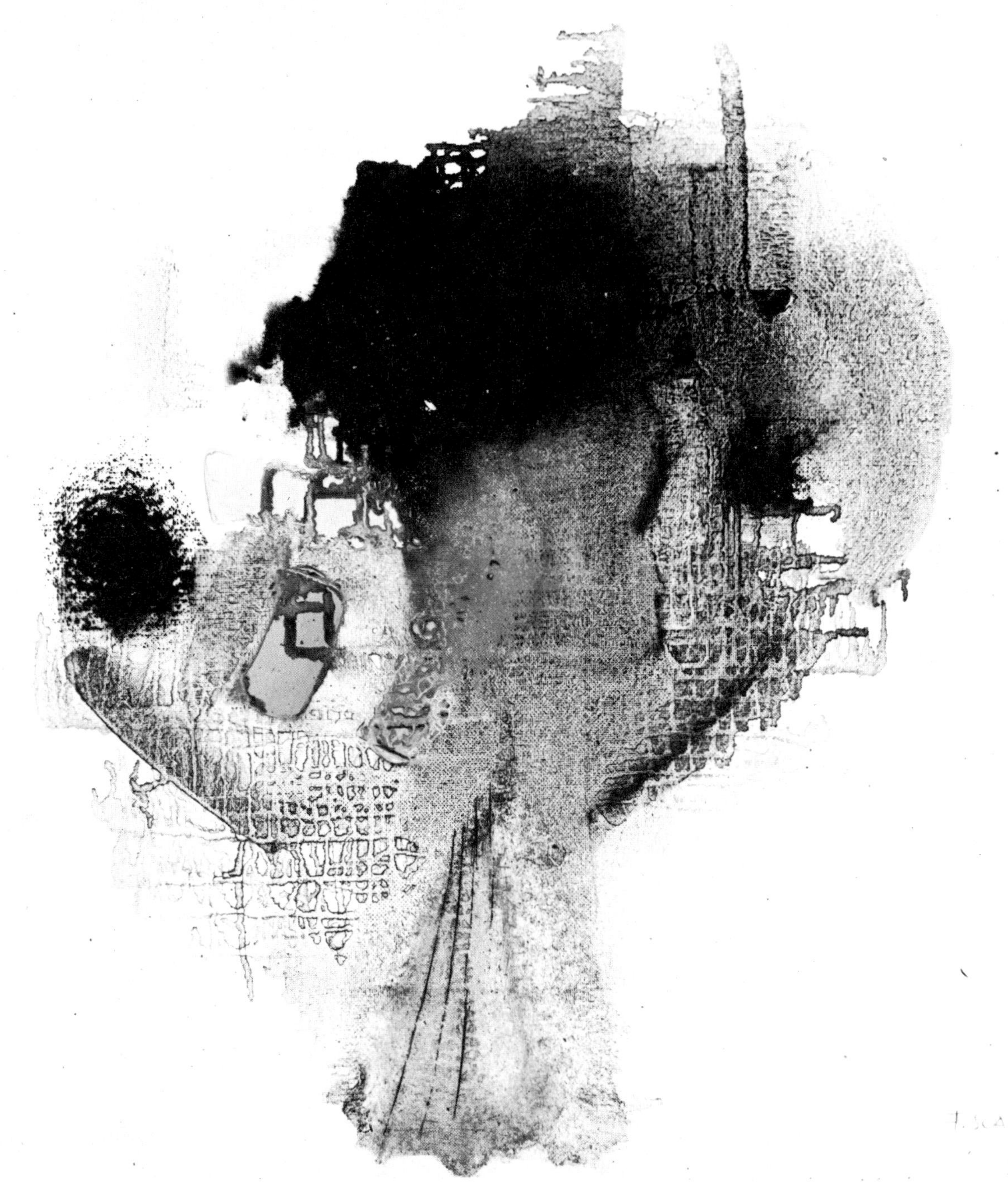

F. SLANA

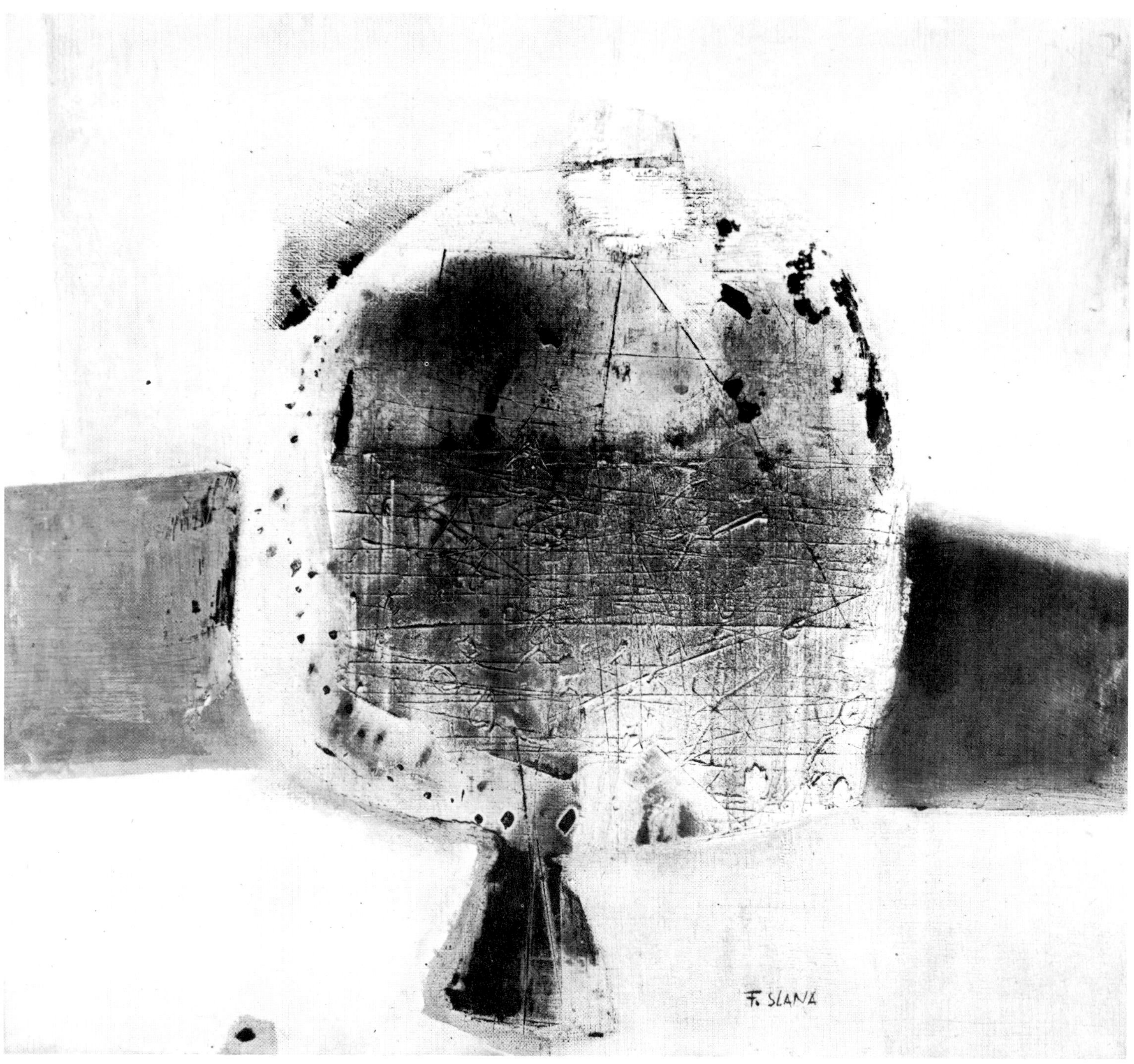
F. SLANA

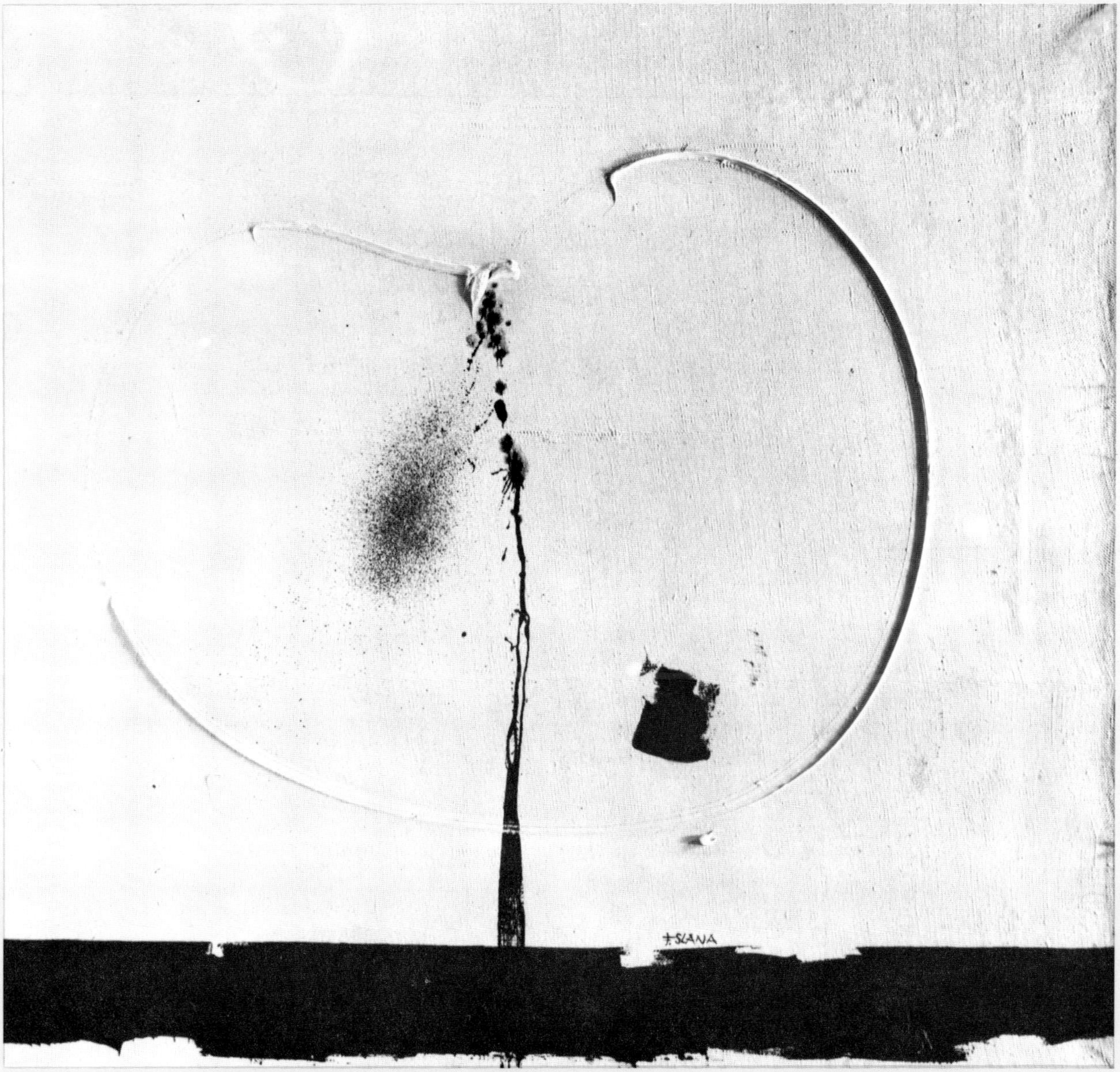

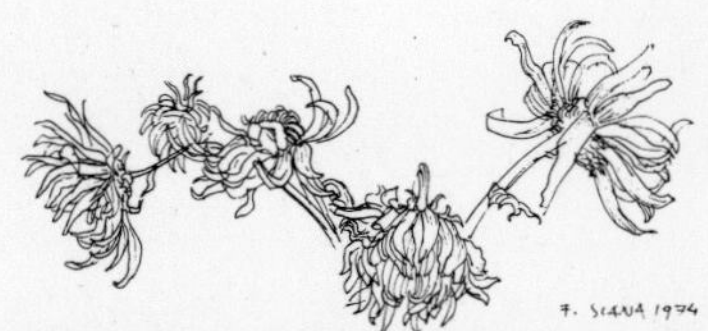

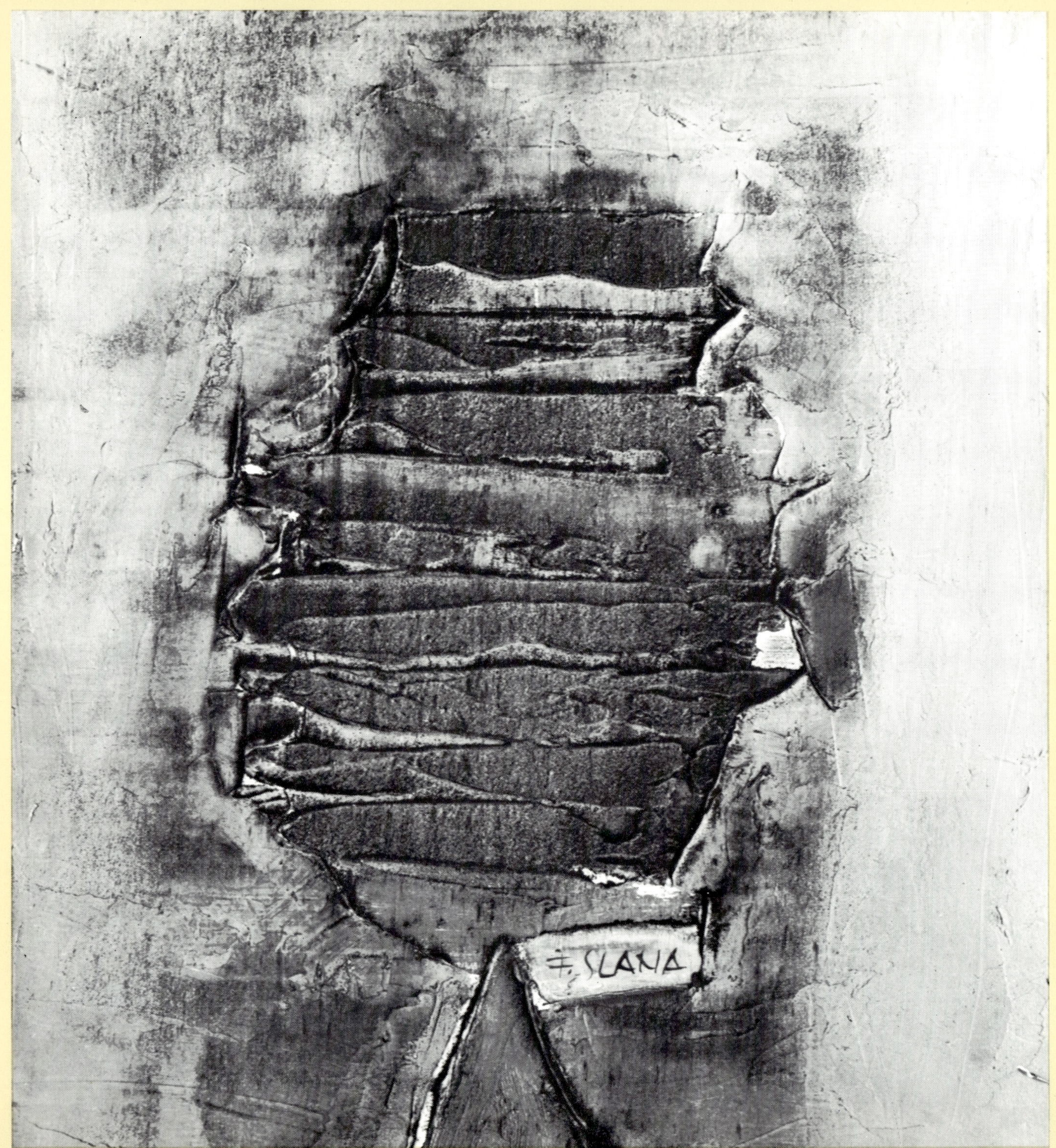
F. SLANA

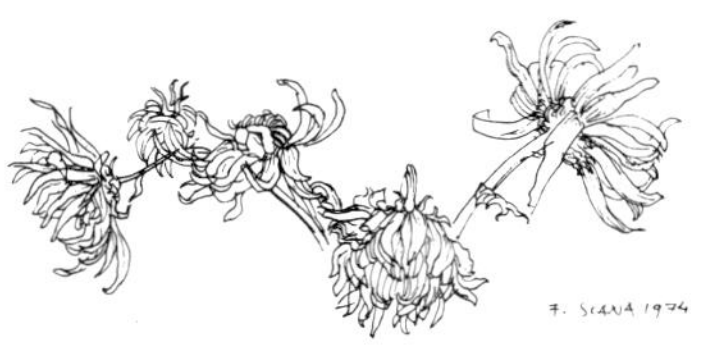

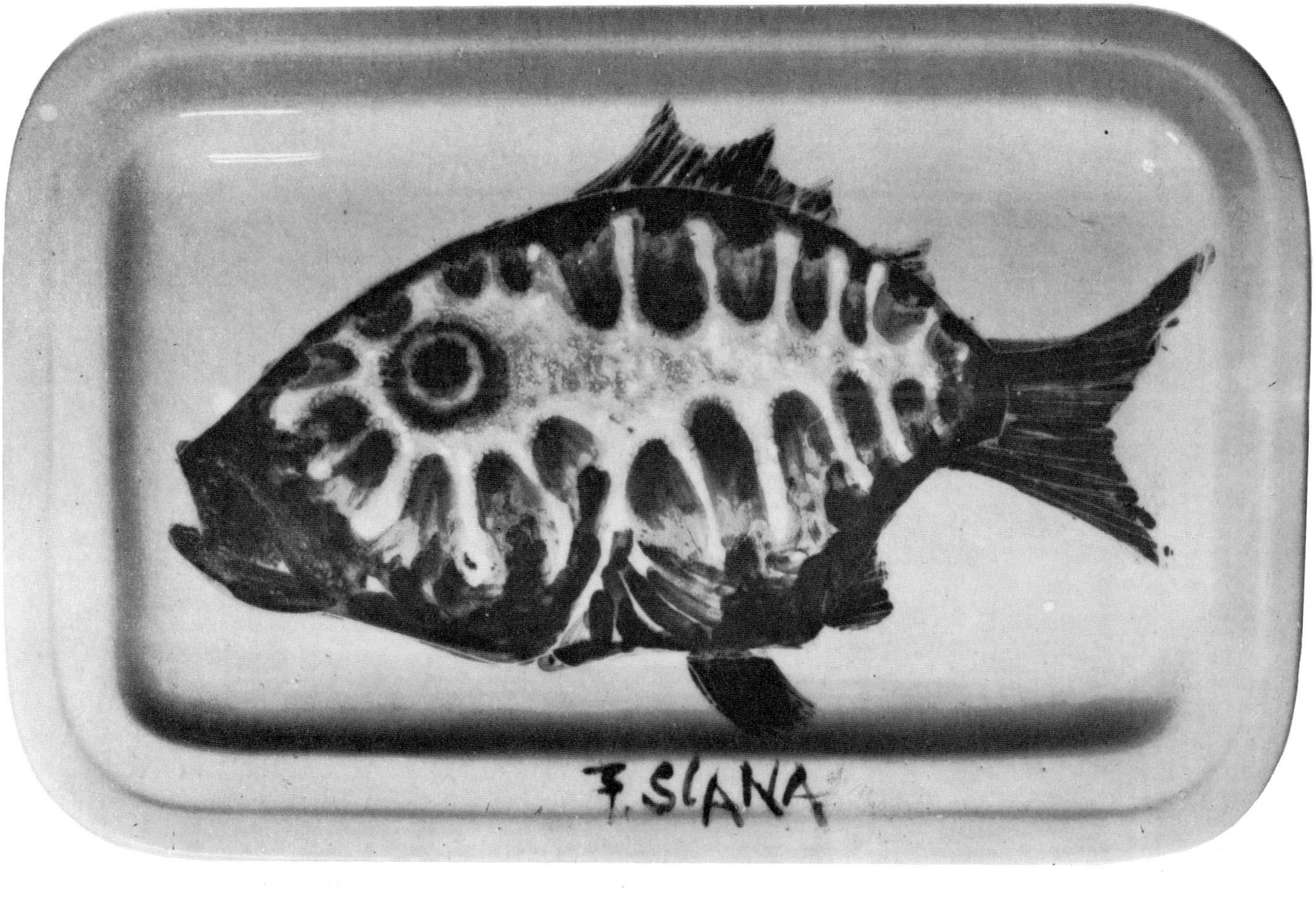

110

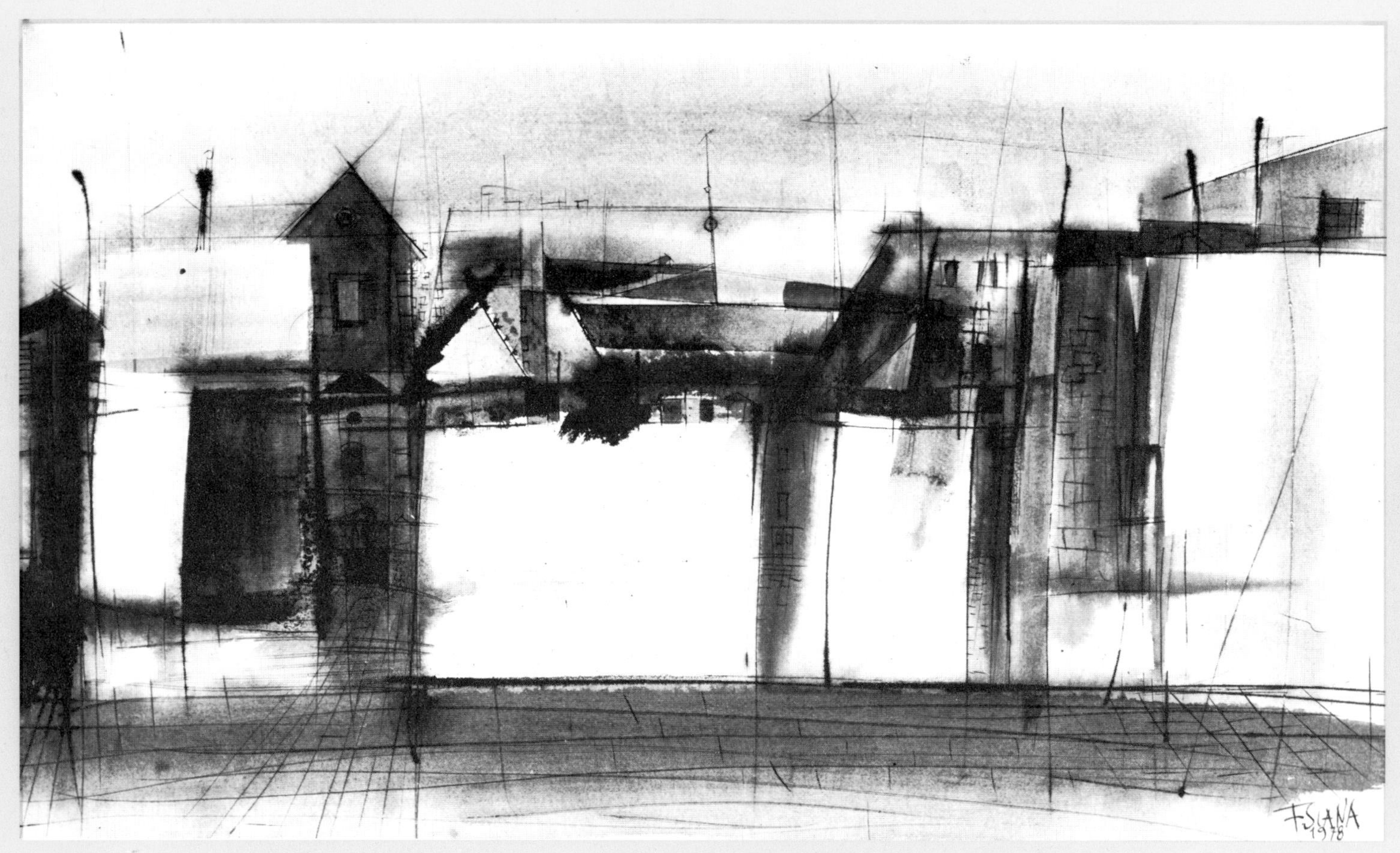

111

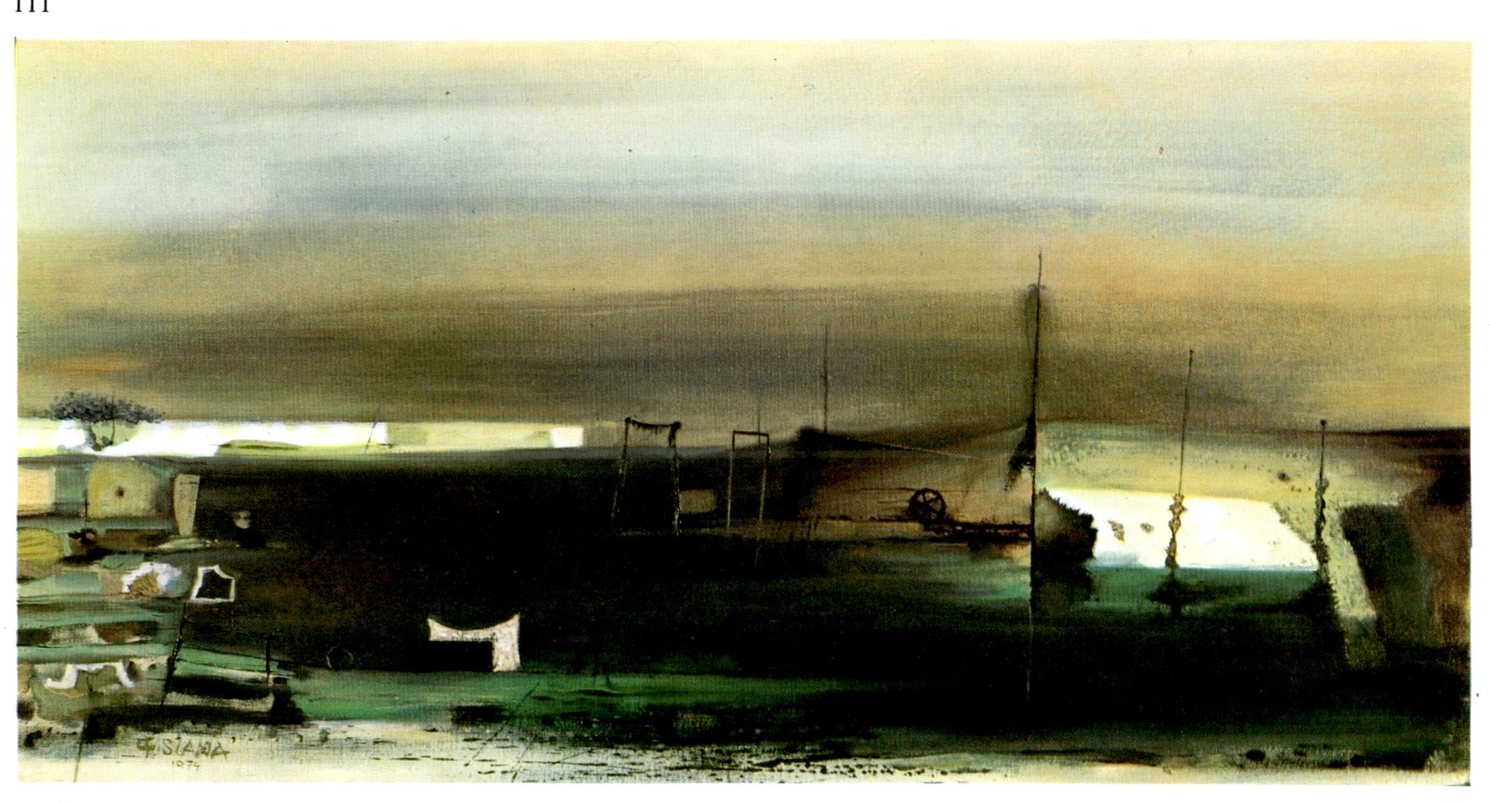

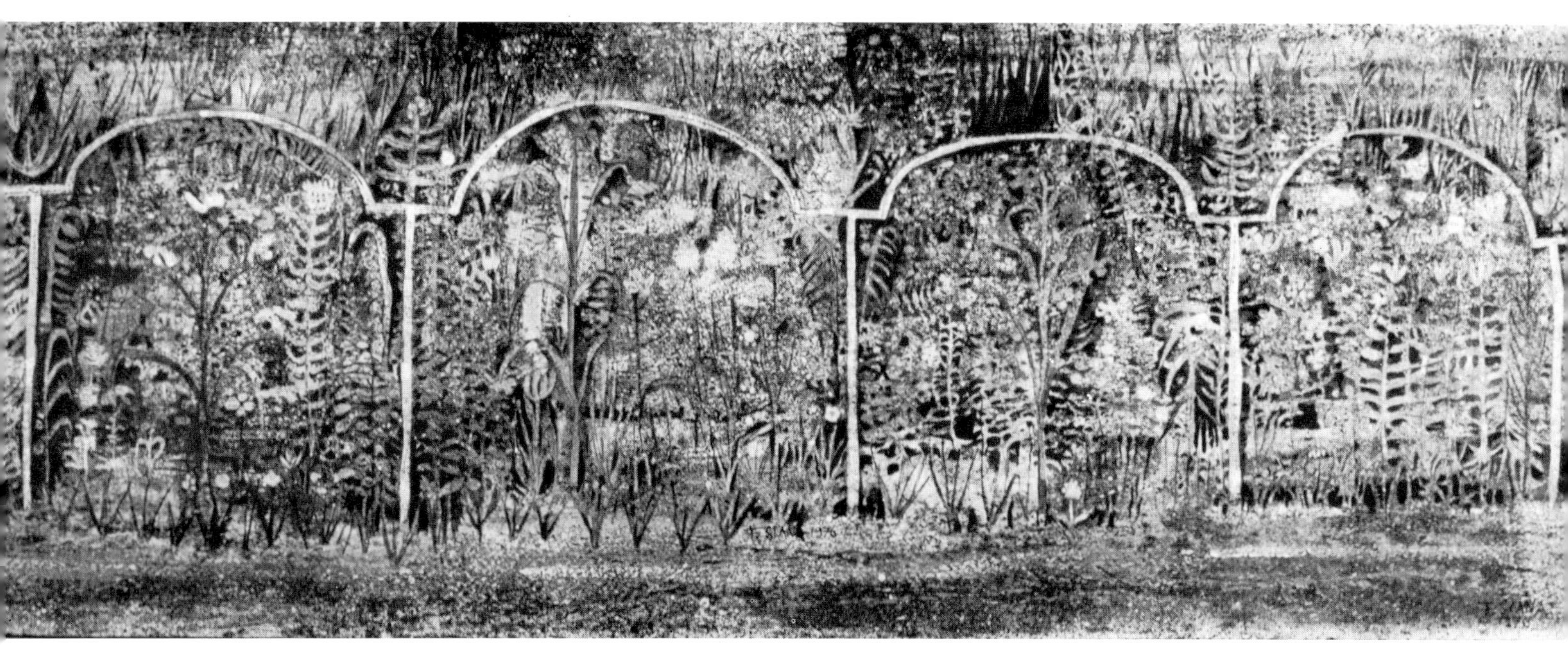

113

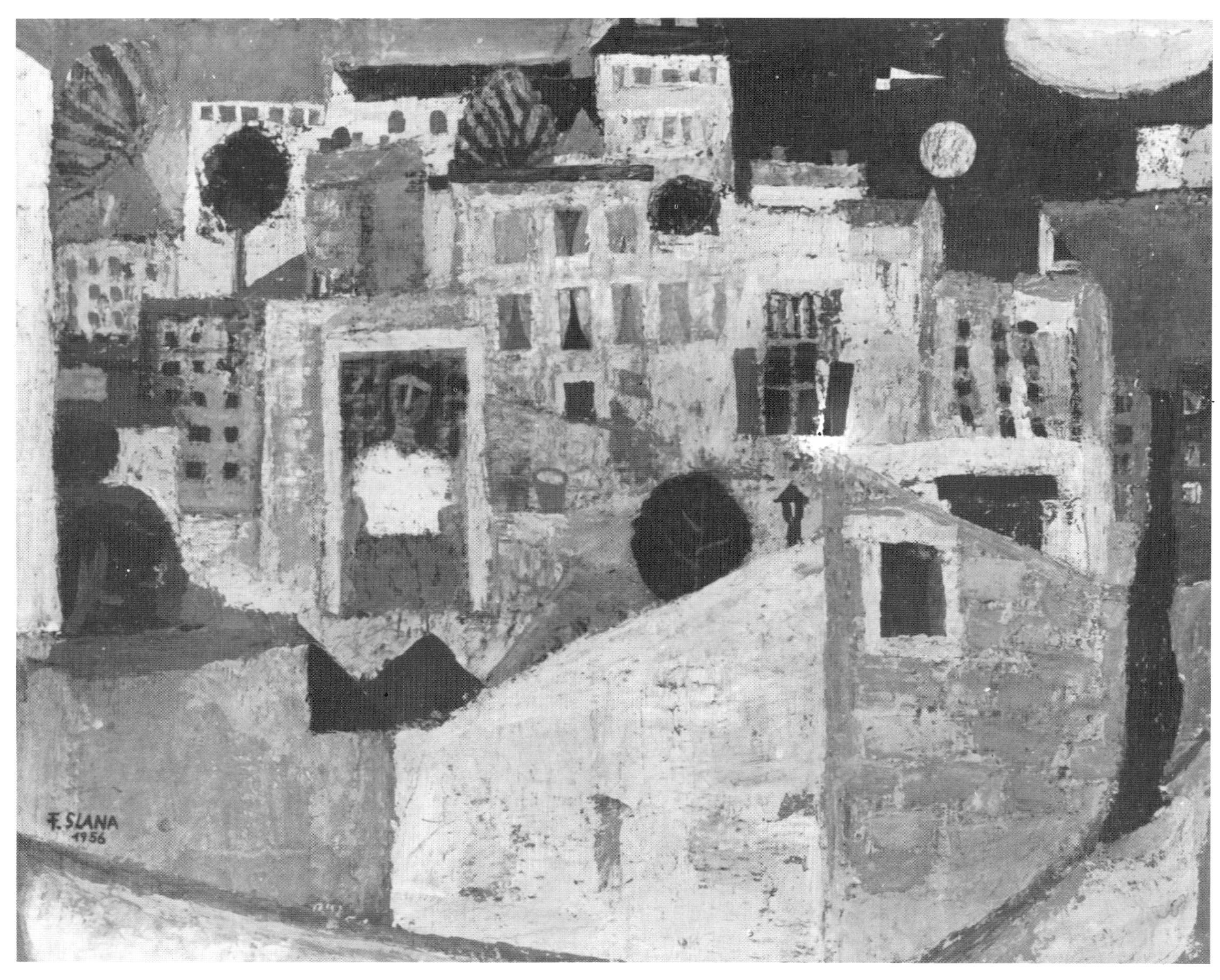

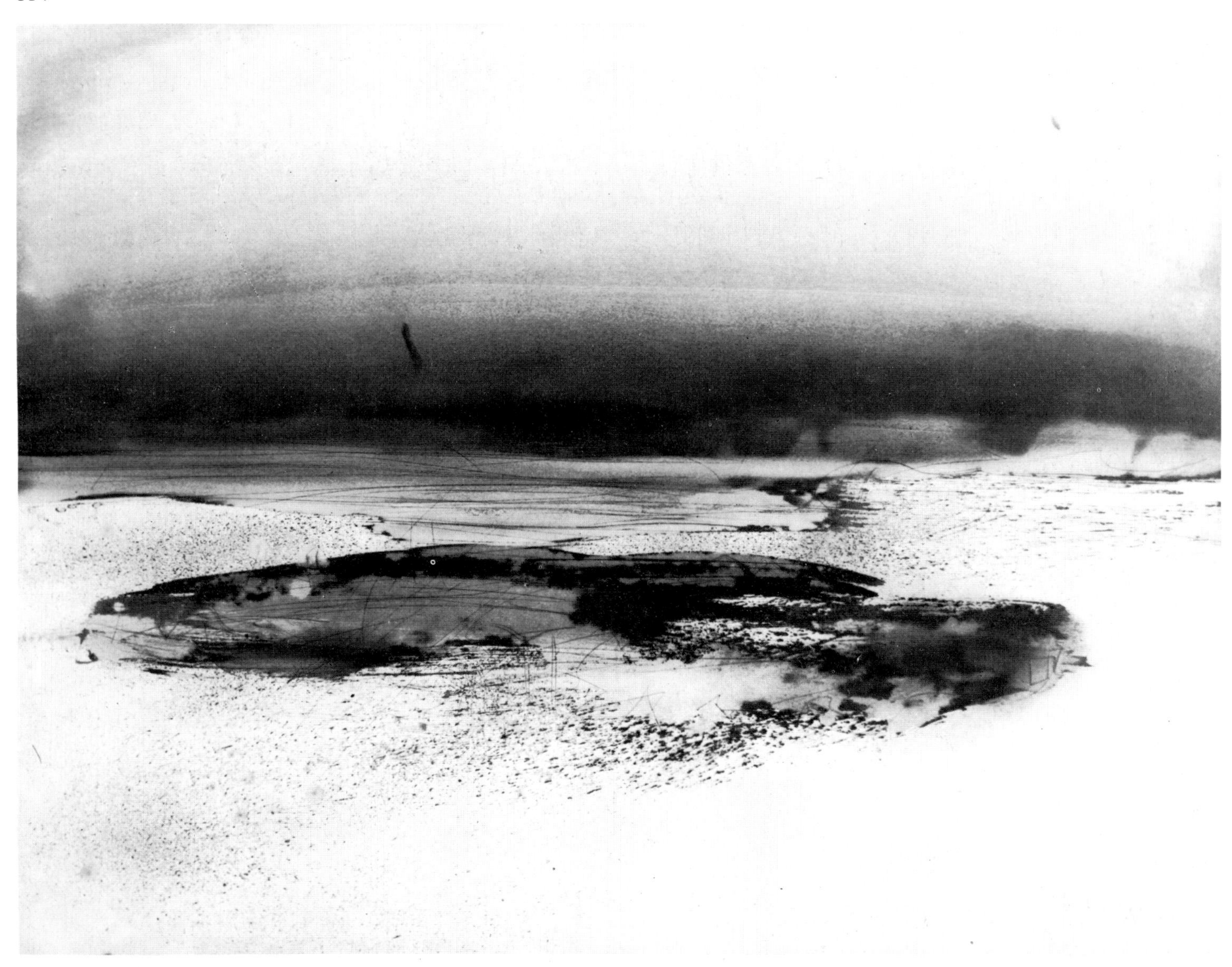

115

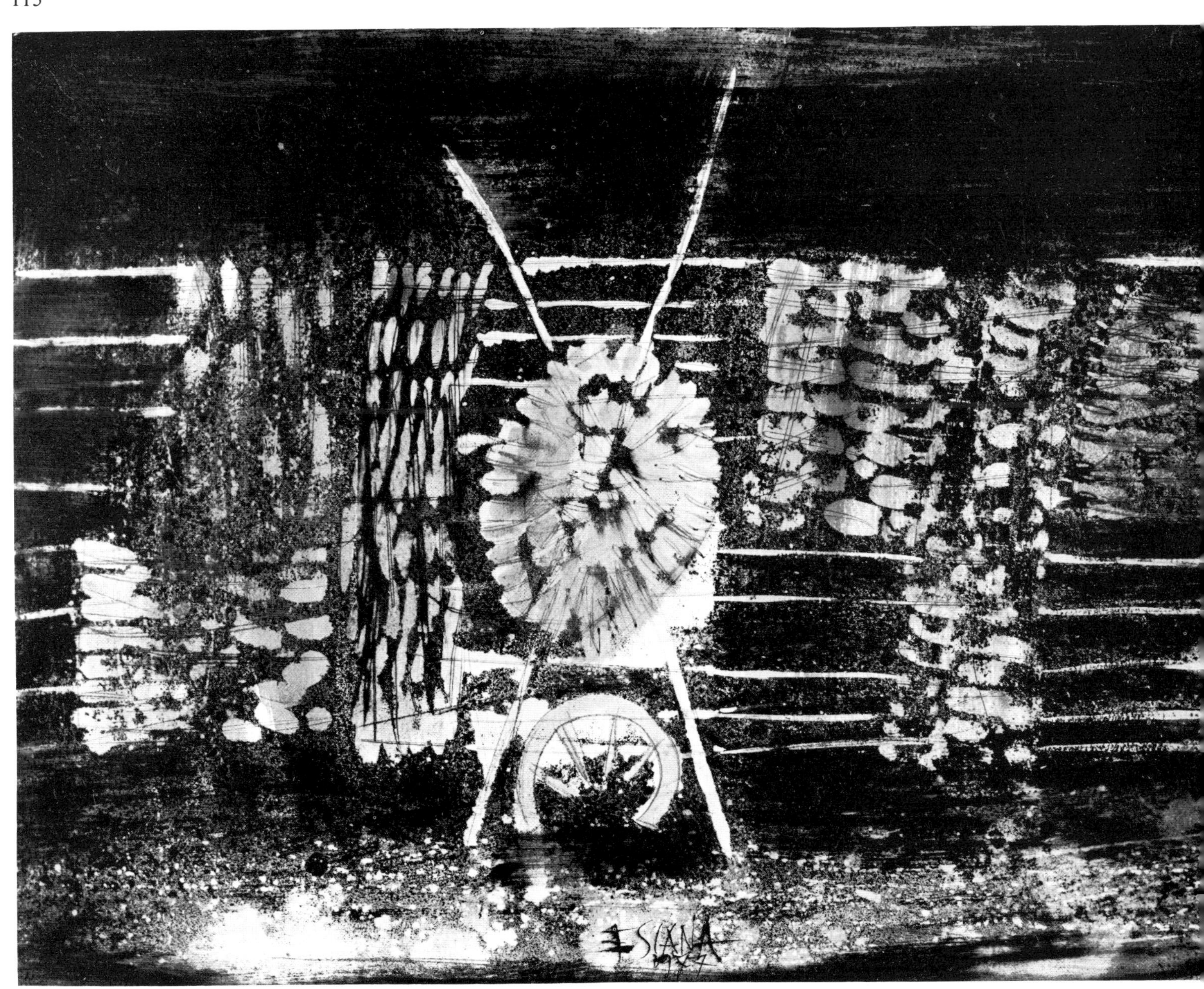

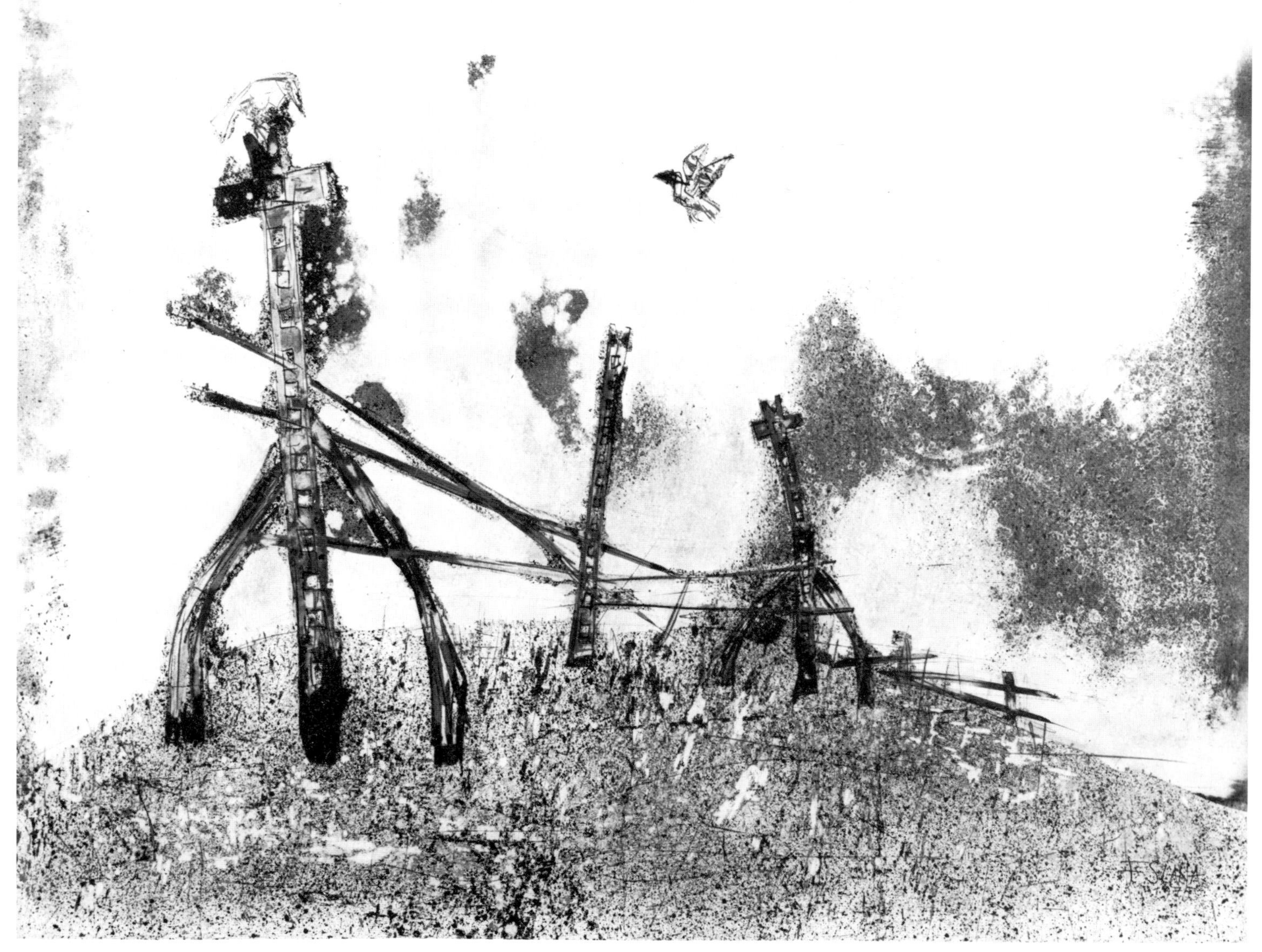

117

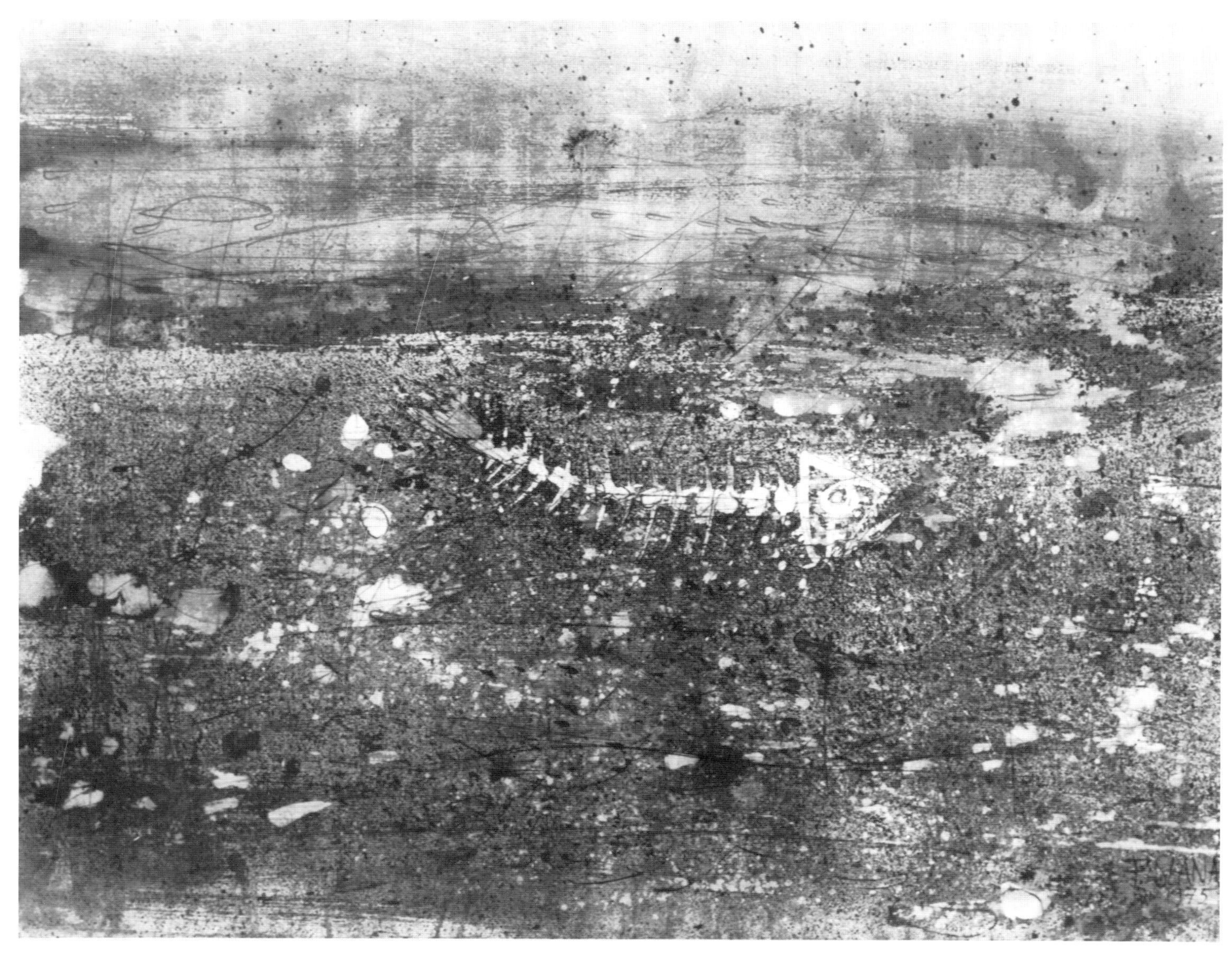

LIST OF REPRODUCTIONS

Note: Dimensions were not available for some of the works.

A. *House at Ručetna Vas,* 1944
Pencil

B. *Karlo Klemenčič,* 1945
Pencil

C. *Partisan,* 1944
Pencil

D. *Portrait,* 1944
Watercolor

E. *In Action,* 1945
Linocut

F. *Portrait,* 1945
Pencil

G. *Portrait,* 1944
Pencil

H. *Sketch from the Jazz Festival at Bled,* 1962
Ink

I. *Girl,* 1974
Ink

1. *Milena Dolgan,* 1945
Pencil

2. *Fighter from the Gorenjski Odred* (*Highland Commando*), 1944
Pencil

3. *Study of Horses,* 1944
Pencil

4. *At Rest,* 1944
Pencil

5. *Soldier,* 1966
Oil on canvas, 82.5 × 116 cm.

6. *Self-Portrait with Still Life and Nude,* 1955
Oil on canvas, 128 × 98 cm.

7. *Motif from the Collieries,* 1955
Oil on canvas, 70 × 50 cm.

8. *My Mother's Kitchen,* 1958
Ink

9. *Doctor Magajna,* 1964
Ink

10. *Self-Portrait,* 1948
Ink

11. *Houses at Night,* 1958
Oil on canvas, 115 × 85 cm.

12. *Marjan,* 1957
Oil on canvas, 72 × 60 cm.

13. *At the Ljubljanica River,* 1955
Oil on canvas, 85 × 65 cm.

14. *Island at Bled,* 1963
Watercolor, ink, 40 × 25 cm.

15. *Clochards,* 1958
Ink

16. *Louvre,* 1958
Ink

17. *Portrait of Friend Mirček,* 1975
Ink

18. *Island Motif,* 1964
Watercolor, ink, 45 × 35 cm.

19. *Fishing Village,* 1963
Watercolor, ink, 60 × 50 cm.

20. *Skopje Ruins,* 1963
Watercolor, ink, 60 × 50 cm.

21. *Mother,* 1954
Ink

22. *Railway at Zagorje,* 1963
Watercolor, ink, 45 × 40 cm.

23. *Hay Barn in Winter,* 1974
Oil on canvas, 70 × 50 cm.

24. *Edge of the Desert,* 1977
Watercolor, 50 × 35 cm.

25. *Barn in Winter,* 1974
Watercolor, ink, 55 × 41 cm.

26. *Slovenia's Last Totems,* 1975
Watercolor, ink, 76 × 57 cm.

27. *Old Fishing Village,* 1975
Oil on canvas, 100 × 61 cm.

28. *Skopje After the Earthquake,* 1964
Watercolor, ink, 51 × 35 cm.

29. *Ljubljana in Winter,* 1954
Oil on canvas, 45 × 40 cm.

30. *Mill in Winter,* 1970
Oil on canvas, 100 × 67 cm.

31. *Shapes on the Hayrick,* 1975
Ink

32. *Big Band,* 1973
Charcoal

33. *Shapes on the Hayrick I,* 1976
Watercolor, ink, 76 × 32 cm.

34. *Shapes on the Hayrick II,* 1976
Watercolor, ink, 76 × 28 cm.

35. *Suburb,* 1979
Watercolor, ink, 76 × 32 cm.

36. *Wreckage on a Beach,* 1974
Oil on canvas, 100 × 35 cm.

37. *School of Fish,* 1975
Ink

38. *Between Two Jetties,* 1966
Watercolor, ink, 78 × 28.5 cm.

39. *Still Life at a Mine* (not dated)
Oil on canvas, 42 × 40 cm.

40. *Old Houses,* 1965
Watercolor, ink, 62 × 20 cm.

41. *Shallow,* 1966
Watercolor, ink, 56 × 28 cm.

42. *Fish Skeletons on a Beach,* 1977
Watercolor, ink, 76 × 57 cm.

43. *Remains on a Beach,* 1972
Watercolor, 76 × 57 cm.

44. *Remains on a Sandbank,* 1972
Watercolor, 76 × 57 cm.

45. *Wreck,* 1968
Oil on canvas, 75 × 65 cm.

46. *Abandoned Barge,* 1976
Watercolor, ink, 76 × 57 cm.

47. *Remains,* 1976
Oil on canvas, 100 × 80 cm.

48. *Dead Fish,* 1978
Watercolor, ink, 76 × 57 cm.

49. *Wreck,* 1973
Watercolor, ink, 69 × 30.5 cm.

50. *Abandoned Mill,* 1977
Oil on canvas, 214 × 73.5 cm.

51. *Conquerors,* 1980
Oil on canvas, 100 × 106 cm.

52. *Old Town in Winter,* 1958
Oil on canvas, 80 × 102 cm.

53. *Sketch of a Nude,* 1976
Ink

54. *Event,* 1978
Watercolor, ink, 65 × 40 cm.

55. *Dried Poppies,* 1955
Ink

56. *Flowers,* 1976
Ink

57. *Little Anna,* 1979
Ink

58. *Marjan,* 1956
Ink

59. *My Son Bor,* 1978
Ink

60. *Lela,* 1980
Ink

61. *Plant,* 1965
Oil on canvas, 42 × 42 cm.

62. *Sitting Nude,* 1971
Oil on canvas, 42 × 42 cm.

63. *Studies of Fish,* 1977
Ink

64. *Blues,* 1970
Oil on canvas, 130 × 117 cm.

65. *Variation on the Subject of a Bouquet,* 1967
Oil on canvas, 60 × 60 cm.

66. *Wine Cellar at Prlekija,* 1975
Watercolor, ink, 57 × 76 cm.

67. *Child on a Chest,* 1978
Ink

68. *Inn at Stara Loka,* 1957
Oil on canvas, 98.5 × 78 cm.

69. *Marjan at the Window,* 1954
Oil on canvas, 55 × 44 cm.

70. *Fossilized Fish,* 1970
Watercolor, ink, 77 × 56 cm.

71. *Lonely Old Man,* 1977
Oil on canvas, 100 × 81 cm.

72. *Strutting Rooster,* 1976
Watercolor, ink, 57 × 42 cm.

73. *Green Rooster,* 1980
Watercolor, ink, 57 × 32 cm.

74. *Little Bor,* 1978
Ink

75. *Variegated Fish,* 1978
Watercolor, ink, 59 × 38 cm.

76. *Fish in a Net,* 1973
Watercolor, ink, 77 × 56 cm.

77. *Woman with Child,* 1978
Ink

78. *Sleeping Child,* 1978
Ink

79. *Bor,* 1978
Ink

80. *Mother and Son,* 1980
Ink

81. *Bor and Anna,* 1979
Ink

82. *Enclosed by Walls,* 1975
Watercolor, ink, 66 × 50 cm.

83. *Old Cat,* 1979
Oil on canvas, 50 × 65 cm.

84. *Brother and Sister,* 1979
Ink

85. *Two Children Asleep,* 1979
Ink

86. *Masks,* 1979
Watercolor, ink, 65 × 38 cm.

87. *Adventurer,* 1977
Oil on canvas

88. *Parade,* 1979
Oil on canvas

89. *Old Jade,* 1978
Watercolor, ink

90. *Dried Peasant Bouquet,* 1974
Oil on wood fiberboard, 62 × 55 cm.

91. *Bouquet in an Old Vase,* 1979
Oil on canvas, 55 × 50 cm.

92. *Bouquet in a Glass Vase,* 1964
Oil on canvas, 70 × 70 cm.

93. *Withered Blossoms,* 1977
Oil on canvas, 66 × 70 cm.

94. *Dried Bouquet on an Azure Background,* 1980
Oil on canvas, 50 × 50 cm.

95. *Bouquet on a Brown Background,* 1978
Oil on canvas, 50 × 50 cm.

96. *Krka River,* 1978
Watercolor, 69 × 50 cm.

97. *Bouquet of Wildflowers,* 1976
Watercolor, 59 × 42 cm.

98. *Autumn Bouquet,* 1974
Oil on canvas, 35 × 35 cm.

99. *Large Bouquet,* 1977
Oil on canvas, 121 × 121 cm.

100. *Dried Bouquet on a Dark Background,* 1977
Watercolor, ink, 76 × 57 cm.

101. *Small Golden Bouquet,* 1977
Oil on wood fiberboard, 26 × 22.5 cm.

102. *Remains of a Bouquet,* 1967
Oil on canvas, 41 × 30 cm.

103. *Flowers in Grey,* 1978
Watercolor, ink, 54 × 41 cm.

104. *Remembrance of a Bouquet,* 1964
Oil on canvas, 42 × 42 cm.

105. *A Memorial Bouquet,* 1966
Oil on canvas, 50 × 40 cm.

106. *Rhythms in a Dried Bouquet,* 1964
Oil on canvas, 44 × 42 cm.

107. *Withered Blossom,* 1967
Oil on canvas, 42 × 42 cm.

108. *Plant,* 1968
Oil on wood fiberboard, 20 × 21.5 cm.

109. *Fish,* 1975
Enamel on ceramic, 30 × 20 cm.

110. *Suburban Walls,* 1978
Watercolor, ink, 60 × 35 cm.

111. *Gloomy Landscape,* 1974
Oil on canvas, 84.5 × 42.5 cm.

112. *Flower Garden,* 1975
Watercolor, 76 × 27 cm.

113. *White Walls,* 1956
Egg tempera, 85 × 66 cm.

114. *Sandbank,* 1972
Watercolor, 60 × 40 cm.

115. *Waste Shore,* 1971
Watercolor, 60 × 40 cm.

116. *Remains of a Hayrick,* 1975
Watercolor, ink, 76 × 57 cm.

117. *Remains of a Fish,* 1975
Watercolor, ink, 55 × 42 cm.

Cover: *Large Bouquet,* 1977
Oil on canvas, 121 × 121 cm.

CHRONOLOGY

1926 — France Slana is born on October 26 at Bodislavci in the Gorice region of Slovenia. He is the first of four children of Franc and Ivana (neé Kunšič) Slana.

1929 — The family moves to Split, where France's father finds a new job.

1934 — France enters elementary school in Split.

1935 — Enrolls in the Split grammar school and remains there only one scholastic year.

1939 — Transfers to the 4th State Grammar School in Ljubljana.

1940 — His father finds new employment in Maribor.

1941 — France works at odd jobs to help support his family in Italian-occupied Ljubljana. Establishes his first contacts with the Liberation Front.

1942 — The family joins the father in German-occupied Maribor.

1943 — To avoid mobilization by the Germans, France moves to Graz, Austria. There he frequents the local Kunstgewerbenschule (arts and crafts school).

Contacts the Maribor section of the Liberation Front and decides to join the Partisans.

1944 — In early February, on the same day on which France plans to leave Graz to join the Partisans, the local branch of the Liberation Front is broken up by the Germans.

Moves to Gorje in the Gorenjsko region of Slovenia and renews contact with the Front there. Becomes an active member of the National Liberation Forces on April 12. Serves first as a messenger and later works in the printing office of the Gorenjski Odred (Gorenjsko High Command).

Moves to Kokrško and works in the printing office of the High Command there prior to volunteering for active duty.

Completes a number of drawings.

1945 — Paints his first watercolor, *Pred dežjem* (*Before the Rain*), in Črnomelj, the Partisan capital of Slovenia. In February, his linocut, *A Partisan,* appears in an exhibition there. This is the first public showing of his work.

At the time of the liberation, he is in Prezid in the Gorski Kotar region.

Spends May in Trieste.

In autumn, he enrolls in the newly-founded Academy of Figurative Arts in Ljubljana.

1947 — Does voluntary labor on the Brčko-Banoviči railway.

1948 — Does voluntary labor on the Šamac-Sarajevo railway.

1949 — Graduates from the Painting Department of the Ljubljana Academy in the class of Professor Gabrijel Stupica. Illustrates the book, *Mi gradimo,* by Vera Albreht.

In autumn, he joins the Mladinska Knjiga publishing firm as an illustrator for the children's magazine, *Pionirski list.* Remains at this post for over a year.

1950 — Illustrates Boromir Magajna's tale, *Brkonja Čeljustnik,* for publication in *Pionirski list.*

1951 — Joins the Society of Slovene Figurative Artists. Decides to become a free-lance illustrator. Moves into a room at 4 Miklošič Street, where he lives until 1961.

1953 — Is mobilized during the Trieste dispute and sent to the coastal region, where he remains for two and one-half months. While there he creates a series of drawings, *Iz vojaške skicirke* (*From a Soldier's Sketchbook*).

1954 — The *Iz vojaške skicirke* drawings are exhibited at Ljubljana's City Gallery.

Illustrates the book, *Sayo and Her Beavers,* by Vesha Kvonezin. Produces a set of illustrations for a Yugoslavian edition of *Uncle Tom's Cabin.* Begins to paint in oils.

1956 — Organizes his first one-man show at Jakopič Pavilion in Ljubljana; the show receives considerable attention from both critics and the public.

During the summer, he devotes himself to watercolor painting.

Illustrates two more books: *Partizanček* (*The Little Partisans*) by Stanko Semič-Daki and *Zlata ptica (The Golden Bird*) by Tone Pavček.

Bogomir Magajna's tale, *Brkonja Čeljustnik,* which Slana illustrated in 1950, is published in book form.

Travels to Norway.

1957 — Exhibits at the Second Mediterranean Biennial in Alexandria, Egypt, and receives first prize for painting.

1958 — Illustrates two more books: *The Closing Nets* by Alberto Manzi and *Secret of the Sea* by Robb White.

Travels to Paris.

1959 — Travels again to Paris.

1960 — Travels to Egypt and remains there for two months. Exhibits in Cairo.

1961 — Acquires a new studio at 8 Breg Street in Ljubljana.

1962 — Participates in a competition celebrating the anniversary of the revolution and wins first prize for his painting, *The Burnt Village* (which is now at the Gorjup Gallery in Kostanjevica).

Together with Ive Šubic and Jože Ciuha, he takes part in an exhibition in Wuppertal, Germany.

Is married on June 26.

In autumn, receives first prize at the exhibition "Gozd in les" in Slovenj Gradec.

1963 — Leaves for Skopje in Macedonia a few days after its catastrophic earthquake. Creates a series of 60 watercolors which later wins a prize from the Prešeren Foundation.

Moves into an apartment at 8 Komenski Street in Ljubljana.

1964 — Is awarded the Prize of the City of Čačak. Paints a new series of watercolors about the island of Dugi Otok.

Travels to Rome, where he exhibits his oil paintings and watercolors at the Studio Margutta 13 gallery.

1965 — Holds a one-man show of his oil paintings at the Modern Gallery in Ljubljana.

Exhibits in Sombor and is awarded the prize for tapestry at the Likovna Jesen festival.

Paints a new series of watercolors on motifs drawn from the Kornati Islands.

1967 — His first son, Domen, is born.

Wins the Kunstverein Prize at the INTART exhibition in Klagenfurt, Austria.

1968 — Is awarded a prize at the "Plavi Salon" exhibition in Zadar.

1970 — Holds a one-man show of his watercolors in Stuttgart, Germany.

1971 — In November, exhibits at the Palace Hotel in Parma, Italy.

1972 — In September, organizes an independent exhibition at the Likovni Salon in Celje.

1973 — Paints a series of watercolors about the Dalmatian island of Krapanj.

1974 — Holds a one-man exhibition at the Salon JNA in Belgrade in April and another at the Salon JNA in Rijeka in June.

1975 — Travels to Kuwait and holds an exhibition of his oil paintings and watercolors.

Exhibits in Cologne, Germany.

Organizes a retrospective show of 120 of his watercolors at the Lamutov Likovni Salon in Kostanjevica.

Is divorced from his first wife.

1976 — Marries Alenka Žagar, a medical student.

His second son, Bor, is born.

1977 — Travels by ship to Libya, Algeria, and Italy. Paints a comprehensive series of watercolors on themes drawn from the journey.

His daughter, Anna, is born.

1978 — Participates in the first Painters' Colony, organized by the Krka pharmaceutical firm, and the ensuing exhibition.

Takes part in another Painters' Colony and exhibition at Borl Castle.

Exhibits his paintings in Ptuj.

1979 — Paints more watercolors on themes drawn from the island of Krapanj.

Participates in the second Painters' Colony and exhibition organized by the Krka pharmaceutical firm.

1980 — Participates in the third Krka-sponsored Painters' Colony.

Completes another series of watercolors on themes drawn from the island of Krapanj.

Today France Slana lives and works in Ljubljana, in the same apartment he has occupied since 1963.

ONE-MAN EXHIBITIONS

1953 — Mala Galerija, Ljubljana

1954 — Mala Galerija, Ljubljana

1956 — Jacopičev Paviljon, Ljubljana (March)

1961–
1962 — Mala Galerija, Ljubljana (December-January)

1962 — Galerie 61, Klagenfurt (June)

1963 — Foyer Slovenskega Ljudskega Gledališča, Celje (June)
Avla Delavskega Doma, Velenje (July)
Gorenjski Muzej, Kranj (October)
Mestna Galerija, Ljubljana (November)

1964 — Galerija Doma JNA, Belgrade (January)
Studio Margutta 13, Rome (February-March)
Izložbeni Salon Doma JNA, Rijeka (April-May)

1965 — Moderna Galerija, Ljubljana (April-May)

1966 — Likovni Salon, Ravne na Koroškem (May)
Festivalna Dvorana, Bled (June)

1968 — Mestna Galerija, Ljubljana (May-June)

1968–
1969 — Dolenjska Galerija, Novo Mesto (October-January)

1969 — Koncertni Atelje Društva Slovenskih Skladateljev, Ljubljana (December)

1970 — Muzej na Gradu, Škofja Koka (January-February)
Bolnišnica za Duševne Bolezni, Ljubljana (May)
Galerija Krsko, Krsko (May-June)
Likovni Salon, Kocevje (October)
Stuttgart

1971 — Preddverje Križank, Ljubljana (June)

1972 — Likovni Salon, Celje (September)

1974 — Galerija Doma JNA, Belgrade (April)
Izložbeni Salon Doma JNA, Rijeka (June)

1975 — Artists' Hall, Kuwait (May)
Yugoslav Information Center, Cologne (June)
Lamutov Likovni Salon, Kostanjevica na Krki (June-September)
Razstavni Salon Rotovž, Maribor (September-October)
Stadtbücherei, Stuttgart (October-November)

1975–1976 — Dolenjski Muzej-Galerija, Novo Mesto (December-January)

1976 — Galerija ARS, Ljubljana (January-February)
Galerie 15, Graz (January-February)
Aula Slovenica, Klagenfurt (January-February)
Galerie Burkhardshof, Neukirch-Egnach (February)

1977 — Jelovškova Galerija, Ljubljana (April)
Savinov Razstavni Salon, Žalec (November-December)

1978 — Ljubljanska Banka, Ljubljana (March-April)
Galerija Labirint, Ljubljana (May-June)
Tovarna Lek, Ljubljana (November-December)

1979 — Studio Galerije Forum, Zagreb (May-June)
Galerija Josip Račić, Zagreb (May-June)

1980 — Duplje
Gradič

GROUP EXHIBITIONS

1945 — Razstava Slovenskih Umetnikov: Partizanov;
Jakopičev Paviljon, Ljubljana
Izložba Slovenačkih Umjetnika Partizana;
Moderna Galerija, Zagreb

1954 — Razstava del Upodabljajočih Umetnikov Slovenije;
Umetnostna Galerija, Maribor

1955 — Slovenska Umetnost po Osvoboditvi 1945–1955;
Moderna Galerija, Ljubljana

1956 — Razstava Zveze Likovnih Umetnikov Jugoslavije;
Moderna Galerija, Ljubljana
Razstava Ilustraciji Knjig;
Jakopičev Paviljon, Ljubljana
Salon 56—Savremeno Slikarstvo i Kiparstvo;
Galerija Likovnih Umjetnosti, Rijeka
Savremeno Slikarstvo Jugoslavije. Izložba Povodom
Glavne Godišnje Skupštine AICA;
Umjetnička Galerija, Dubrovnik
Ljubljana v Podobi. Razstava Umetniških del Ljubljana;
Jakopičev Paviljon, Ljubljana

1957 — Savremena Jugoslovenska Umjetnost;
Dubrovnik
Second Mediterranean Biennial;
Alexandria, Egypt

1957–
1958 — Jugoslavisk Natidskunst;
Bergen
Oslo
Stavanger
Trondheim

1958 — Savremeni Slovenački Likovni Umetnici;
Mali Kalemegdan, Belgrade
Sodobna Slovenska Umetnost;
Moderna Galerija, Ljubljana

VII. Razstava Ilustracij Mladinske Knjige;
Jakopičev Paviljon, Ljubljana
Mostra d'Arte Slovena Contemporanea;
Museo Civico, Pistoia
Mostra d'Arte Slovena Contemporanea;
Casa della Cultura, Livorno
Avtoportret na Slovenskem;
Moderna Galerija, Ljubljana

1959–
1960 — Izložba Društva Slovenskih Likovnih Umetnikov;
Skopje
Novi Sad

1960 — Exhibition with Bernik, Boljka, Borčić, Kranjc, Makuc, Rogelj, Sovre, Tihec, Tršar, and Zelenko;
Jakopičev Paviljon, Ljubljana
Exhibition with Bernik, Boljka, and Rogelj;
Galerija Doma JNA, Belgrade
Exhibition with Ciuha and Šubic;
Galerie Palette-Röderhaus, Wuppertal-Barmen
Exhibition with Plestenjak;
L'Atelier du Caire, Cairo

1961 — Risbe. Razstava Risb Slovenskih Likovnih Umetnikov (1941–1961);
Jakopičev Paviljon, Ljubljana
I. Trijenale Likovnih Umetnosti;
Beogradski Sajam, Belgrade
Dvaintrideset del Jugoslovanskega Slikarstva iz Zbirke Moderne Galerije;
Salon Moderne Galerije, Belgrade
Zeitgenössische Slowenische Malerei und Bildhauerei;
Künstlerhaus, Klagenfurt
Salon 61—Slikarstvo, Kiparstvo, Tapiserija;
Galerija Likovnih Umjetnosti, Rijeka
Neue Jugoslawische Kunst;
Städtisches Museum-Gemäldegalerie, Wiesbaden
Städtisches Museum, Braunschweig
Museum Folkwang, Essen
Suermondt Museum, Aachen
Badischer Kunstverein, Karlsruhe

Narodno Oslobodilačka Borba u Delima Likovnih
Umetnika Jugoslavije;
Dom JNA, Belgrade

1961–
1962 — L'Art Contemporain en Yugoslavie;
Musée National d'Art Moderne, Paris
Premio Morgan's Paint: III.
Biennale Internazionale per la
Pittura e la Scultura, Italy-Yugoslavia;
Palazzo dell'Arengo, Rimini
Moderna Galerija, Ljubljana
Moderna Galerija JAZU, Zagreb

1962 — L'Arte Contemporanea in Jugoslavia;
Palazzo delle Esposizioni, Rome
Bari
Contemporary Yugoslav Painting;
Bombay
Ahmadabad
New Delhi
Zeitgenössische Jugoslawische Malerei, Graphik und
Plastik;
Neue Galerie, Linz
Graz
Vienna
Exhibition with Dovjak and Šubic;
Gradska Izložbena Sala, Novi Sad
8 Slikara
Galerija Likovnih Umjetnosti, Dubrovnik
Dela Jugoslovanskih Umetnikov iz Fundusa Moderne
Galerija v Ljubljani;
Galerija Piran, Piran
Slovenačka Umetnost. Dela iz Zbirke Moderne Galerije;
Salon Moderne Galerije, Belgrade
Zeitgenössische Kunst in Slowenien;
Kulturring, Spittal d. Drau
I. Jugoslovanska Razstava Gozd in les v Likovni
Umetnosti;
Umetnostni Paviljon, Slovenj Gradec
Contemporary Yugoslav Painting;
Svea Galleriet, Stockholm
La Peinture et la Sculpture Yougoslaves Contemporaines;
Comptoir Suisse, Lausanne

1962–
1963 — Gruppe rbk;
Wuppertal
Kiel
Welzlar
Heilbronn
Nüremberg
Utrecht

1963 — Arte Jugoslava Contemporânea;
Museu Nacional de Belas Artes, Rio de Janeiro
XIII. Premio Lissonne—Biennale Internazionale di Pittura;
Milan
Akvizicije 1;
Galerija Suvremene Umjetnosti, Zagreb
Likovna Umetnost s Tematiko NOB:
Šeškov Dom, Kočevje
Mestna Galerija, Ljubljana
Mladi Jugoslovanski Slikarji;
Galerija Piran, Piran
Die Moderne im Slowenischen Kulturbereich;
Forum Stadtpark, Graz
Sammlung Röder;
Galerie Palette-Röderhaus, Wuppertal
Crteži, Grafike i Akvareli iz NOB;
Vojni muzej, Belgrade
Razstava Jugoslovanske Tapiserije;
Moderne Galerija, Ljubljana
Atelje 61—Tapiserije;
Muzej za Umjetnost i Obrt, Zagreb
II. Izložba Tapiserija "Atelje 61;"
Galerija Doma JNA, Belgrade
III. Likovna Jesen. I. Trijenale Savremenog Jugoslovenskog Crteža;
Gradski Muzej, Sombor
22nd International Watercolor Biennial. Yugoslavia, Sweden, United States;
The Brooklyn Museum, New York
Društvo Slovenskih Likovnih Umetnikov;
Moderna Galerija, Ljubljana

1964 — Razstava Društva Slovenskih Likovnih Umetnikov;
Moderna in Mestna Galerija, Ljubljana
III. Memorial Nadežde Petrović;
Gimnazija, Čačak
Exhibition of Contemporary Yugoslav Painting;
Morocco
Plavi Salon. 3. Biennale Jugoslavenskog Skilarstva;
Moderna Galerija, Narodnog Muzeja, Zadar
2. Trijenale Likovnih Umetnosti;
Beogradski Sajam, Belgrade
IV. Jugoslovanska Likovna Jesen;
Gradski Muzej, Sombor
Izlake 64. Razstava I. Slovenske Kolonije Izlake 64;
Foyer Delavskega Doma, Trbovlje
Exhibition with D. Plestenjak;
Ljudska Knjižnica, Skofja Loka
Vajont-Skopje;
Umetnički Paviljon Mali Kalemegdan, Belgrade
La Collettiva;
Studio S.M. 13, Rome
Grabados y Tapices Yugoslavos;
Instituto Nacional de Bellas Artes, Mexico

1965 — Mostra Delle Opere Donate Degli Artisti Jugoslavi per le Zone Sinistrate del Vajont;
Galleria Nazionale d'Arte Moderna, Rome
V. Biennale Internazionale d'Arte Contemporanea;
Palazzo del Kursaal, San Marino
Partizanska Grafika;
Delavski Dom, Zagorje
Razstava Umetniških Tapiserij (Atelje 61);
Galerija Piran, Piran
Izbor iz Galerijske Zbirke Moderne Galerije;
Festivalna Dvorana, Bled
Povojna Generacija Slovenskih Slikarjev in Kiparjev;
Moderna Galerija, Ljubljana
Grabados, Tapices Yugoeslavos;
Instituto Nacional de Cultura ya Bellas Artes, Caracas
Jugoszláv Szőnyeg és Kisplasztika;
Ernest Muzeum, Budapest

V. Likovna Jesen. Jugoslovanska Tapiserija;
Gradski Muzej, Sombor
Četvrti Likovni Susret u Subotici: Slikarstvo Umetničkih Kolonija;
Velika Terasa—Izložbena Sala; Subotica—Palić
Umetniške Kolonije v Jugoslaviji;
Mestna Galerija, Ljubljana
Deseta Izložba Umjetničke Kolonije Ečka;
Ečka
Tapiserije—Atelje 61
Novi Sad
Gore v Podobi;
Umetnostni Pavoljon, Slovenj Gradec
Berge im Bild;
Künstlerhaus, Klagenfurt
II. Biennale Internationale de la Tapisserie;
Musée Cantonal des Beaux-Arts, Lausanne
Mostra di Pittura Contemporanea Jugoslava;
Civica Residenza, Pasaro
Razstava Društva Slovenskih Likovnih Umetnikov;
Moderna Galerija, Ljubljana
Društvo Slovenskih Likovnih Umetnikov;
Mali Kalemegdan, Belgrade
Subotica

1966 — Exhibition of Yugoslav Tapestry and Small Sculpture;
Bucharest
Razstava Društva Slovenskih Likovnih Umetnikov;
Moderna Galerija, Ljubljana
Društvo Slovenskih Likovnih Umetnikov;
Umetnostna Galerija, Maribor
Razstava Društva Slovenskih Likovnih Umetnikov;
Kabinet Grafike JAZU, Zagreb
II. Trijenale Savremenog Jugoslovenskog Crteža;
Gradski Musej, Sombor
Razstava Slikarske Kolonije Izlake 65;
Avla Delavskega Doma, Zagorje

1966–
1967 — Mir, Humanost in Prijateljstvo med Narodi;
Umetnostni Paviljon, Slovenj Gradec

1967 — Mir, Humanost in Prijateljstvo med Narodi;
Umetnostni Paviljon, Slovenj Gradec

1967 — Prešernove Nagrade za Likovno Kulturo;
Moderna Galerija, Ljubljana
Razstava del Nagrajenih s Prešernovo Nagrado za Likovno Kulturo;
Razstavni Salon Rotovž; Maribor
Iz Zbirke Galerije Doma JNA Beograd;
Moderna Galerija, Ljubljana
Art in Yugoslavia, Contemporary Trends;
Adria Art Gallery, New York
I. Zagrebačka Izložba Jugoslavenskog Crteža;
Kabinet Grafike JAZU, Zagreb
INTART;
Künstlerhaus, Klagenfurt
23 Artisti Jugoslavi;
Museo Civico Revoltella-Palazzo Constanzi, Trieste
French and Yugoslav Tapestries;
Adria Art Gallery, New York
Salon d'Automne, Paris
"Forma," Bratislava

1968 — 5. Plavi Salon
Moderna Galerija Narodnog Muzeja, Zadar
Malíři, Sochaři, Grafici Socialistické Republiky Slovenie;
Galeria Vincence Kramáře, Prague
Galerie Uměni, Karlovy Vary
Savremena Slovenačka Umetnost;
Muzej Savremene Umetnosti, Belgrade
Moderna Galerija, Zagreb
Moderna Galerija, Ljubljana
Vila Bled, Bled

1969 — 2. Zagrebačka Izložba Jugoslavenskog Crteža;
Kabinet Grafike JAZU, Zagreb

1970 — Razstava del Članov 3. Groharjeve Slikarske Kolonije 1969;
Galerija, Škofja Loka

1971 — III. Razstava Narodnoosvobodilni boj v Delih Likovnih Umetnikov Jugoslavije;
Dom JNA, Belgrade

Deseto Likovno Srečanje: Razstava Slikarstva
Udeležencev Umetniških Kolonij v Jugoslaviji;
Salon i Galerija Likovnih Susreta, Subotica
Exhibition with Plestenjak;
Palace Hotel, Parma
Exhibition with M. Sedej, senior, and M. Sedej, junior;
Mestna Galerija, Ljubljana

1972 — Narodnoosvobodilna borba v Delih Likovnih Umetnikov
Jugoslavije;
Dom JLA, Ljubljana
7. Plavi Salon;
Moderna Galerija Narodnog Muzeja, Zadar
NOB v Delih Likovnih Umetnikov Jugoslavije;
Muzej Revolucije, Celje

1973 — Izbor iz Stalne Zbirke Moderne Galerije;
Mestna Galerija, Ljubljana

1974 — Društvo Slovenskih Likovnih Umetnikov;
Moderna Galerija, Ljubljana
'74 Društvo Slovenskih Likovnih Umetnikov;
Izložbeni Paviljon Masarikova 4, Belgrade
Novi Sad
Tapiserije;
Atelje 61, Novi Sad
Salon Narodnog Pozorišta Bosanske Krajine, Banja
Luka

1975 — Partizanska Grafika in Risba;
Moderna Galerija, Ljubljana
Mestna Galerija, Ljubljana
Dolenjski Muzej-Galerija, Novo Mesto

1976 — Nagrajenci INTART;
Moderna Galerija, Ljubljana
Izložba Likovnih del iz Forda Zbirke Slikarske Kolonije
Izlake;
Mala Galerija, Bačka Topola
Zlati Oktober. Kulturna Akcija ob 20-Letnici Dolenjskega
Kulturnega Festivala v Kostanjevici na Krki,
1956–1976;

Lamutov Likovni Salon in Restavracija Pod Gorjanci, Kostanjevica na Krki
Razstava Stalne Zbirke Celjskega Likovnega Salona; Razstavni Salon, Rogaška Slatina

1977 — Likovna Zbirka Bernardin;
Moderna galerija, Ljubljana
Atelje 61;
Umetniški Paviljon "Cvijeta Zuzorić," Belgrade
XV. Likovni Susret Subotica 1977. Izlake;
Galerija Likovnog Susreta, Subotica
Slovensko Slikarstvo od Realizma do Danes;
Pokrajinsko Narodno Pozorište (Foyer), Priština
Exhibition with Arzenšek;
Savinov raztavni, Žalec
Razstava Prve Generacije Študentov ALU v Ljubljani-Udeležencev NOB;
Moderna Galerija, Ljubljana

1978 — Razstava Prve Generacije Študentov ALU v Ljubljani-Udležencev NOB:
Umetnostna Galerija, Maribor
NOB u Delima Likovnih Umetnika Jugoslavije;
Galerija Doma JNA, Belgrade
Exhibition with Jakelić, Mišević, Prodanović, and Šiško;
Galerija Doma JNA, Belgrade
Exhibition of Yugoslav Applied Art;
Leipzig
2nd Biennale INTART:
Udine
Klagenfurt
Ljubljana

1979 — Slovenska Likovna Umetnost, 1945–1978;
Moderna Galerija, Ljubljana
Razstava Tapiserij Slovenskih Likovnih Umetnikov;
Tovarna Dekorativnih Tkanin, Ljubljana
BAJ-Biennale Akvarela Jugoslavije;
Galerija Vjekoslav Karas, Karlovac
Galerija Umjetnosti, Vinkovci

PRIZES AND AWARDS

1957 — First prize for painting, Second Mediterranean Biennial, Alexandria, Egypt

1962 — First prize for painting, The Committee for the Celebration of the Twentieth Anniversary of the Revolution, 1962

Prize at the exhibition, "Gozd in les," Slovenj Gradec

Prize of the Prešeren Foundation

1964 — Prize of the City of Čačak

1965 — Prize for tapestry at the exhibition, "Likovna jesen," Sombor

1967 — Prize of the Kunstverein, INTART exhibition, Klagenfurt, Austria

1968 — Prize at the exhibition, "Plavi salon," Zadar

SELECTED BIBLIOGRAPHY

Adanja, Katarina. "France Slana, Galerija Doma JNA." *Umetnost,* no. 39 (1974), pp. 62–63.

Baldani, Juraj. "'Od angažiranog do zavičajnog' France Slana—izložba akvarela u Studiju galerije 'Forum' u Zagrebu i izložba ulja u galeriji 'Josip Račič' u Zagrebu." *Studio* (Zagreb), no. 793 (1979), p. 83.

Baloh, Vera. "France Slana." *Enciklopedija likovnih umjetnosti* (Zagreb), no. 4 (1966), p. 221.

Bassin, Aleksander. "France Slana," (introduction to catalog for exhibition at Moderna Galerija). Ljubljana, 1965.

______. "France Slana." *Umetnost,* no. 3/4 (1965), p. 183.

______. "France Slana." *Umetnost,* no. 16 (1968), p. 99.

______. "France Slana: Skopska mapa," (introduction to catalog for exhibition at Mestna Galerija). Ljubljana, 1963.

______. "Ob razstavi Franceta Slane." *Sodobnost,* no. 6 (1965), pp. 629–631.

______. "Stari mlin—Slikarstvo Franceta Slane." *Umetnost,* no. 8 (1966), pp. 83–88.

Bihalji-Merin, Oto. "L'Art contemporain en Yougoslavie," (introduction to catalog for exhibition at Musée National d'Art Moderne). Paris, 1961.

Cevc, Emilijan. "Barve zemlje (Ob razstavi Frenceta Slane)." *Nasa sodobnost,* no. 3 (1962), pp. 278–279.

______. "France Slana," (introduction to catalog for exhibition at Dolenjska Galerija). Novo Mesto, 1968.

______. "France Slana," (introduction to catalog for exhibition at Mestna galerija). Ljubljana, 1968.

Čopič, Spelca, in *Slovensko slikarstvo* (Ljubljana: Cankarjeva založba, 1966), pp. 208–209.

Čorak, Željka. "France Slana. Izložba slika," (introduction to catalog for exhibition at Galerija "Josip Račič"). Zagreb, 1979.

Denegri, Ješa. "Beograjska likovna kronika. Sodobna slovenska umetnost." *Sinteza,* no. 10/11 (1968), p. 147.

______."Suvremena slovenska umjetnost." *Život umjetnosti,* no. 6 (1968), p. 140.

Kermauner, Taras. "Maksim Sedej sen., France Slana, Maksim Sedej jun.," (introduction to catalog for exhibition at Mestna Galerija). Ljubljana, 1971.

Kržišnik, Zoran. "Bernik, Boljka, Rogelj, Slana," (introduction to catalog for exhibition at Galerija Doma JNA). Belgrade, 1960.

______. "Ciuha—Slana—Šubic," (introduction to catalog for exhibition at Galerie Palette). Wuppertal-Barmen, 1960.

———. "8 slikara," (text on Slana for catalog for exhibition at Galerija Likovnih Umjetnosti). Dubrovnik, 1962.
———. "France Slana," (introduction to catalog for exhibition at Galerie 61). Klagenfurt, 1962.
———. "France Slana," (introduction to catalog for exhibition at Mala Galerija). Ljubljana, 1961.
———. "France Slana," (introduction to catalog for exhibition at Studio Margutta 13). Rome, 1964.
———. "Mostra d'arte slovena contemporanea," (introduction to catalog for exhibition at Museo Civico). Pistoia, 1958.
———. "Neue jugoslawische Kunst," (introduction to catalog for exhibition). Wiesbaden, 1961.
———. "Savremeni slovenački likovni umetnici," (introduction to catalog for exhibition at Mali Kalemegdan). Belgrade, 1958.
———. "Zeitgenössische slowenische Malerei und Bildhauerei," (introduction to catalog for exhibition at Künstlerhaus). Klagenfurt, 1961.
Maleković, Vladimir. "France Slana," (text for brochure for exhibition at Galerija Labirint). Ljubljana, 1978.
Maležič, Matija. "Pripovedi treh partizanskih likovnikov: Ive Subic, Ivan Seljak-Čopič, France Slana." *Borec,* no. 5 (1965), pp. 472–485.
Menaše, Ljerka. "Savremena slovenačka umetnost," (text for catalog for exhibition at Muzej Savremene Umetnosti). Belgrade, 1968.
Menaše, Luc. "Avtoportret na Slovenskem," (introduction to catalog for exhibition at Moderna Galerija). Ljubljana, 1958.
———. "Avtoportret v zahodnem slikarstvu." *Slovenska Matica* (Ljubljana, 1962), p. 220.
———. In *Evropski umetnostnozgodovinski leksikon.* (Ljubljana: Mladinska Knjiga, 1971), p. 1990.
Mesesnel, Janez. "France Slana," (introduction to catalog for exhibition at Jakopičev Paviljon). Ljubljana, 1956.
———. "France Slana, 1945-1975," (introduction to catalog for exhibition at Lamutov Likovni Salon). Kostanjevica na Krki, 1975.
———. "France Slana: Črpam iz domačega okolja." *Elle-Ona,* no. 36 (1970), pp. 74–76.
———. "Ljubljanska likovna kronika." *Sinteza,* no. 23 (1972), p. 74.
———. "Ljubljanska likovna kronika. France Slana—koncertni atelje." *Sinteza,* no. 17 (1970), p. 55.
———. "Ljubljanska likovna kronika. France Slana—Mestna galerija, June." *Sinteza,* no. 12 (1968), p. 66.
———. "Marjan Dovjak—France Slana—Ive Šubic," (introduction to catalog for exhibition at Gradska Izložbena Sala). Novi Sad, 1962.
———. "Razstava slikane keramike Franceta Slane in razstava marksistične in leposlovne literature Cankarjeve založbe ob akciji 'Družba in knjiga' tednika Komunist," (introduction to catalog for exhibition at Ljubljanska Banka). Ljubljana, 1978.

Mikuž, Jure. "Partizanska grafika in risba," (introduction to catalog for exhibition at Moderna Galerija). Ljubljana, 1975.

Pavlovec, Andrej. "France Slana," (introduction to brochure for exhibition at Galerija Krško). Krško, 1970.

———. "France Slana," (introduction to catalog for exhibition at Likovni Salon). Kočevje, 1970.

———. "France Slana," (introduction to catalog for exhibition at Muzej na Gradu). Škofja Loka, 1970.

———. "Gorenjska likovna kronika." *Sinteza,* no. 17 (1970), p. 60.

Rebolj, Ida. "Keramika Franceta Slana." *Ljubljanska banka,* no. 1 (1978), p. 14.

Sabol, Željko. "France Slana," (introduction to catalog for exhibition at Studio Galerije Forum). Zagreb, 1979.

Sedej, Ivan. "Malíři, Sochaři, grafici socialistické republiky Slovenie," (introduction to catalog for exhibition at Galerie Vincence Kramáře). Praha, 1968.

———. "Slikar France Slana." *Obzornik,* no. 2 (1970), pp. 112–122.

Šijanec, Fran. "Sodobna slovenska likovna umetnost." *Založba Obzorja* (Maribor, 1961), p. 230.

Stele, France. "II. Bienale tapiserije v Lausanne." *Sinteza,* no. 4 (1966), pp. 88, 91.

———. "Slovenija—Slikarstvo." *Enciklopedija likovnih umjetnosti,* no. 4 (1966), p. 245.

Stele-Možina, Melita. "Razstava 'Slovenska umetnost—dela iz zbirke Moderne galerije v Beogradu.' " *Likovna revija,* no. 4/5 (1962), p. 24.

Znidaršič, Asta. "France Slana." *Slovenski biografski leksikon* 10 (1967): 345–346.